CRAFTS

FROM AROUND THE WORLD

CRAFTS
FROM AROUND THE WORLD

B. J. Casselman

Creative Home Library®
In Association with Better Homes and Gardens®
Meredith Corporation

Designed by Allan Mogel
Photography by William N. Hopkins

CHL Creative Home Library
© Meredith Corporation, 1975
All rights reserved
Printed in the United States of America
Library of Congress Catalog Card Number: 75-952
SBN: 696-17900-8

About the Author

A graduate of UCLA with a degree in art, B. J. Casselman is a well-known designer and art teacher. She has taught crafts to both children and adults for the Los Angeles city schools and for the Assistance League of La Canada, California, and she lectures widely on crafts to women's organizations. During the past eight years she has contributed more than 200 designs to Better Homes and Gardens special interest publications and countless more to *Better Homes and Gardens* magazine. Her works have been displayed at the Brand Library in Glendale, California, and the highly acclaimed Descanso Gardens annual show. Married and the mother of four children, Ms. Casselman loves to travel, having made several trips to Europe and Mexico on which she garnered a number of the craft ideas presented in this book.

Contents

Preface

As the world grows smaller and nations become more interdependent, we all need to develop an understanding of people whose cultures and backgrounds are different from our own. Folk art is the expression of people who, with limited resources and a desire to beautify their surroundings, create out of necessity. In all areas of the world and from time immemorial, such people have taken what few tools and materials were at hand and made useful, beautiful things that filled real needs.

By studying the handmade items with which native people surround themselves, we gain valuable insight into their needs, their religious beliefs, their fantasies, sense of humor, and love of beauty. This knowledge enables each one of us to understand and appreciate all people, everywhere. It is my hope that this book will spark new interest in folk art—particularly in the different artistic expressions and design motifs—taken from all parts of our world.

I have tried throughout to keep intact the naïve charm of each project and to maintain the authentic designs along with the simple tools and equipment that were used to make them. In some cases, the original use of the item is applicable today, while in other cases, the designs have been adapted to a more modern, practical use. Please try to be flexible, to use what you have available, to adapt to your needs, just as the people did who originated and developed these design motifs. Most of all, enjoy the pride of accomplishment, just as each craftsman has done since the beginning of time.

Chapter 1

Living Room

Mirror-Cloth Valance

Discussions of the crafts of India always include such words as *exotic*, *diverse*, and *vibrant*. Probably no other nation can top India for its wide variety of arts. In this huge, heterogeneous land of fourteen basic languages, countless dialects, and some seventy thousand villages, art and religion are woven inseparably into daily life.

Of particular interest is the tradition of wedding hangings. These embroidered hangings usually feature "Ganesh," the elephant god, who is also the god of luck and the overcomer of obstacles. Part of a young girl's dowry and a display of her artistry and quality of upbringing, these hangings are made to be worshipped by the newlywed couple and are placed in their domestic shrine after the wedding.

From Kathjawar, Gujaràt, come two traditions used in our hanging—the making of *torans*, a particular type of traditional hanging, and the use of mica mirrors in embroidery work. *Torans* are made in squares or rectangles and are then filled with all types of embroidered animals, flowers, and other decorative motifs set off by tiny mirrors.

This mirror-cloth valance is an adaptation of a *toran*. Although the materials are different—felt instead of cotton and wool instead of silk—our valance displays a traditional Indian color scheme and motif. Small mirrors for this project can be purchased in hobby or crafts stores; however, circles cut from aluminum pie tins will serve just as well.

Materials

½ yard felt, 72 inches wide, in yellow
orange

Persian-type needlepoint and crewel
yarn* (approximate amounts):
2 ounces, in green
1 ounce, in red purple
2 ounces, in hot pink

embroidery floss, 6-strand:
2 packages, in red purple
3 packages, in green

21 mirrors, each ½ inch in diameter

9 mirrors, each ¾ inch in diameter

11 mirrors, each 1 inch in diameter

Tools

yardstick
brown wrapping paper
ruler
pencil
dressmakers' carbon
tracing wheel
yarn needle
scissors

* Four-ply yarn may also be used if split in half.

Procedure

1. Measure area where valance is to be
placed. Adjust pattern to fit space by
adding or subtracting birds and flowers
or triangles on border rows.

2. On brown wrapping paper, draw 1-
inch grid and enlarge pattern (see
"Helpful Hints"). To complete other half
of pattern, lay over carbon, face up, and
trace over all lines. Transfer pattern to
felt by placing dressmakers' carbon face
down on fabric, placing pattern on top,
and drawing over all lines with tracing
wheel. Use carbon side of pattern for
transferring second half.

3. Start to work design pattern by attaching mirrors. Following color arrangement shown in photograph, thread
needle with six strands of embroidery
floss. Following figures on next page,
attach mirrors to felt with framing stitch.
To do this, hold mirror in place on fabric
with thumb and index finger of left hand.
With right hand, bring needle up at point
A, right next to mirror. Bring needle over
mirror and insert through fabric at point
B. Bring needle up at point C, over mirror, and down at point D (Figure 1). Keep
thread drawn up snugly. Next (Figure 2),
bring needle up at point E, around (over
and then under) AB, around CD, and

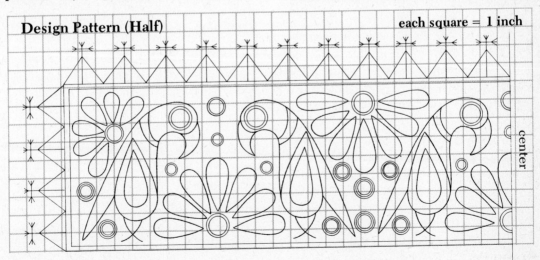

Design Pattern (Half)   each square = 1 inch

center

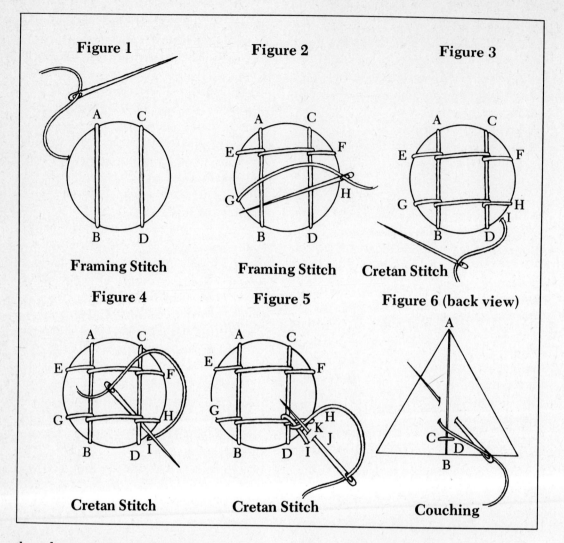

Figure 1

Framing Stitch

Figure 2

Framing Stitch

Figure 3

Cretan Stitch

Figure 4

Cretan Stitch

Figure 5

Cretan Stitch

Figure 6 (back view)

Couching

then down at point F. Bring thread up at point G, around AB, around CD, and then down at point H.

4. Using same color floss, border mirrors with Cretan stitch. Begin by bringing thread up at point I (Figure 3). With I directly facing you and thread under and to right of needle, bring needle over and then under intersection CDGH (Figure 4). With thread under and to right of needle, go in at point J and up at point K (Figure 5). Point K now becomes point I for next stitch. In this manner, repeat

Cretan stitch all the way around mirror, working stitches so that they resemble spokes of a wheel, with inner stitching closer together than the outer stitching. As you work around mirror, Cretan stitches will pull framing stitches back to form a rounded frame around mirror.

5. To embroider remaining design, follow photograph for colors and work with two strands of yarn. Because felt has a tendency to stretch, an embroidery hoop will not be helpful. Keep work flat, however, and do not draw stitches.

The design is done in a standard closed herringbone stitch (see embroidery-stitch section in "Helpful Hints"), except for outer frames around those mirrors that have double frames. These are done in a chain stitch (see embroidery-stitch section in "Helpful Hints"). To work triangles, fill shape with closed herringbone stitch, working from base to point. On the last stitch, bring yarn to back of fabric; bring up at point A and down at point B (Figure 6). Work AB in couching (see embroidery-stitch section in "Helpful Hints"). Triangle tops are done with straight stitches.

6. When design is completed, place valance, face down, on padded board and press with iron set for wool. Finished valance may be lined and hung on a rod or mounted on a padded valance board.

Alternate Design Pattern

Mother-of-Pearl Mirror

A land of contrasts, Morocco offers the visitor the best of two worlds—Africa with European overtones. Here, one is immediately attracted by the skill of the craftsmen and the beauty of their wares. Shopping for these wares—carpets, leathergoods, silver, and furniture—is done in the *souks*, which are located in the medieval parts of the cities, called *medinas*. One is expected to bargain in the *souk* or he will disappoint the vendors.

The craftsmen who make small furniture are traditionally from Essaouira, on the Atlantic seaboard. Founded in pre-Roman days, Essaouira was once a supplier of the rich purple mollusk dye used by the Roman patricians. The Portuguese followed the Romans, and then, in the eighteenth century, a sultan arrived with a prisoner who just happened to be a French architect. Together they constructed a port and fortifications. The sultan welcomed all to trade, and soon it was a prosperous seaport.

Today, Essaouira looks like a Mediterranean village, with white houses accented by deep blue shutters and Portuguese-style doors. Once in town, one can see the inlayers hard at work, encrusting their highly polished furniture with designs of silver mother-of-pearl and wood to create marvelous stylized floral decorations. Although woods are scarce, yew, cedar, arar, walnut, oak, lemon, and ebony are available to an extent.

Our easily constructed mirror uses sequins to create the illusion of mother-of-pearl.

Materials
plywood:

1 piece, ⅜ × 19 × 23 inches, for mirror
frame

1 piece, ⅜ × 12 × 18 inches, for
decorative top

pine:

1 piece, ½ × 1 × 17 inches, for detail
strip

2 pieces, each ¼ × 1 × 6 inches, for
braces

10 mirror clips and small screws, for
mounting mirror

mirror, 9½ × 15 inches

white glue

brads, each ¾ inch long

flat paint, in black

300 mother-of-pearl-finish round
bangles, each 20 millimeters

300 mother-of-pearl-finish cupped
sequins, each 8 millimeters

low-gloss plastic varnish

2 screw eyes

wire, for hanging

Tools
brown wrapping paper

pencil

ruler

carbon paper

scissors

masking tape

jigsaw *or* coping saw

sandpaper, medium and fine grades

screwdriver

hammer

nailset

paintbrush, medium

6 or 7 file cards

small box or dish, for holding cutouts

varnish brush

Procedure
1. On brown wrapping paper, draw 1-
inch grid and enlarge patterns, including
all design lines (see "Helpful Hints").
To make other halves, lay over carbon
paper, carbon side up, and trace over
lines to produce reverse design. Cut out
patterns, tape to wood, and mark outlines; flip patterns over to complete.

2. With jigsaw or coping saw, cut out
pieces. Sand edges and attach mirror
clips with screws, locating them on the
back of the frame in the positions indicated on pattern.

3. Glue and, using brads and nailset, nail
detail strip to top edge of mirror frame.
Horizontal dotted line on pattern indicates proper position for bottom edge.

4. Glue and nail both braces to top back
of frame, following vertical dotted lines
on pattern for proper positioning.

5. With black paint, paint frame parts and
allow to dry completely.

6. Tape pattern to frame and go over design lines with a hard, sharp pencil, indenting the pattern into wood. Turn patterns over to complete other half.

7. Using carbon paper, transfer patterns
for all design shapes except wedge to
file cards; cut out. Hold leaf shape
over bangles and cut out 132 leaf shapes.
Reserve leftover bits of bangles to fill in
large units. (A small box or dish is helpful
for holding cutouts.)

8. Spread even layer of white glue on patterns for vase and large flowers and cover
with leftover pieces of bangles, fitting
pieces as closely together as possible so
that card is completely covered. Set aside.

9. Glue vase and large flowers in place
on mirror top. Cut small petals from bangles and glue in position on frame. Position and glue leaves in place.

10. Cut each cupped sequin into 6 pie-
shaped wedges. (The sequins are marked
in a hexagon pattern at the edges, so cut
from the edge to the center hole.) Keep

cutouts in a small box or dish. Glue wedges to frame along pattern lines. For small flower designs, assemble circular shapes with 5 wedges.

11. When complete design is glued in place, apply a coat of plastic varnish. Follow manufacturer's directions for drying time and apply as many coats as necessary so that sequins are sunk below level of finish. Allow drying time.

12. Attach mirror to back of frame, and add screw eyes and wire for hanging.

13. Slip decorative top of frame in place between detail strip and top two braces.

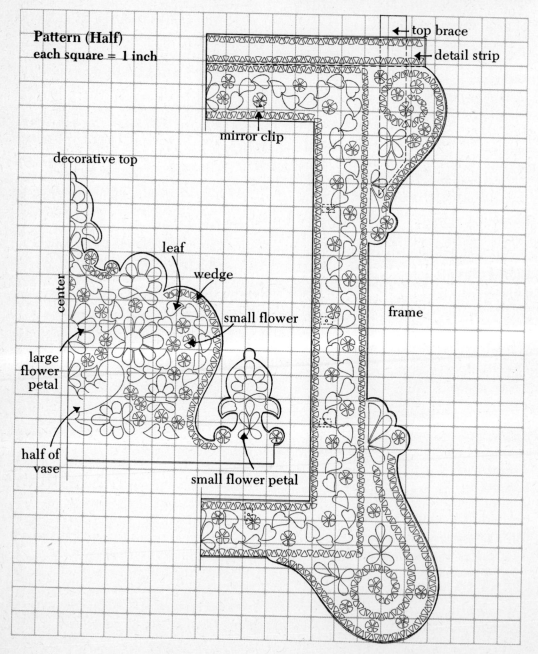

Pattern (Half)
each square = 1 inch

top brace
detail strip
mirror clip
decorative top
center
leaf
wedge
small flower
frame
large flower petal
half of vase
small flower petal

Dolphin Mosaic Table

Mosaic work may very well be the oldest craft of all, dating as far back as 3500 B.C. when Egyptians composed geometric mosaic designs. Before that, it is safe to assume that people arranged patterns in the mud with rocks and bits of wood. Mosaic work was particularly popular in ancient Greece. There, mosaics made of colored stones and sometimes outlined with metal strips are found in fourth-century Macedonian palaces. The Hellenistic age featured *tesserae*—little cubes of colored stone or glass—which can still be seen in the fine mosaic floors at Delos. The Romans then took the mosaic floor to all parts of their empire. The freshness of their landscapes, farm scenes, marvelous animals, and human figures can still be seen today.

Early Christian art found its fullest expression in mosaic, particularly during the Byzantine era, which married Eastern and Western cultures. Serving as a poor man's Bible, mosaics were well-suited for churches and more outstanding than paintings, for the tiny squares of glass and gold, tilted at various angles, caught the light in all its moods.

The small dolphin mosaic in this project was influenced by floors at Delos, Greece. For this table, ceramic tiles on net backing were used. However, stones, broken crockery, and bits of glass and mirror could also be used for more exciting and innovative results.

Materials

table commercially prepared for mosaic top, with 12½ × 12½-inch center opening on top*
ceramic tiles**, each ½ × ½ inch (approximate amounts):**
   575 tiles, in white
   180 tiles, in dark brown
   60 tiles, in light brown
   130 tiles, in black
white glue
1 bag tile grout
stain *or* finish of your choice

Tools

masking tape
brown wrapping paper
pencil
ruler
carbon paper
tile nippers
file
sandpaper, coarse and fine grades
mixing bowl
paintbrush (optional)
sponge
soft cloth
modeling tool

*You may also make your own table with four pieces of picture-frame molding, four prefab legs, and 1 piece plywood, ½ × 12½ × 12½ inches, for tabletop.

**Available in 12 × 12-inch net-backed sheets, by the strip, or by the bag and sold in craft and hobby stores.

Procedure

1. Cover molding of table with masking tape to protect surface.
2. On brown wrapping paper, draw 1-inch grid and enlarge design pattern(see "Helpful Hints"). Place carbon paper, face down, on tabletop and tape pattern over it; trace over all lines. Remove pattern and check to make sure all lines have been transferred. Retrace if necessary.

3. Tiles for dolphins are cut in half either horizontally to form strips or diagonally to form triangles. Cut enough black, dark brown, and light brown tiles for one dolphin, following color code on pattern. To cut tile, grasp in tile nippers about halfway across at the center and squeeze jaws together. Tile will snap in half. File or rub cut edges on coarse sandpaper if necessary.
4. Working on a small section at a time, spread even coat of white glue on one dolphin outline. Glue black tiles in place, leaving about 1/16 inch between them. Following same procedure, glue remaining tiles to dolphin. Cut tiles for second dolphin and, following same procedure, glue in place.
5. Spread glue over background areas and fit white tiles in place. Position tiles in straight horizontal and vertical rows. Allow glue to dry overnight.
6. Place grout in a mixing bowl, add a small amount of water, and stir until mixture is the consistency of very heavy cream. Add about a teaspoon of white glue to mixture so that it will stick better and produce a smoother surface.
7. Spoon or pour grout over tiles, using your hand or a brush to work grout into spaces between. If grout dries while you are still working with it, add water with hands or brush to soften. Rub grout thoroughly for at least 15 minutes, or until the air bubbles are all worked out. Allow grout to set up for at least 30 minutes.
8. Fill mixing bowl with water and dip in sponge. Wring most of the water out of sponge and wipe over mosaic surface, removing surplus grout. If too much grout comes off, allow more drying time. Rinse sponge occasionally in water. Let grout dry for additional 45 minutes and remove grout film by wiping with a soft,

dry cloth. Clean tile surface again with slightly moistened sponge. Cover tile with wet cloth and allow to dry overnight.

9. When grout is completely dry, remove masking tape from wood molding. Clean up edges with modeling tool, if necessary. Polish tile surface with soft cloth.

10. Sand table frame and legs with fine sandpaper and then finish as you wish.

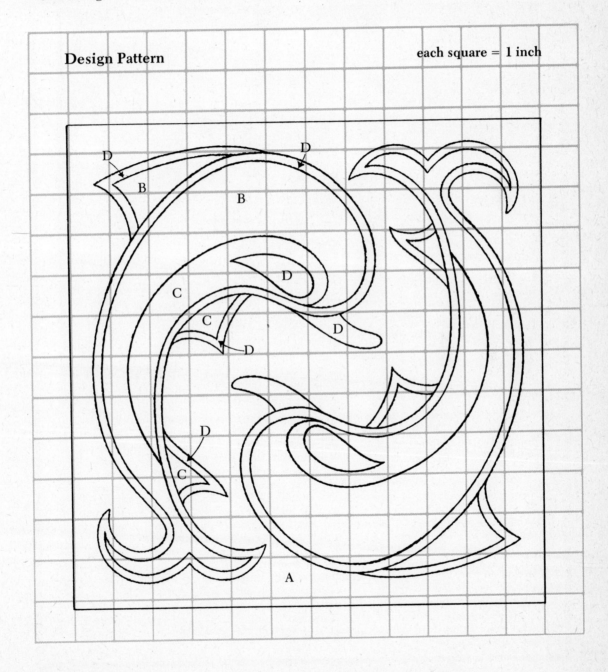

Design Pattern

each square = 1 inch

Color Code: A = white B = dark brown C = light brown D = black

Australia

Aborigine Rug

Aborigines are known for the unique design work they have painted on rock faces and eucalyptus bark. The designs are of two styles. The first, known as the "X-ray" style, depicts stylized internal organs as well as the outstanding external characteristics of animal or human figures. These are usually done in more than one color. The second style, known as the "Spirit," or "Mimi," style, depicts stylized human figures and are painted in only one color. Many aborigines claim that the Mimi paintings are not painted at all but are simply shadows of passing spirits caught on the cliffs; others say that they were caused by the Mimi's unique ability to melt into cliff faces by blowing upon a rock. In any case, these two styles of aborigine art exist side by side on the rocks. Renewed from time to time by passing bands of aborigines, the designs fascinate the contemporary eye.

Oftentimes, designs of kangaroos, wallabies, and emus are found painted on the rocks near watering places. Usually done by hunters whiling away the hours waiting for game to appear, these paintings function as sympathetic magical charms, ensuring the prompt return of game to the area. The paintings also serve as signposts for other hunters, indicating what type of game is in the area.

The kangaroo figures used as the main design element for our easy punch-hooked rug project shown here were taken from rock paintings on the Rawlinson range of Australia.

Materials

1 piece jute rug backing
   of your choice, 36 × 40 inches
rug yarn, 3-ply (approximate amounts):
   8 ounces, in rust
   24 ounces, in eggshell
   4 ounces, in blue
latex rug backing*
carpet thread, in eggshell
4 yards rug binding, 1½ inches wide
   (optional)

Tools

brown wrapping paper
pencil
ruler
dressmakers' carbon
masking tape
tracing wheel
indelible felt-tipped pen
rug frame, approximately 36 × 40
   inches**
staple gun or hammer and tacks
punch needle***
paintbrush
needle, large

*A liquid bonding agent used to seal rug loops in place and available at art needlework departments and stores.
**Standard rug frames are available inexpensively in variety stores and art needlework departments and stores. You may also use a quilting frame or any other frame that is sturdy enough to withstand rug punching If frame is not large enough to accommodate backing, simply work rug in sections, repositioning as necessary.
***Standard punch needles are available at variety stores. Adjustable punch needles, which automatically regulate the length of the loops being made, are available at a slightly higher cost in art needlework departments and stores.

Procedure

1. On brown wrapping paper, draw 1-inch grid and enlarge design pattern (see "Helpful Hints"). Place dressmakers' carbon face down on backing; center and tape pattern over it. Transfer pattern to fabric by going over lines with tracing wheel. Remove pattern and join dots with indelible felt-tipped pen. Make sure that the pen you use is indelible or the design will bleed into the yarn. A hot-iron transfer pencil may also be used for this operation (see section on transferring patterns in "Helpful Hints").

2. Machine-stitch around edges of backing; then lay over the rug frame, with design face up and outer edges of design at least 1 inch from inside of frame. Using staple gun or tacks, fasten at center of each side. Continue stapling from the centers to corners, first on one side and then on the opposite side, keeping fabric taut and even. Backing must be mounted straight or stitching will be crooked.

3. Following manufacturer's directions, thread needle of punch hook with rust yarn, leaving a 2-inch tail of yarn to extend beyond needle. Yarn should move freely from needle. Work on a small test area of backing to decide on how dense to make your stitches. This will depend on thickness of yarn, closeness of weave on backing, and desired height of pile. The rug in this project was made with a ⅜-inch pile. Experiment with your materials to find the desired stitching gauge.

4. Follow color code on pattern for color scheme. Then, following design lines on backing, begin stitching outlines of all figures with rust yarn. The 2-inch tail will be run through later to front of fabric. Although there are no fixed rules, it is best to outline all figures first and then to work small inner areas, then outer areas, and then background areas. Always follow contours of outlines and work toward center. When you wish to change colors, hold last stitch down in front and withdraw needle. Cut yarn, leaving a 1-

24

inch tail. Stitch background area last, using straight line, wave, zigzag, or curve pattern. Leave enough space along outer edges for two rows of closely spaced loops. These will keep the rug edges flat.
5. When hooking has been completed, turn work over and examine carefully for bare spots. Fill in bare spots with a few loops or rows, if necessary. Run all yarn tails through to the front, and cut off even with pile.
6. With completed rug still on frame, paint latex backing over back of rug. Allow to dry overnight. This will seal loops.
7. Remove rug from frame. Trim backing all the way around to leave a 1-inch border around edges of design. Make

diagonal cuts across each corner, ½ inch from corner of design. Run a thin line of rug backing on all cut edges to prevent raveling. Allow to dry. Turn under diagonal edge at each corner and turn down adjoining sides over diagonal, to miter the corners. Whip mitered edges together. Turn under raw edges along sides and tack hem to back of rug. If you wish, you can use rug binding instead of tacking the hem: Machine-stitch one edge of binding as close as possible to last row of stitches on front side. Bring binding around to back. At corners, tack excess binding under and sew mitered corner seam. Do not cut binding at corners. Tack binding down to back of rug.

Design Pattern   **each square = 1 inch**

Color Code:
A = rust
B = eggshell
C = blue

Alternate Design Patterns

Alternate Design Patterns

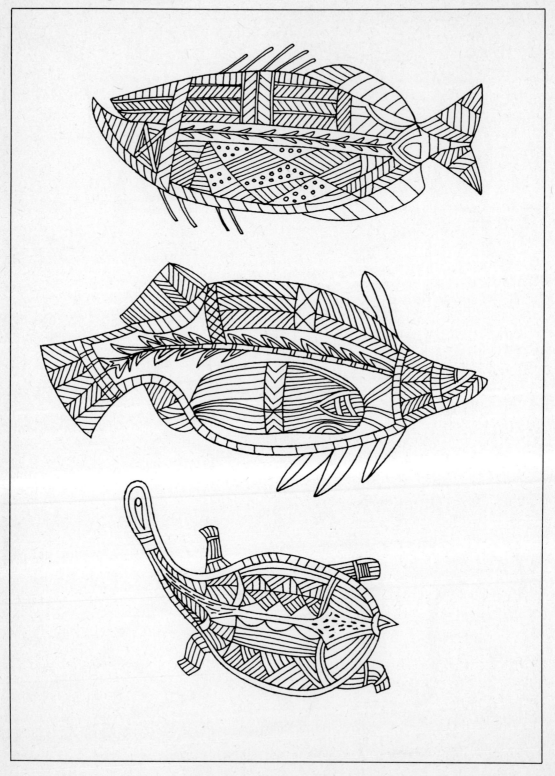

Pakistan

Macramé Plant Holder

Macramé, the art of knot tying, is probably as old as paleolithic or neolithic man. The first time that man tied two cords together to form a single piece, he was practicing macramé.

The oldest known examples of macramé have been found in Egypt, where knots were used to make nets. Macramé is a universal art, stretching from Peru, where Incas used knot tying to record and convey messages, all the way to Greece, where knots were used to form slings for broken arms. Macramé was also popular throughout the Victorian era, when society folk adorned everything from gowns to clocks with knot designs.

With the renaissance of interest in macramé today, this macramé plant holder will add a contemporary as well as exotic touch to your living room. The essential procedures for this ancient art are explained in "Helpful Hints"; read the section before you begin.

28

Materials
approximately 900 feet hemp cord
spool wire, medium weight
glass or plastic container
6 wooden curtain rings, in black, with
   screw eyes removed
24 small beads, in black (optional)
24 large beads, in black (optional)
ceramic pot
2½ feet plastic tubing*, ¼ inch in
   diameter

Tools
scissors
hook
white glue

*An item used to equip aquariums and available in large pet stores.

Procedure
1. Cut twelve pieces of hemp cord, each 70 feet long, and fold each cord in half. Wire together at point 5 inches below this fold, forming a 5-inch loop (not shown in photograph).

2. Hold bundle together. With another cord, wrap over wire around the loop. Continue wrapping down cord bundle, about 2 inches below wire. Run cord end in under wrapping. Then suspend loop from hook.

3. *Rows 1–15:* Divide cords into four groups of six cords each and make a fifteen-knot square-knot sennit in each group. The center two cords are the knot bearers; knots are tied with outer two cords on each side.

4. *Rows 16–20:* Working around glass container, make five rows of alternating square knots.

5. *Row 21:* Holding wooden ring horizontally, add ring by putting knot bearers inside ring, knotting cords outside, and

tying one row of square knots below ring.

6. *Rows 22–54:* Divide cords into four groups of six again and make a thirty-three-knot square-knot sennit in each group.

7. *Rows 55–58:* Holding wooden rings vertically, add one to each group, putting knot bearers inside ring and knotting cords outside ring. Make three square knots in center of each ring, or as many as space allows.

8. *Rows 59–63:* With knot-bearing cords inside ring and knotting cords outside, tie a five-knot square-knot sennit under each ring.

9. *Rows 64–68:* Holding wooden ring horizontally, add ring in same manner as before and tie five rows of alternating square knots.

10. To connect side rings, cut twenty-four 30-inch pieces of hemp. For both sides of all four rings, fold three cords in half, so that you now have six, and tie onto ring in lark's-head knot. There should now be a lark's-head knot on both sides of all four rings. Insert ceramic pot. Bring cords together between rings, and, using the three innermost cords of the two groups as knot bearers and the three outermost cords of the two groups as knotting cords, make a square knot. Cut off ends and apply white glue to back of knot.

11. If you wish, thread black beads onto fringe and hold in place with overhand knots.

12. Insert plant of your choice into pot. To water plant, fill glass or plastic container with water. With one end of plastic tubing pinched together, fill tubing with water and place open end in container; insert other end 1 inch into plant soil.

Macramé Doormat

Sailors, while at sea, oftentimes spent their free time doing macramé, or "square knotting," as they called it. Although the sailors used the familiar combinations of square knots and hitches in their pieces, they often embellished them with such knots as the Oriental, monkey's fist, Turk's head, and marine plaits. It is interesting to note that in 1940, *The Bluejackets' Manual* of the U.S. Navy published instructions for making square-knotted porthole covers out of rope. To this day, it is mentioned in the naval manuals as part of the class 4 knots.

In addition to being used for porthole covers, MacNamara's lace, as it was sometimes called, was used to make bellpulls, mast skirts, table mats, bunk pockets, and sea-chest covers. Elaborate purses, knotted from cotton or silk cord, made lovely gifts for sweethearts, wives, or a pretty face waiting in the next port of call. Macramé objects were occasionally used as barter.

The rug in this project is based upon a table-mat pattern and requires only three knots—the double half hitch, the square knot, and the lark's head. You will find instructions for all of these in the macramé section of "Helpful Hints." Read it before you begin.

Materials
approximately 2,100 feet sisal cord,
    3/16 inch in diameter
1 plywood board, 30 × 40 inches
5 dozen nonrusting nails
white glue

Tools
hammer
ruler
scissors
cotton gloves (optional)
needle-nosed pliers *or* crochet hook
mixing bowl
paintbrush

Procedure
1. Hammer in one nail at each top corner of 40-inch side of board. Cut a 4-foot holding cord from sisal and tie to nails. Cord should be taut. If you wish, wear cotton gloves to protect hands. Cut 104 cords, each 19 feet in length.
2. *Row 1:* Fold cords in half, and tie on the holding cord in lark's-head knots. There is now a total of 208 single cords on holding cord.
3. *Rows 2–4:* Cut a 3½-yard-long cord for knot-bearing cord, tie one end temporarily to lefthand nail, and make three rows of horizontal double half hitches. Then bring end of knot-bearing cord down with first two cords of next row. Knot over all cords, thus running ends into work.
4. *Rows 5–15:* Tie cords 1 through 4 in vertical double half hitches, with cords 3 and 4 serving as knotting cords and cords 1 and 2 as knot bearers. Repeat for last four cords in row, incorporating the end of the knot-bearing cord from row 4 with the knot bearers of the vertical half hitches. Divide the remaining cords into ten groups of twenty cords each. Work two rows of diagonal double half hitches in each group to form a chevron or V pattern. This is done by using the first cord in each group as the knot-bearing cord for next nine cords (cord 5

Knotting Diagram (Quarter of Mat)

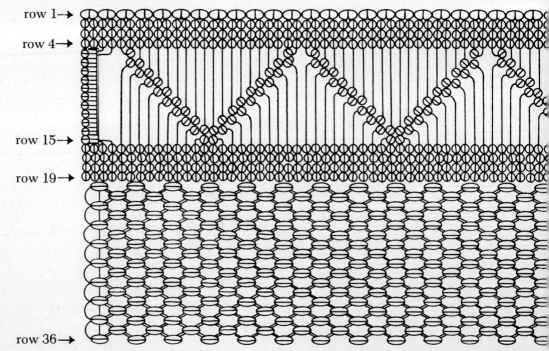

row 1→
row 4→
row 15→
row 19→
row 36→

for cords 6 through 14) and then using the last cord in each group as knot-bearing cord for preceding nine cords (cord 24 for cords 23 through 15). Repeat pattern for remaining nine groups. Tie as many vertical half hitches as necessary to make sennit length match depth of chevron pattern.

5. *Rows 16–19:* Cut 4½-yard-long cord for knot bearer and tie one end temporarily to lefthand nail. Then tie four rows of horizontal double half hitches. The end of the knot-bearing cord will be run into the knots on back side of piece when knotting is completed.

6. *Rows 20–53:* Tie thirty-four rows of alternating square knots.

7. *Rows 54–57:* Repeat step 5.

8. *Rows 58–67:* Repeat step 4, but this time you should reverse the working order so that you begin with row 15 and work back to row 5. Use the tenth cord in each group as knot-bearing cord for preceding nine cords (cord 14 for cords 13 through 5) and the eleventh cord in each group as knot-bearing cord for next nine cords (cord 15 for cords 16 through 24).

9. *Rows 68–71:* Repeat step 5.

10. *Row 72:* To end piece, knot cord 1 in horizontal double half hitch over knot bearer. Hold cord 1 with knot bearer and knot cord 2 over both. Drop cord 1 and pull it through to back of piece. Hold cord 2 with knot bearer and knot cord 3 over both. Drop cord 2 and pull through to back. Hold cord 3 with knot bearer and knot cord 4 over both. Drop cord 3; pull through to back. Continue across row. Remove rug from board.

11. Untie cord ends around nails and run into knots on the back side of rug, using pliers or a crochet hook. Cut off excess cord. Nail mat to board, spacing nails approximately 1 inch apart all around. Mix 1 part glue to 4 parts water and coat back of rug thoroughly with solution. This will hold ends in place. Let mat dry completely; then remove mat from board.

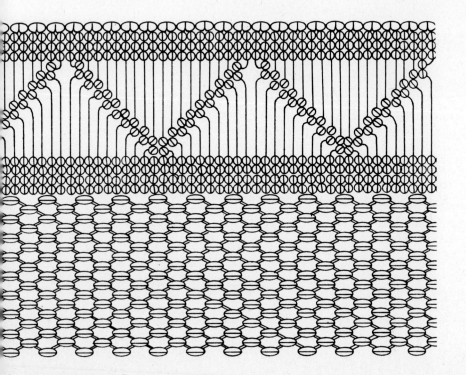

Mexico

Sun Fern Stand

If one had to choose the most dominant theme of world art, it would have to be the sun, for the sun is the center of life—it is the source of energy, power, and even eternity. It is feared and adored in hot countries, revered and welcomed in cold countries.

In Mexico, the sun was worshipped, and, in the Aztec world, it was a privilege for a man to be sacrificed as an ambassador to the sun. In the cruelly cold Northern countries, rites were conducted to lure the sun's return. Sun worship was also practiced by the American Indians, as documented by John Smith's expeditions in Virginia, and by other records. All around the world, sun symbols can be found carved on houses, furniture, tools, and rocks; embroidered on cloths; and painted on walls. Hindu temples even stand on wheels, the spokes of which symbolize the sun's rays. Because of man's dependence on the sun, it is the most popular design of all.

For this reason, suns have been chosen to decorate this fern stand, done in the warm tones of copper and brass. The design patterns themselves have been compiled from many different representations of the sun, as depicted by many different cultures.

Materials
plywood:
  4 pieces, each 1 × 11 × 41½ inches, for sides of stand
  2 pieces, each 1 × 12 × 12 inches, for top and bottom of stand
finishing nails, each 1½ inches long
wood putty
4 casters
covering metal for stand:
  3 pieces aluminum sheeting*, each 36 × 36 inches
  4 pieces brass**, each 2 × 12 inches, for top of sides
  4 pieces brass**, each 5½ × 12 inches, for bottom of sides
  4 pieces aluminum right-angle edging*, each ½ x ½ x 1/16 inches and 6 feet long
metal for sun faces:
  9 feet brass**, 28 gauge
  9 feet tooling copper**, 36 gauge
  9 feet tooling aluminum**, 36 gauge
contact cement
plastic spray
paint for metal, in black

Tools
hammer
nailset
sandpaper, medium grade
ruler
tin snips, small
wood block, terry cloth, string or rubber band, and wooden mallet
rubber brayer (optional)
hacksaw
miter box
lightweight cardboard
pencil or ballpoint pen
scissors
file
steel wool, 000 grade
bone folder*** or flat background tool

craft knife
soft cloth or cotton glove
paintbrush (optional)
newspapers

*Right-angle aluminum edging (item #2406) and 36 × 36-inch aluminum sheets are made by the Reynolds Aluminum Company and are available at hardware stores.

**Brass, tooling copper, and tooling aluminum come in 12-inch-wide rolls and are sold by the foot. Tooling metals are sold at craft stores; brass is sold at sheet-metal shops and hardware stores.

***Used primarily in bookbinding work and available at art-supply stores.

Procedure
1. To build stand, nail four sides together with butt joints. Nail top and bottom pieces in place. Use nailset to sink nails below surface.
2. Sand piece, and fill with wood putty where necessary.
3. Add casters to bottom, positioning them 1 inch in from corners.
4. Mark aluminum sheets into 12 × 36-inch pieces; cut out with tin snips.
5. Fit metal pieces to sides, mark placements on wood, and following manufacturer's instructions for using contact cement, cement to all sides of stand: Turn stand on its side on a pad of newspaper. Beginning at top edge, cement on brass followed by aluminum followed by brass. Make sure fit is tight on edges where metals butt together. To ensure good bond between metal and wood surfaces, use a wood block padded with several layers of terry cloth held in place with string or a large rubber band. Place padded surface on metal and, with wooden mallet, pound block over metal surfaces. You may also roll over surface with hard rubber brayer, applying even pressure over area. Wipe off excess glue.
6. Cement 12 × 12-inch piece of alu-

minum sheeting to the top in same manner as described in step 5.

7. On one 6-foot piece of right-angle aluminum edging, mark height of side of stand minus the width of both top and bottom aluminum edging strips; do not cut yet. From the remainder of the strip, cut two 12-inch sections for top and bottom edges. Miter corners using hacksaw and miter box. Repeat same procedure with other three lengths of edging.

8. Fit top trim pieces around top edge and cement, using padded block of wood and mallet to ensure obtaining a good cement bond. Add bottom trim in the same way. Measure length of each side between top and bottom trim, cut aluminum edging to this measurement, and cement in place as before.

9. On lightweight cardboard, draw 1-inch grid and enlarge face patterns (see "Helpful Hints"). Cut out patterns and mark features according to type of metal from which they will be cut and to which face they belong (see photograph). You will decorate all faces before cementing them to stand (see following steps). Cut brass with tin snips, as it is quite stiff and the hardest of tooling metals. Tooling aluminum and copper can be cut with ordinary scissors. Since aluminum and copper are soft, take care not to scratch surfaces.

10. Using cardboard pattern, cut 10½-inch-diameter brass circles for backgrounds of all faces. File edges smooth. Place circles on flat work surface and clean with steel wool.

11. Place tooling copper on flat work surface, smooth with bone folder or flat background tool, and clean with steel wool. On copper, place cardboard ray pattern for face #2 and mark outlines.

With craft knife, start cutout for face center, and then use scissors to cut out inner circle, which will be used for face #1. Cement copper ray pattern to brass circle.

12. Carefully smooth tooling aluminum on flat surface. For face #1, mark and cut ray pattern but do not cut out central circle. Spread even coat of contact cement on copper circle (cut in previous step), and on center of aluminum ray pattern. Cement copper face to rays; then cement face to brass circle.

13. Smooth aluminum and cut circle for face #3; cement to center of brass circle. Smooth and steel-wool copper for forehead and nose pattern; mark, cut, and cement in place.

14. Mark and cut remaining facial patterns from scraps of metal, and cement to faces. Rays on face #3 are cut from copper and aluminum and are evenly spaced on brass background so that all three metals are part of edge design. You can cement all pieces flat or, if you wish, you can tool the aluminum and copper with ballpoint pen and soft pencil. (Refer to "Helpful Hints" for notes on tooling metal.)

15. To apply finish, read metal-tooling section in "Helpful Hints." Then, holding metal with soft cloth or cotton glove, clean and polish faces with steel wool. If you wish a shiny surface, spray with clear plastic. If you wish an antique surface, apply coat of black paint, allow to dry partially, and then rub paint off highlights with terry cloth; finish with spray.

16. Before adding faces to stand, lay stand on its side on newspaper pad to avoid scratching metal. Position faces and mark on stand with soft pencil.

17. Apply cement to faces and stand; glue

in place. Using padded block and mallet, pound faces lightly but firmly to ensure complete bond. Pay particular attention to all edges. Clean off any excess cement.

Design Patterns

each square = 1 inch

face 1

face 2

face 3

Chapter 2

Dining Room
Kitchen

Sunburst Inlay Table

The art of inlaying, or *intarsia*, as they say in Italian, has long been a tradition in Italy. In ancient times, inlay work came from the Far East. The art reached its peak of popularity in Europe, particularly in Italy, during the early Renaissance. Inlay work still represents big business in Italy, as can be affirmed by anyone who has ever taken a tour bus to Sorrento. Several stops are made at shops that specialize only in the sale of inlaid articles.

When inlay work is done, part of a surface is cut out and another material inserted in its place so that the resulting surface is smooth and flat. Obviously, this requires a great deal of skill. Strictly speaking, the top of our table is an *overlay*. With the advances in technology that have made it possible to cut wood in very thin, even sheets of veneer, the inlay effect can now be achieved simply by gluing prefitted pieces of veneer to any suitable surface. You can easily obtain this look in any number of attractive designs by cutting pieces of veneer of different shades or colors to fit your design pattern and then applying them to the surface you have prepared.

The "inlay" portion of our project requires only two sheets of veneer, glue, and a precut disk of plywood. A rolling pin and a craft knife are the only hand tools necessary.

Materials

folding wooden campstool*, with canvas
    seat removed
1 plywood disk, ¾ inch thick, 18 inches
    in diameter**
wood veneer***:
    1 piece, 9 × 18 inches, in light shade
    1 piece, 9 × 18 inches, in dark shade
white glue
4 pipe straps, each 1 inch, and 8 wood
    screws, ½ inch long, diameter to
    fit holes in pipe straps
satin-finish plastic varnish

Tools

sandpaper, medium and finishing grades
brown wrapping paper
pencil
ruler
scissors
craft knife *or* single-edged razor blade
rolling pin, hard rubber squeegee, *or*
    veneer roller
wax paper
newspapers
2 C-clamps
scrap wood, for cushion blocks
screwdriver
varnish brush
lint-free cloth .

*A set of prefab legs and two-position top plates may be substituted for the campstool, pipe straps, and wood screws. Two-position top plates are manufactured by Gerber, St. Louis, Mo., and available inexpensively at most hardware stores. A kit that contains both the legs and double brackets is available through Legs Unlimited, Emco Specialties, P.O. Box 864, Des Moines, Iowa 50304.

**Available precut at lumberyards.

*** The type used in this project is available in rolls, manufactured by U.S. Plywood, P.O. Box 17183, Louisville, Ky. 40271, and sold under the name Handi-wood Genuine Wood Veneer. Also available through Albert Constantine & Son, Inc., 2050 Eastchester Road, Bronx, N.Y. 10461.

Procedure

1. With medium-grade sandpaper, sand all surfaces and edges of campstool and plywood disk.

2. On brown wrapping paper, draw 1-inch grid and enlarge pattern (see "Helpful Hints"). This represents half the pattern; to complete other half, use pattern in reverse. Number and code sections (*light* or *dark*) for ease in assembling. Carefully following the lines, cut out various sections of pattern.

3. Read manufacturer's instructions for applying veneer. Then place each pattern section on appropriate veneer sheet, trace around border, and cut out with craft knife or single-edged razor blade. Number each to correspond with pattern-section numbers.

4. Following numerical sequence, glue veneer sections to tabletop and press firmly in place. Roll firmly over entire area with a rolling pin, a hard rubber squeegee, or a veneer roller to force out all excess glue and to ensure good glue bond. Wipe off excess glue with damp cloth.

5. Cover tabletop with wax paper (to prevent glue from sticking) and top with a drawing board, a piece of plywood, or several boards (to distribute weight evenly). Then weight tabletop with books, flat irons, etc., until glue has thoroughly dried.

6. Continue the pattern of the tabletop around the edge, still alternating the shades but using a dark shade on the edge when the adjoining top piece is light, and vice versa. Cut veneer pieces required for edge and glue in place, using same procedure as for top. Using firm pressure, roll edge with roller, squeegee, etc., and wipe off excess glue remaining on the edge with a damp cloth.

7. To attach tabletop to stool, turn top upside down on a pad of newspapers. Lay out and mark exact position desired for two top bars of stool. Then, clamp middle of bars to tabletop to prevent shifting, using cushion blocks in clamps to protect tabletop. Fasten top bars to tabletop with pipe straps, each held by two screws. As an alternate method, prefab legs may be attached by means of two-position top plates, installed according to manufacturer's instructions.

8. Sand top lightly with finishing paper, and apply four coats satin varnish, sanding and dusting with a lint-free cloth between each coat.

Edge View

Pattern (Half)

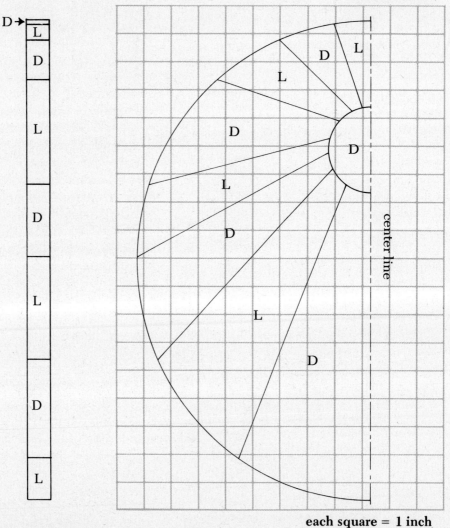

each square = 1 inch

Color Code:
D = dark
L = light

Russia

Candleholder

This brightly painted candleholder is typical of Russian folk art in three ways—color scheme, design motif, and shape. If one were asked to single out the one characteristic of Russian folk art that it bests represents, it would have to be its wealth of ornamental effects. Today, these seem purely decorative, but they probably were an outgrowth of popular superstition. All kinds of exotic beasts—unicorns, griffins, basilisks, and mermaids—appear with amazing regularity in traditional Russian designs.

The fun in assembling this candelabra is in being able to use up your scrap wood and other odds and ends. Use what you have on hand and don't be restricted by our list given below. In fact, if you are a scrap wood saver, you probably have this candleholder in your wood box right now. Just follow the general instructions for assembling and adjust your pieces to fit. If you don't have a supply of scrap wood, you can begin with a turned newel post from a lumberyard or you can turn the base yourself if you have a lathe.

42

Materials

1 piece plywood, ¾ × 13½ × 14½ inches, for top section

1 plywood circle, ¾ inch thick, 6¾ inches in diameter, for base

6 inches dowel, 1½ inches in diameter

6 plywood circles, each ¼ inch thick, 2 inches in diameter

26 inches dowel, ⅛ inch in diameter

10 wooden beads, each 1 inch in diameter with ⅛-inch-diameter center holes

wood odds and ends for stem section:
   small wooden candleholder with diameter of base approximately 6 inches
   2 wooden drapery rings, each approximately 2½ inches in outside diameter
   3 wooden paper-roll cores**, each approximately 2 to 2½ inches in outside diameter

wood putty

wood sealer

white glue

broomstick

acrylic paint, in color of your choice, for base coat

acrylic tube paints, in blue, green, red, and yellow

watercolor brushes, small

1 felt circle, 6¾ inches in diameter, in color of your choice

Tools

brown wrapping paper

pencil

ruler

carbon paper

masking tape

jigsaw *or* coping saw

file

sandpaper, medium and fine

center punch

drill with ⅛-inch bit

vise

brace

nails *or* C-clamps

scrap wood

U-gouge (optional)

Styrofoam sheet *or* cardboard-box lid

*A solid piece of wood, approximately 2 inches in outside diameter and 6 inches long, shaped to suitable contour with a lathe may be substituted for odds and ends. You may also use a portion of a turned newel post purchased from a lumberyard. If using either of these, you must drill a hole in one end to accommodate top section and another hole in bottom end to accommodate top of small wooden candleholder.

**Suitable cores come at the ends of rolls of brown wrapping paper, butcher paper, etc. If you have none on hand, ask any store that uses wrapping paper to save them for you.

Procedure

1. On brown wrapping paper, draw 1-inch grid and enlarge pattern, including all design lines and vertical dotted line extending down to top of wooden candleholder but excluding candlestick assembly at top (see "Helpful Hints"). To make other half of pattern, lay pattern over carbon paper, carbon side up, and trace over all lines, producing pattern in reverse on back of sheet. Cut out on outline and tape to plywood; mark around outline of entire top section and transfer vertical dotted line. Flip pattern over to complete other half of outline. Remove pattern and saw out wood on outline and vertical dotted line; smooth edges with file. Sand piece well with medium and then fine sandpaper, and fill surface and edges with wood putty. Sand again. Following pattern for wooden bead placement, center-punch each position and, with ⅛-inch bit, drill holes for dowels to a depth of 1⅛ inches.

2. Apply wood sealer to plywood.

3. To make candleholder stem, assemble

odds and ends of wood as described below or use shaped piece described in footnote. If you are using odds and ends, cut top off small wooden candleholder to reduce height to approximately 4½ inches and then glue to center of 6¾-inch plywood circle. Check to make sure that each odds-and-ends piece will fit over stem of small candleholder. If not, enlarge centers with file or drill. If it is necessary to enlarge gluing surfaces of pieces, rub over sandpaper laid flat on table. Then, following pattern for assembling if desired, glue pieces over small

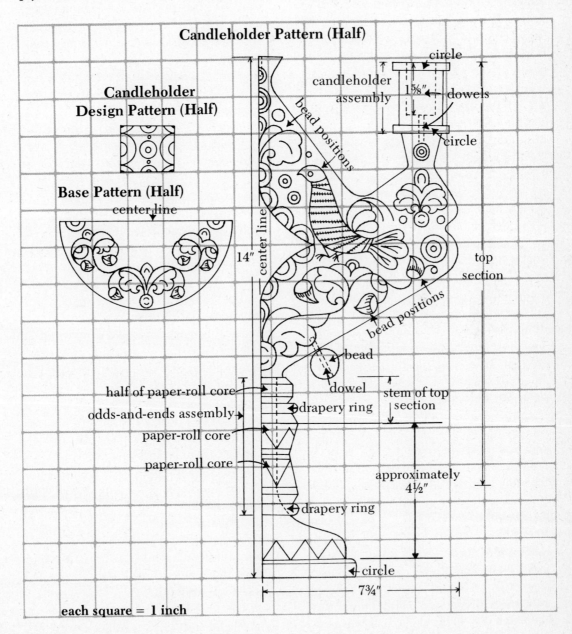

Candleholder Pattern (Half)

Candleholder Design Pattern (Half)

Base Pattern (Half)
center line

candleholder assembly

circle

1⅝" dowels

circle

bead positions

14"

center line

top section

bead positions

bead

dowel

half of paper-roll core

odds-and-ends assembly

paper-roll core

paper-roll core

drapery ring

stem of top section

approximately 4½"

drapery ring

circle

7¾"

each square = 1 inch

candleholder. As you glue on each piece, fill spaces between cores of pieces and candleholder with wood putty. Continue in this manner until all pieces have been assembled; allow glue to dry. Then insert stem of top section into center of odds-and-ends stem, resting it on top of wooden candleholder. From a length of broomstick or thick dowel, cut half-round wood shims to fill spaces within cores on both sides of top stem; glue shims in place inside stem, and remove top plywood section.

4. To make the three candleholders, cut 1½-inch-diameter dowel into three 2-inch lengths (see doweling procedure in woodworking section of "Helpful Hints"). Working one at a time, place in padded vise and, in the center, center-punch hole for bit of brace. Drill holes about 1⅝ inches deep and large enough in diameter to accommodate candles of your choice. Then, temporarily nail or clamp each of three of the 2-inch plywood circles to a piece of scrap wood, center-punch at centers, and, with brace, drill holes of the same diameter. Matching holes, glue one circle to each dowel. File and sand inside edges smooth and even. If you wish holes to have flat bottoms, use a U-gouge. Glue each of remaining three 2-inch circles to other end of 1½-inch dowels, center-punch the circle centers, and drill ⅛-inch-diameter holes, continuing holes through bottoms of dowels (see dotted lines on pattern). For each assembly, drill ⅛-inch-diameter hole into plywood base (part of top section). Cut ⅛-inch-diameter dowel into three 2-inch lengths. Apply glue to one end of each dowel and insert into hole of bottom circle piece; insert other dowel end into candleholder base to check fit; if too long, cut off as re-

quired. Then set all candleholders aside.

5. Apply base coat of paint to all parts of candleholder and allow to dry.

6. Place enlarged design pattern made in step 1 over top section of candleholder. With a sharp pencil, trace over all lines of the design, using enough pressure to dent the wood. (Do not use carbon paper, as it will rub off on the paint.) Turn pattern over and use reverse pattern to complete remaining half of design. Do not attempt to trace designs on rounded surfaces; see step 6 for this procedure. Remove pattern sheet and paint design, following color photograph on page 36 for color arrangement or using your own color scheme. Check base pattern for fit on your base, adjust if necessary, and transfer and paint in same manner.

7. To figure spacing for triangular motifs, circles, and half circles on rounded sections, cut a strip of paper long enough to fit exactly around the piece. Fold paper in half, thirds, quarters, fifths, etc., depending upon the desired size of motif and number of repeats. Wrap paper strip around the wood, and mark on wood at these folds. Using marks as guides, draw design elements—triangles or circles, etc.—freehand on wood. Following color scheme, paint. For ease in painting and drying project pieces that have dowel attachments, push dowel ends into a piece of Styrofoam or a cardboard-box lid.

8. From ⅛-inch-diameter dowel, cut ten 2-inch-long pieces. Glue into beads, with ends projecting slightly. After glue has dried, file and sand ends flush with surface of bead. Paint beads and push ends into Styrofoam while paint is drying. When dry, glue dowel ends in holes drilled in candleholder.

9. Glue three candleholder assemblies in place; glue felt circle to bottom of base.

Tablecloth

When one is a Lapp, he has the unusual distinction of living in a country that doesn't actually exist. In fact, the area that we call Lapland is made up of the northernmost sections of four other countries—Norway, Sweden, Finland, and Russia. This area is inhabited by the descendants of the most ancient nomadic tribe of Europe—the Lapps—who spend a good portion of the year following the migration of their reindeer herds. Spotting a group of Lapps wandering across the dazzling white snow would be easy, as their clothing is often of the brightest blue, bordered with brilliant red and yellow felt bands. Even the hats of the tribesmen are distinctive and colorful. One may feature four points representing each of the four winds, while another may be topped by an enormous red pom-pom.

Our tablecloth is made of Lapp blue felt and is bordered with an authentic design taken from a design on a tunic that belonged to a member of the Karesuando group.

46

Materials
felt:

2¼ yards, 72 inches wide, in blue

⅔ yard, 72 inches wide, in red

1 strip, 7 × 72 inches, in yellow

rickrack:

4 packages, in yellow

2 packages, in blue

soutache braid:

2 packages, in red

1 package, in yellow

thread, in blue, red, and yellow

Tools
straight pin, wire, and pencil, for
   compass

brown wrapping paper

scissors

straight pins

yardstick

Procedure
1. Assemble compass with pin, wire, and pencil; on brown wrapping paper, draw a half circle having a 36-inch radius. Cut out. This is half the tablecloth pattern.

2. Fold blue felt in half lengthwise. Matching straight edge of pattern to fabric fold, pin pattern to felt. Following pattern line, cut felt and unfold to make complete circle.

3. From leftover blue felt and following circular shape left by cutting out the circle, cut enough 3-inch-wide strips to piece together a facing for edge of tablecloth. (You will need a strip approximately 6⅓ yards long.) Set aside for now.

4. From remaining blue felt, cut enough ½-inch-wide strips to make a 6-yard-long band. Set aside.

5. Fold paper pattern into quarters and cut on folds so that you will have four pie-shaped sections, each of which is one-eighth the size of the tablecloth. You will use only one of these. From point of wedge, measure and mark off 27 inches and then 34 inches. With point of compass on point of wedge, construct an arc at the 27-inch mark. Repeat for 34-inch mark. Cut out this 7-inch arc strip. Using this as a pattern eight times, cut out a total of eight strips from red felt. Sew strips together with ¼-inch seams; press seams open.

6. Pin red band (made in step 5) to tablecloth so that bottom edge is about 3½ inches up from bottom edge of tablecloth. Machine-stitch at top and bottom edges.

7. On brown wrapping paper, draw yellow triangle band, as shown on red band pattern, making each triangle approximately 3 inches high and 2 inches wide at the base; cut out. Cut yellow felt so that it is 7 by 72 inches. Pin pattern along 72-inch length of yellow felt, matching straight edges. Trace around triangles. Move pattern over and continue to trace triangles for entire length of felt. Cut out. Place triangles on red band 1¼ inches up from bottom edge. Machine-stitch around points and bottom edge, overlapping joins very slightly. By hand, blindstitch joins together.

8. Pin ½-inch-wide blue felt band (made in step 4) to red band so that its top edge is about 1¼ inches down from top of red band. Machine-stitch top and bottom edges.

9. Following pattern, center yellow rickrack on red area above blue band and machine-stitch; center remaining yellow rickrack on red area below bottom edge of yellow triangles, and machine-stitch. Place blue rickrack on yellow triangle band so that it is ¼ inch up from lower yellow edge, and machine-stitch. Machine-stitch red soutache braid just

below blue rickrack. Machine-stitch yellow soutache ¼ inch below blue band. 10. Pin facing to right side of bottom edge of tablecloth; machine-stitch with a ¼-inch seam. Turn facing to the back, press, and hand-stitch top edge in place.

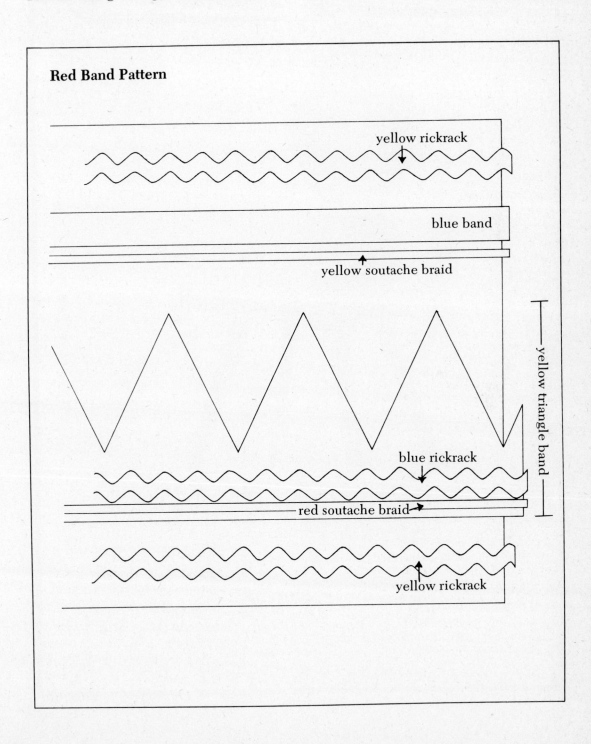

Red Band Pattern

yellow rickrack

blue band

yellow soutache braid

yellow triangle band

blue rickrack

red soutache braid

yellow rickrack

Wedding Chair

The house of the central European peasant was a riot of color. Brightly colored and beautifully embroidered handwoven hangings covered their walls, while embroidered bedcovers and pillow covers adorned their beds and decorated pottery filled the cupboards. When it came to painting, they often designed scenes for the walls that intermingled flowers with biblical and legendary scenes. The furniture was also decoratively painted and, oftentimes, carved, as well.

In Upper Austria, weddings called for a specially painted chair—the *Hochzeitsstuhl*, or "wedding chair." On the backs of these chairs were painted wedding scenes that might feature the bride and groom, the members of the wedding, or the musicians and dancers taking part in the festivities.

Our *Hochzeitsstuhl* is designed in the typical peasant-chair shape found throughout Central Europe and is painted in a wedding merrymakers' scene. To simplify construction of the chair, prefab legs have been used, attached by two-position top plates.

Materials
pine:
- 1 piece, ¾ × 11½ × 18 inches, for chair back
- 1 piece, 1¼ × 14¼ × 17 inches, for chair seat
- 1 set two-position top plates*, for leg attachments

16 flat-head wood screws, #5, each 1 inch long

4 round prefab legs, each approximately 19 inches long

wood primer

semigloss or flat enamel, in yellow

acrylic tube paints, in blue, white, black, green, and red

white glue

low-gloss plastic varnish

Tools
brown wrapping paper
pencil
ruler
scissors
masking tape
jigsaw
drill with any size bit
pattern file, half-round
sandpaper, medium and fine grades
scrap wood, for jig
C-clamps
chisel
screwdriver
paintbrush
watercolor brushes, small
varnish brush
lint-free cloth

*Made by Gerber, St. Louis, Missouri, and available inexpensively at most hardware stores. A kit that contains both the legs and double brackets is available through Legs Unlimited, Emco Specialties.

Procedure
1. On brown wrapping paper, draw 1-inch grid and enlarge patterns for chair back and seat (see "Helpful Hints"). Cut out patterns, tape to appropriate wood pieces, and draw over lines, pressing hard enough to indent wood. To complete other half of chair-seat pattern, flip pattern over. Saw out pieces on outlines. To cut out heart shape in chair back, drill a hole in the center of the outline. Remove blade from jigsaw, insert in hole, and reassemble saw around it. Cut out shape on outline, remove wood plug, and file cut edges. Sand all edges and surfaces with medium and then fine sandpaper.

2. Referring to chair-seat pattern, mark proper positions for groove and tab slots for chair back. Cut both tab slots, each 1¾ inches, all the way through wood so that sides of the slots are continuations of the groove sides. Then cut groove: As indicated by dotted lines on side view of chair (Figure 1), groove must be cut at an angle. If you don't have the necessary power tools, make a 98-degree jig and an 82-degree jig from scrap wood, as shown in Figure 2. Matching edge of jig to line for groove (as shown in Figure 2), clamp jigs to chair seat (see clamping section in woodworking section of "Helpful Hints"). Keeping flat side of chisel held against the jig, cut groove. Finished groove should measure ¾ inch wide by ¾ inch deep by 10 inches long. Fit chair back into groove and tab slots and make any necessary adjustments. Remove chair back and set aside.

3. To mark positions for top plates, first construct diagonals shown on chair-seat pattern: On pattern, measure 6¼ inches up from front edge and mark off on center line. Fold pattern at this point, matching top portion of center line with bottom (fold 1 on pattern). Open pattern up and align center line of front portion of seat with the fold you have just made; crease

Figure 1

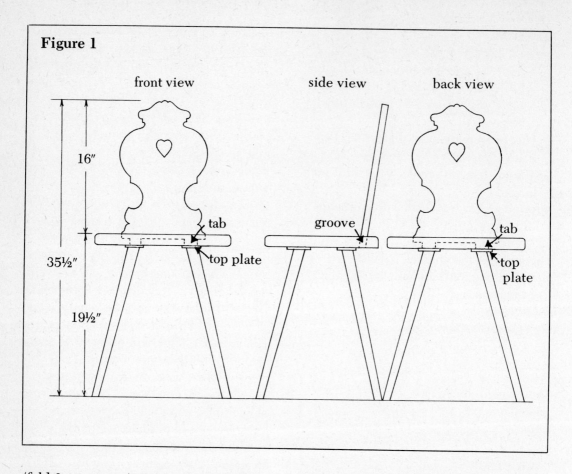

front view   side view   back view

16"

35½"

19½"

tab

top plate

groove

tab

top plate

(fold 2 on pattern). Repeat for back diagonal by aligning center line of back portion of seat with fold 1. Then, with pencil, mark along folds of pattern on underside of chair seat. For each front leg, place length of top plate alongside front diagonal, with end 2⅜ inches in from intersection of diagonals and with

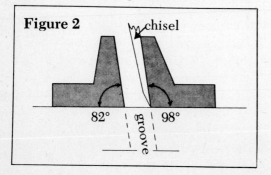

Figure 2

chisel

82°   98°

groove

"angle" portion of plate slanting toward the front edge. Screw in place. For each back leg, center plate *over* diagonal, with end 3 inches in from intersection of diagonals and with "angle" portion slanting toward the back edge. Screw in place. Then screw legs into holes in plates.

4. Apply wood primer to entire chair except groove and tabs. After primer coat has dried, paint chair with yellow paint; again, do not paint groove and tabs.

5. On brown wrapping paper, draw 1-inch grid and enlarge chair-back design (see "Helpful Hints"). Transfer design by taping pattern to chair back and tracing over lines with a pencil, using enough pressure to indent the surface of the wood. (Do not use carbon as it will

Chair-back Pattern

each square = 1 inch

cutout

tab

tab

rub off on the paint.) Remove pattern sheet and, if necessary, go over pattern lines lightly with a sharp pencil. Paint in design, using acrylic paints and water-color brushes and following photograph on page 36 for color arrangement. When paint is dry, glue the chair back into place. 6. Finish chair with two coats of varnish. With finishing paper, sand very lightly between coats, sanding just enough to give finish a "tooth" to hold the next coat. Dust with lint-free cloth between coats.

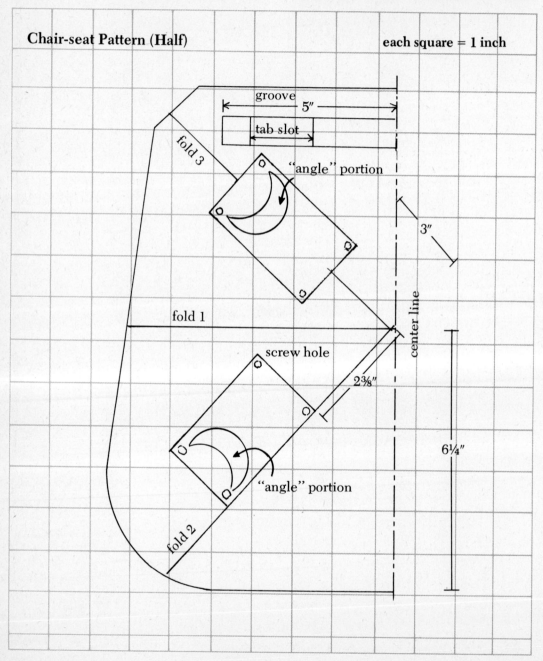

Chair-seat Pattern (Half)   **each square = 1 inch**

groove

5"

tab slot

fold 3

"angle" portion

3"

fold 1

center line

screw hole

2⅜"

"angle" portion

6¼"

fold 2

Romania

Crockery Cupboard

A crockery cupboard was a necessary item in every European peasant home. Although the geometric designs on our cupboard are typically Romanian, they somehow convey a "today" feeling, as well. To make this Romanian design, we will use an ancient—in fact, prehistoric—method of decoration. Called by many different names—pyrographing, *brandmalerei*, poker painting, and wood burning—it is a process of burning a design into wood with a piece of heated metal, such as a poker. Although poker painting is often thought of as being a craft practiced mainly by herdsmen, examples of it are found on household items throughout the world.

We can simplify the process of poker painting by using an electric wood-burning tool. Wood stain, varnish, and acrylic paints provide the Romanian light-on-dark effect.

Materials

clear pine:

  2 pieces, each ¾ × 7½ × 39 inches, for
    sides

  3 pieces, each ¾ × 7½ × 26 inches, for
    shelves and base

  2 pieces, each ¾ × 2½ × 27½ inches,
    for plate rails

  1 piece, ¾ × 5½ × 22 inches, for center
    door divider

  2 pieces, each ¾ × 11 × 22 inches, for
    doors

white glue

finishing nails

2 lengths piano hinge, each 22 inches
  long, with screws

satin-finish plastic varnish

wood stain, nonbleeding, dark

acrylic tube paints, in white and
  necessary colors to mix to natural wood
  shade

wood putty, to match natural wood

2 "Tutch" latches*, for door catches

Tools

hammer
nailset
file
screwdriver
brown wrapping paper
pencil
ruler
compass
wood-burning tool
scrap wood (optional)
varnish brush
watercolor brush, small
sandpaper, finishing grade
lint-free cloth

---

*"Tutch" latches, which are made by National
Hardware Co., and are available at some hardwares
and builders' hardware-supply houses, enable
doors to be opened or closed with a slight push.

Procedure

1. Following pattern, glue and nail base and shelves of cabinet to sides. Use nail set to drive nails slightly below wood surface. Wipe off excess glue with damp cloth. (Horizontal dotted lines on pattern indicate proper placement of base and shelves.)

2. Position plate rails and center door divider. Nail temporarily to check fit.

3. File cut ends of piano hinge smooth. Fit doors and set hinges, putting a hinge screw in every other hole.

4. Remove plate rails, divider, and doors of cabinet. On brown wrapping paper, draw 1-inch grid and enlarge design patterns (see "Helpful Hints"). To transfer pattern to wood, measure radius of each circle and arc on pattern. Set compass appropriate for each, and draw on wood pieces. Flowers can be transferred by constructing arcs with compass.

5. Heat wood-burning tool. (If you have never done wood burning before, try a few lines and curves on scrap wood before starting project.) Burn in all lines on pattern except for those that separate dark from light areas.

6. Apply plastic varnish on all areas designated on pattern as *light*. Paint carefully up to the lines and allow adequate drying time.

7. Test stain on scrap wood before applying to cabinet to become familiar with the way in which stain flows from brush and to determine time required to develop to the shade you want. Using varnish brush, apply stain carefully onto areas designated on pattern as *dark*. Allow drying time. Apply a second coat if necessary. Stain entire frame of cabinet.

8. Apply plastic varnish to entire cabinet.

9. Mix acrylics to match unstained wood as closely as possible. With this shade,

use watercolor brush to paint burned lines within dark areas. Remove any excess paint with a damp cloth, and allow paint to dry.

10. Reassemble cabinet: Using a screw in each hole, hinge doors to cabinet. Set nails slightly below wood surface with nailset. Fill nail holes with wood putty, and touch up with stain where necessary.

11. Apply varnish to entire cabinet. When completely dry, sand lightly with finishing paper and dust carefully with lint-free cloth. Apply a final coat of varnish.

12. Install "Tutch" latches, according to manufacturer's directions on the package.

Pattern   **each square = 1 inch**

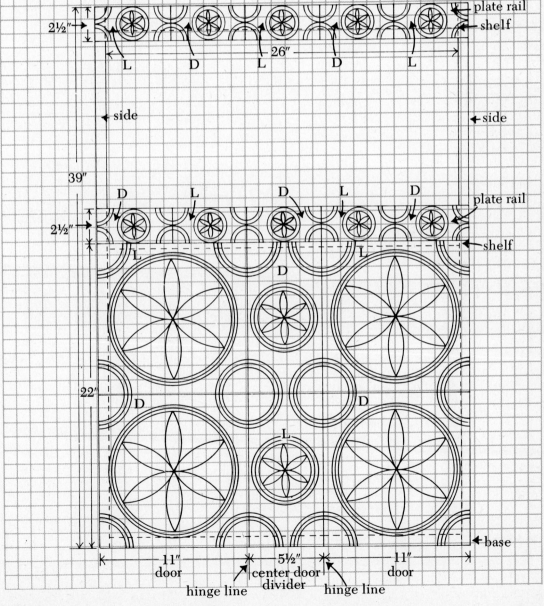

Color Code: D = dark L = light

Metal-tooled Cabinet

The Mexican tradition of tinworking is actually a result of the Spanish influence. Because of the extreme difficulty experienced by the Indians in mining and refining tin in preconquest Mexico, tin was used only for currency. When the Spaniards arrived and banned the Indian use of precious metals, the Indians were forced to substitute tin in their decorative handiwork.

Nowadays, commercially produced tin is used for making boxes, mirrors, trays, and many other items. Mexican artisans, however, often utilize discarded tin cans. Sometimes the manufacturer's lithographed design forms an integral part of the overall design for the piece. Much of the tin design work of Mexico is characterized by curliques, scallops, helixes, and undulating borders highly reminiscent of the baroque style that was introduced by the Spaniards many years ago.

Our cabinet design motif and shape were taken from a colonial tin cabinet seen in Tlaquepaque, a town just outside of Guadalajara. We have substituted tooling aluminum for tin, however, since it is softer and therefore allows for more freedom in design work.

Materials
pine:
    4 pieces, each ¾ × 7¾ × 24½ inches,
      for sides, top, and bottom
    1 piece, ¾ × 6¾ × 23 inches, for shelf
    2 pieces, each ¾ × 11¼ × 24⅜ inches,
      for doors
    1 piece, ¾ × 10½ × 30 inches, for
      decorative top
    1 piece plywood *or* hardboard, ¼ ×
      24½ × 26 inches, for back
tooling aluminum, 36 gauge:
    4 pieces, each 10 × 27 inches, for sides,
      top, and bottom
    2 pieces, each 12 × 25 inches, for doors
    1 piece, 12 × 33 inches, for decorative
      top
    4 pieces, each 1 × 12 inches, for top
      and bottom door edges
    4 pieces, each 1 × 25 inches, for side
      door edges
    2 pieces, each 1 × 25 inches, for
      decorative top edges
white glue
finishing nails in two sizes: 1 inch and
  1¾ inches long
2 pairs butt hinges, each ¾ × 1½ inches
flat enamel paint, in black
contact cement
Sculptamold
2 corner braces, each with 1½-inch legs,
  for attaching decorative top
magnetic door catches
2 wooden knobs, small
2 screw eyes
wire, for hanging
fast-drying spray paint for metal, in black
  (optional)
kitchen appliance wax

Tools
hammer
ruler
screwdriver
sandpaper, medium and fine grades
paintbrush
small, flat stick, for spreading cement
soft cloth
single-edged razor blade
wooden modeling tools
newspaper
masking tape
brown wrapping paper
pencil
ruler
carbon paper
tracing wheel, leather tool, stylus, *or* any
  other tool suitable to stipple
  background

Procedure
1. On brown wrapping paper, enlarge pattern for decorative top piece (see "Helpful Hints"); cut out. Tape to appropriate wood piece, outline, and saw out. Then assemble cabinet: Following assembly diagram, butt top and bottom to sides; attach with white glue and 1¾-inch finishing nails. Attach back to cabinet frame with 1-inch finishing nails. Nail and glue in shelf, flush with back, 13 inches up from bottom.

2. Inset hinges on doors and cabinet so that they are flush (read about mortising in woodworking section of "Helpful Hints"). Try doors for fit; then remove.

3. With medium and then fine sandpaper, sand inside of cabinet and doors; paint inside with black flat enamel.

4. Starting with top, bottom, and sides and working on one piece at a time, use small, flat stick to spread contact cement over aluminum sheets; line up edges of sheets with back edge of cabinet. Smooth down aluminum with hands and soft cloth. Fold over front edge and cement in place. Mark corners for mitering, cut miters, and trim off any excess aluminum

58

overhanging front edge with single-edged razor blade. Rub down edges well with modeling tool to ensure good bond.

5. Tape a pad of newspapers to a drawing board or tabletop. On brown wrapping paper, draw 1-inch grid and enlarge design patterns (see "Helpful Hints"); cut out. Place one of aluminum panels on newspaper-covered surface; center pattern over it and tape down two edges. Slide carbon paper, face up, between metal and pattern (to make reverse pattern on back of paper for other door panel) and tape down remaining two edges of pattern. Trace over design lines with soft, blunt pencil. Turn metal over to make sure that all details have been marked. Remove pattern and carbon.

6. Refer to metal-tooling instructions in "Helpful Hints." With modeling tool, begin modeling on the back side. Following photograph, push out areas to be raised. Occasionally, turn work face up on smooth, hard surface and, working around the outside of the outlines, flatten the background areas. Remember that aluminum is soft enough to push sharp edges through and will scratch easily. Handle with a reasonable amount of care.

7. When entire pattern has been completed, work the background. Turn work right side up on hard smooth surface and stipple all background areas, using a tracing wheel, leather tool, or stylus.

8. Turn tooled aluminum face down. Mix Sculptamold according to manufacturer's directions. Pour into all depressions and smooth off with a straight edge so that it is flush with the background. Let dry.

9. Cement panel to door. Bend excess metal over edges; with razor blade, cut out spaces for hinges, and cement metal to sides. Pinch corners together and cut off excess. Cement on strips to cover door edges. Burnish all edges with wooden

modeling tool to ensure good glue bond.

10. Repeat steps 5 through 9 for second door. Remember to reverse the pattern so that the two birds will be facing each other. To do this, turn pattern over and work from back side.

11. Follow same procedure for decorative top piece.

12. Screw corner braces to back of decorative top; slide onto cabinet flush with front. Screw braces to top of cabinet.

Design Pattern (Half)

each square = 1 inch

Assembly Diagram

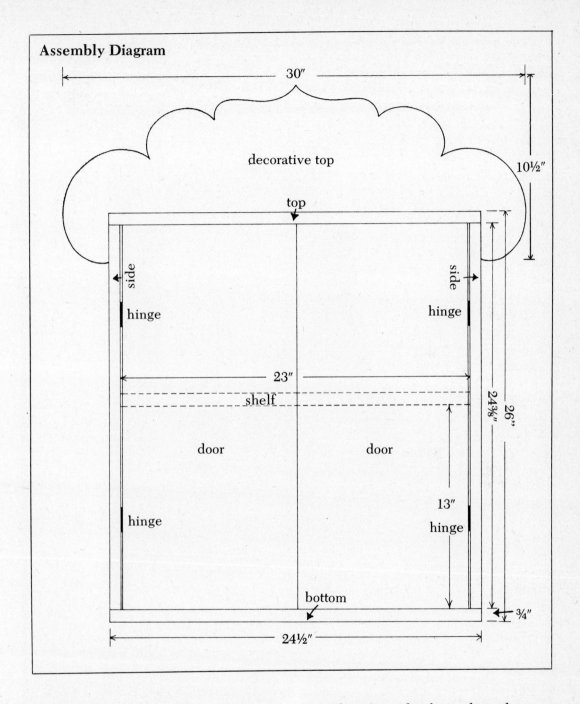

13. With screws, hinge doors to cabinet. Position magnetic catches under shelf and inside doors in appropriate position. Attach knobs to doors; attach screw eyes and wire to cabinet back, for hanging.

14. If antique finish is desired, spray door panels with fast-drying black paint, wipe off high spots, and allow paint to dry. Polish with a soft cloth. For even higher shine, apply kitchen appliance wax.

Chip-carved Shelf

Chip carving has been practiced by people in all parts of the world. As evidence of the wide distribution of this technique, examples from all European countries, as well as from Egypt and China, can be found in most museums. Probably the reason for chip carving's being one of the oldest and most widespread crafts in the world is that the only tool needed to accomplish even the most intricate designs is a carving knife.

Chip-carving designs are geometric in form. The design is first blocked out in geometric shapes, which are then divided into sloping triangular areas to form an interesting three-dimensional arrangement.

To chip-carve successfully, use dry, well-seasoned wood that has a fine grain. If this is your first attempt, it would be a good idea to practice first on a piece of scrap wood.

Our chip-carved kitchen shelf will serve nicely for holding your cookbooks and your recipes. With a little knowledge of woodworking, you can complete this shelf easily.

Materials

pine:

1 piece, ¾ × 11¼ × 19¾ inches, for
back

1 piece, ¾ × 8½ × 12¾ inches, for
shelf

2 pieces, each ¾ × 9¼ × 15½ inches,
for sides

1 piece, ¾ × 8½ × 11¼ inches, for
bottom

1 piece, ¾ × 4 × 11¼ inches, for
drawer front (outside)

1 knob, 1½ inches in diameter × ½
inch

plywood:

2 pieces, each ¼ × 3½ × 7⅛ inches, for
drawer sides

1 piece, ¼ × 3¾ × 11 inches, for
drawer back

1 piece, ¼ × 2½ × 7⅛ inches, for
divider

1 piece, ¼ × 3½ × 10½ inches, for
drawer front (inside)

1 piece, ¼ × 11 × 7⅛ inches, for
drawer bottom

1 wooden bead, ½ inch in diameter

63½ inches dowel, ¼ inch in diameter,
for pegs and for knob dowel

white glue

brads, each 1 inch long

4 flat-head wood screws, #7, each ¾ inch
long

low-gloss plastic varnish

Tools

brown wrapping paper
pencil
ruler
scissors
masking tape
jigsaw
pattern file, half-round
sandpaper, medium and fine grades
carbon paper
compass
craft knife, stencil knife, pen knife, *or*
chip-carving knives (an outlining knife
and a slicing knife)
center punch
C-clamps *or* nails
hammer
drill with ⅛- and ¼-inch bits
wooden mallet
hacksaw blade, fine-toothed
2 narrow wood strips (¼-inch plywood,
etc.)
scrap wood, for cushion blocks
screwdriver
vise
varnish brush
lint-free cloth

Procedure

1. On brown wrapping paper, draw 1-inch grid and enlarge pattern pieces for back, shelf, and sides (see "Helpful Hints"); cut out patterns.

2. With masking tape, tape patterns to wood, mark outlines, and saw out. Remove saw marks with pattern file. Then sand all pieces with medium and then fine sandpaper.

3. On brown wrapping paper, draw 1-inch grid and enlarge design patterns (see "Helpful Hints"); cut out.

4. Tape patterns on wood and transfer with carbon paper and pencil, or draw pattern directly on wood using a compass and a ruler.

5. Before you begin carving, study design pattern and note that each area is a triangle or group of triangles that fits into a square, circle, or rectangle. The triangle shape may even be curved to fit a given area. To make well-defined cuts, be sure to keep your knife very sharp. For each triangle pattern, make cuts along design outlines according to one or both of the

Patterns

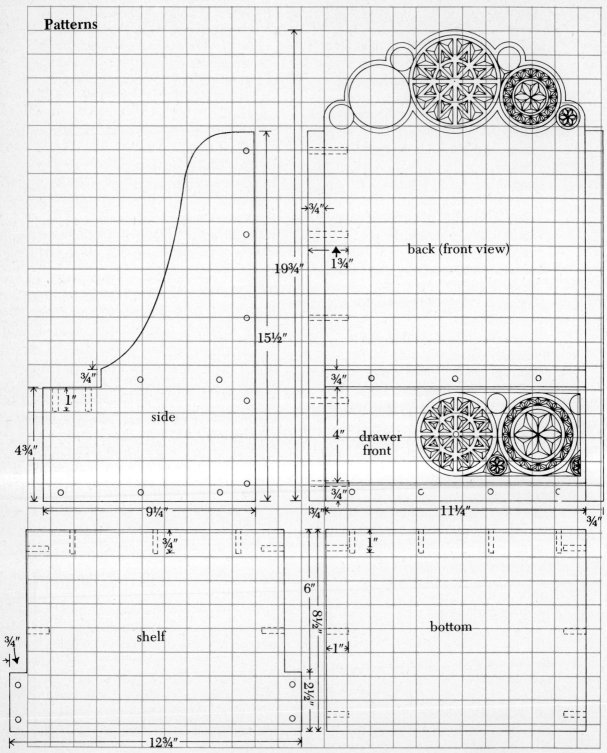

back (front view)

19¾"

¾"

1¾"

15½"

side

¾"

1"

4¾"

drawer
front

4"

¾"

9¼"

¾"

11¼"

¾"

¾"

1"

6"

shelf

8½"

bottom

¾"

1"

2½"

12¾"

each square = 1 inch

following methods:

The single cut (Figure 1):

a. With thumb on top of handle and holding knife vertical to wood, press point of blade in at A to a depth of ⅛ inch. This will be the deepest point of the cut. Then cut line AB, pulling the blade toward you and decreasing the depth of the cut as you approach B (indicated by dotted lines in Figure 1).

b. Repeat to cut line AC.

c. To slice away chip between lines AB and AC, hold knife at an angle on line BC and slope it toward A.

Controlling the blade with the index finger of the left hand, pull blade slowly across triangle from base to apex. When finished, the cut will have a sloped triangular bottom with vertical sides. The deepest point of cut will be at A and will slope upward to base line BC. If you have cut correctly, a triangular, wedge-shaped piece of wood will have been removed. If necessary, repeat cuts. Do not try to pry out chip.

The double cut (Figure 2):

a. With the base of the triangle facing toward you, hold knife vertical to

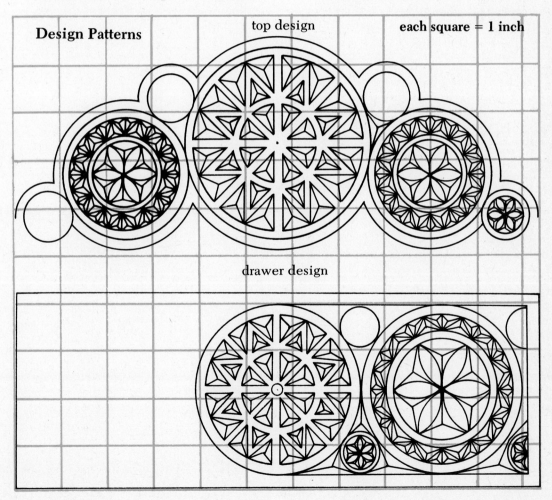

Design Patterns top design **each square = 1 inch**

drawer design

wood at point D. Push point of knife in to a depth of about ⅛ inch and cut to B, gradually decreasing the depth of the cut as you approach.

b. Make a similar cut from D to C. Next, push point of knife in at D and slope cut up to A.

c. Turn work around so that apex A is facing toward you. Hold knife at angle on line BA and, keeping knife point aligned with D, cut along BA, sloping cut downward toward D, so as to remove half of chip BDA. Follow same procedure to remove other half of chip BDA, or make as many cuts as are necessary to make a clean cut.

d. Return work to original position, and remove chip CDA in the same manner. If you wish to remove chip BDC in some areas of your design, follow same steps.

6. From ¼-inch doweling, cut and prepare thirty-one dowels, each 2 inches long (refer to doweling in woodworking section of "Helpful Hints"). Mark positions for dowels on wood pieces (shown on pattern by small circles). Use center punch to dent center of each dowel location, to take drill bit.

7. Join shelf parts together by means of

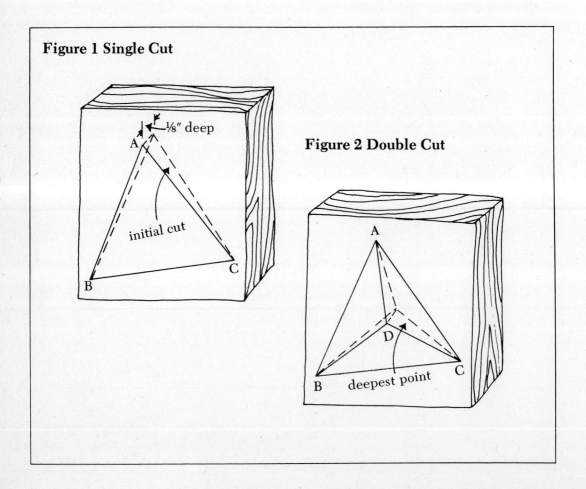

Figure 1 Single Cut

⅛" deep

initial cut

Figure 2 Double Cut

deepest point

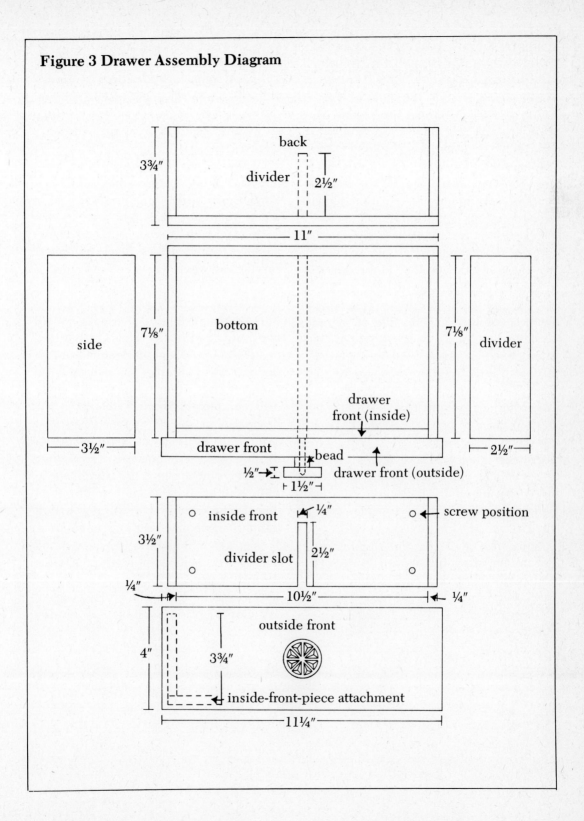

Figure 3 Drawer Assembly Diagram

temporary nailing or clamping (see woodworking section in "Helpful Hints"), making certain that all dowel marks are on the outside of the pieces. Put a piece of masking tape around ¼-inch drill bit, 1¾ inches up from the point. Drill all dowel holes, allowing the bit to penetrate the wood as far as the masking tape. Clear holes of bits of wood.

8. Glue and, using wooden mallet, dowel pieces together in this order: back to bottom, sides to back and bottom, then shelf to sides and bottom. With hacksaw blade, cut off projecting dowel ends smooth with surface and finish with pattern file.

9. Refer to Figure 3 for drawer assembly. Draw center line on both sides of bottom piece to show placement of divider. On one side of the bottom, temporarily tack a narrow strip of wood on each side of the line. These strips will hold divider in place during assembly. Cut slot on inside of front piece to hold divider and insert divider to check for fit.

10. Spread glue on those edges of the sides, bottom, and inside front piece that are to be joined and then assemble by nailing in brads.

11. To set in divider, apply glue to bottom edge and slot. Put divider between temporary strips and slip divider end into slot so that end of divider is flush with outer face of front piece. Holding divider in place, turn drawer upside down. Resting top edge of divider

on a piece of blocking wood, nail along center line on bottom.

12. Apply glue to back edges of drawer that will join with drawer back, and nail back in place. Remove temporary nailing strips and wipe off excess glue with a damp cloth.

13. To join drawer to drawer front, mark holes for screws, center-punch, and, with ⅛-inch bit, drill through inside front piece. Position inside front piece on the back of outside front piece and clamp together, using cushion blocks to protect carving and wood. Then screw together.

14. Clamp bead in vise and enlarge hole with ¼-inch drill bit. To keep vise jaws from marring bead, pad jaws with cloth or corrugated cardboard. Then drill ¼-inch hole ¾ inch deep at center front of drawer. Drill another ¼-inch hole in center back of knob, being careful not to drill completely through the knob. As described in step 7, use masking tape around drill bit as a depth gauge for drilling holes. File one end of remaining dowel (1½ inches long) to a cone shape to fit hole in knob. Glue knob and bead on dowel. The end of the dowel that will fit into the drawer should be a scant ¾ inch. If necessary, cut off dowel end and round off edges on sandpaper or with file. Glue dowel in place.

15. Give completed shelf two coats of low-gloss varnish, sanding and dusting after first coat with lint-free cloth.

Alban Hills, Italy

Miss Frescatti, Barometer

This winsome Miss from Frescatti, Italy, is a real cookie made of dough. This particular cookie is inedible, though, since it is made from a mixture of bread dough, salt, and bits of straw. This dough is then molded—usually into the shape of a woman wearing a long dress—baked, wrapped in cellophane, and sold with a tag plastered on the apron that announces "Miss Frescatti." Often the cookie has also been decorated with a feather headdress, peppercorn eyes and buttons, and a red-pepper mouth.

This delightful doll serves a double purpose—she blesses the vineyards in spring and gives thanks for the harvest in fall. During the Easter season and autumn, she is a popular item in local stores. Miss Frescatti's purpose is more than just decorative, however. She also acts as a barometer. When the air becomes moist, the salt softens the dough, indicating rain. In dry weather, the salt loses its moisture and the dough hardens.

68

Materials

2 cups flour
½ cup salt
¾ cup water
bits of straw
peppercorns (optional)
ribbon *or* **gummed-tape picture hanger**

Tools

1 piece corrugated cardboard, about 10 ×
** 14 inches**
aluminum foil, enough to cover
** cardboard**
rolling pin *or* **large bottle with rounded**
** sides**
table knife
orangewood stick *or* **pencil**

Procedure

1. With aluminum foil, cover corrugated cardboard to serve as baking pan.

2. Prepare dough by mixing flour, salt, water, and straw bits. Knead very well.

3. On a floured surface, roll out dough to a ⅜-inch thickness, using either a rolling pin or a large bottle. Cut cookie to desired shape with table knife, and place on aluminum-covered cardboard. For hair, skirt, belt, and details, roll pieces of dough between palms or on table, forming rounded rope shapes. For cheeks, nose, and bosom, roll small pieces of dough between palms to form balls. With water, dampen areas on cookie where details are to be added and press on dough shapes. To make indentations in dough, use an orangewood stick or a pencil point. If you wish to add peppercorns or other decorative material, press them into dough before baking.

4. Bake in 300-degree oven until dough is lightly tanned.

5. Remove cookie from oven and let cool. To hang cookie, tie a ribbon around her neck or attach picture hanger to the back.

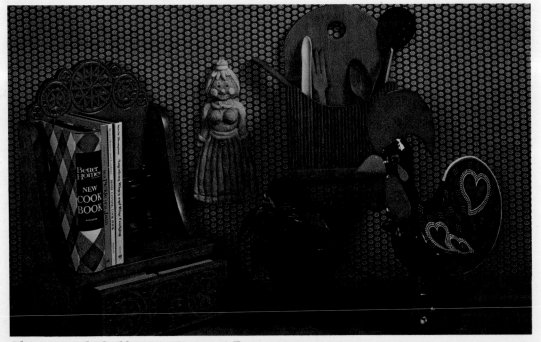

Chip-carved Shelf, Miss Frescatti Barometer,
Spoon Holder, and Good-Luck Rooster

Scotland

Spoon Holder

The arts and crafts of Scotland tend to be utilitarian, showing skill in fabrication rather than in ornamentation. Perhaps this is partially because of the fact that timber has been in short supply since the late seventeenth century. In any event, the contribution of the tartans and kilts alone have set the Scots apart from other peoples.

Our utility spoon box hails from an open-hearth cottage. It lives up to tradition in that it is functional and roomy enough to hold all your wooden tools. The simple trim on the holder front is easily made by gluing dowels side by side. Since your wooden tools will be displayed in such an attractive holder, you might wish to carve the tool handles.

Materials

pine:

    1 piece, ¾ × 9¼ × 14 inches, for back

    1 piece, ¾ × 9¼ × 7 inches, for front

    1 piece, ¾ × 9¼ × 4½ inches, for
      bottom

    2 pieces, each ¾ × 3½ × 7¾ inches, for
      sides

22 feet dowel, ¼ inch in diameter,
    for front decoration and pegs

white glue

low-gloss plastic varnish

Tools

brown wrapping paper

pencil

ruler

scissors

masking tape

jigsaw (optional)

coping saw

pattern file, half-round

sandpaper, medium and fine grades

drill

drill bit, ¼ inch in diameter

wooden mallet

4 pieces scrap wood, each approximately
    9 inches long, for cushion blocks

4 C-clamps

varnish brush

lint-free cloth

Procedure

1. On brown wrapping paper, draw 1-inch grid and enlarge pattern pieces (see "Helpful Hints"); cut out patterns.

2. With masking tape, tape patterns to appropriate wood pieces, outline, and, with jigsaw or coping saw, saw out wood parts. Also cut out 1½-inch-diameter hole on back of box for hanging finished piece. To do this, drill hole inside circle large enough to accommodate blade of jigsaw or coping saw. Remove blade from saw, insert into hole, and reassemble saw around blade. Cut around circle outline. Remove saw and wood plug, smooth opening with file, and sand with medium and then fine sandpaper wrapped around a length of large-diameter dowel, broomstick, etc. With medium and then fine sandpaper, sand all wood pieces smooth.

3. Cut four 1½-inch lengths of dowels for attaching box front; cut fourteen 2-inch lengths for attaching remaining pieces. Prepare dowels as described in doweling procedure in woodworking section of "Helpful Hints." Mark dowel hole placements (see pattern) and drill about 2 inches deep. Then glue and dowel bottom to back, and side pieces to back and bottom, using wooden mallet for driving dowels. Wipe off excess glue with a damp cloth. Drill holes needed to attach front to sides, but do not dowel together yet.

4. With ruler, mark vertical line down center of box front. Cover the four dowel holes on front face for attaching front to sides with small pieces of masking tape to keep glue out. Cut first dowel to approximately 5 inches and, aligning it with bottom edge, glue on center line. Working toward outer edge of front piece, cut each remaining dowel about ⅛ inch longer than the preceding one and glue in place, keeping bottom ends of dowels even with bottom edge of front piece. Repeat process, working from center line out to other edge.

5. Using cushion blocks to avoid marring wood and to distribute pressure evenly, clamp dowels in place: Put two cushion blocks on top of dowels (Figure 1). Position C-clamp on end of top block, slip bottom block in place underneath, and tighten clamp. Attach C-clamp at other end of same block. Repeat this procedure

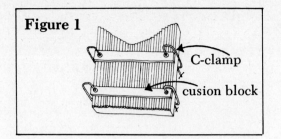

Figure 1

C-clamp

cusion block

for other two cushion blocks. Allow glue to dry completely.

6. Remove clamps and use coping saw to saw off all projecting dowel ends flush with the top curve. Sand edges lightly.

7. Glue and insert dowels into side holes (protruding dowel tips should measure ¾ inch). Join front piece to sides, pushing dowel ends into holes on front. Place protective board over front and tap board with mallet to force joint tightly together. Drill holes in front and bottom for dowels and glue dowels in place.

8. With medium and then fine sandpaper, sand assembled box; dust with lint-free cloth. Finish with two coats low-gloss varnish, sanding and dusting after the first coat with a lint-free cloth.

Patterns

each square = 1 inch

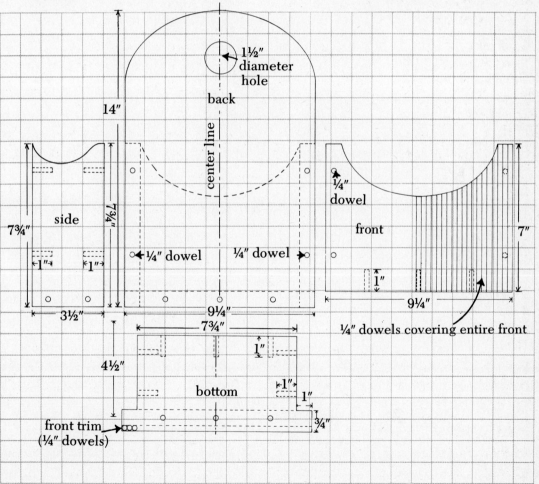

Portugal

Good-Luck Rooster

Once upon a time in Portugal in the region called Barcelos, an accused murderer was saved from the gallows by a rooster. It seems the judge had said that if a particular cooked rooster were to crow, it would prove the man's innocence. Sure enough, as the noose was being prepared, the rooster stood up on its plate and crowed. As you can imagine, the rooster was then proclaimed to be a good-luck charm, and today no Portuguese home is complete without a brightly painted ceramic likeness. The black roosters bring everyday good luck, and the white ones are offered as good-luck wedding gifts.

Portuguese peasants have been making decorative sculpture since the Middle Ages. Working first with stone and then with clay, they have achieved a distinctive and colorful style. The earliest pieces of Portuguese folk sculpture were crib figures, which were often modeled after the sculptor's friends and neighbors. The provinces of Barcelos, Goia, and Estremoz were centers for folk sculpture.

Today, statuettes are molded into figures of musicians, hens and chicks, demons, donkeys, and many others. However, the only figure more popular than the rooster is that of the Madonna. All are colored brilliantly with oil paints or lacquer.

Our rooster is made of Styrofoam, cardboard, and a fast-frying papier-mâché pulp.

Materials

1 cardboard cone, with wide end approximately 2½ inches in diameter, 7 inches long
½ Styrofoam ball, 5 inches in diameter
1 Styrofoam ball, 5 inches in diameter
1 Styrofoam egg, 3 inches in diameter
1 cardboard tube, 2 inches in diameter, 4 inches long
masking tape
straight pins
4 Popsicle sticks
Sculptamold
gesso
acrylic tube paints, in black, red, yellow, blue, and white; or colors of your choice
high-gloss plastic spray

Tools

craft knife
ruler
serrated-edge knife
brown wrapping paper
pencil
scissors
2 pieces lightweight cardboard, each 12 × 18 inches; *or* scrap pieces, large enough to accommodate patterns (see step 7)
spoon
table knife
sandpaper, fine grade
watercolor brushes, small and medium

Procedure

1. With craft knife, cut top 3 inches off cardboard cone and set this top aside.
2. Push wide end of cone into rounded portion of halved Styrofoam ball, forming base and legs.
3. Push whole ball onto narrow end of cone for body. With serrated-edge knife, slice away sides of body to make flat areas for attachment of wings (Figure 1).
4. Cut top of cardboard cone (from step 1) to 2 inches and push into egg to form head and beak (Figure 2).
5. To form neck, push one end of cardboard tube into egg and push the other end into the Styrofoam body (Figure 2).

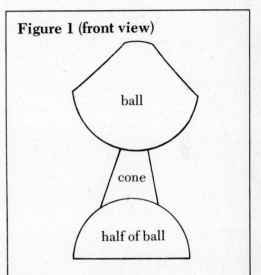

Figure 1 (front view)

ball

cone

half of ball

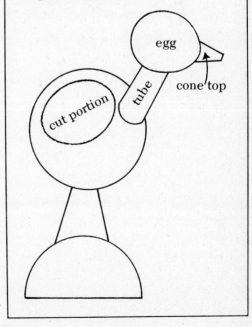

Figure 2 (side view)

egg

cone top

tube

cut portion

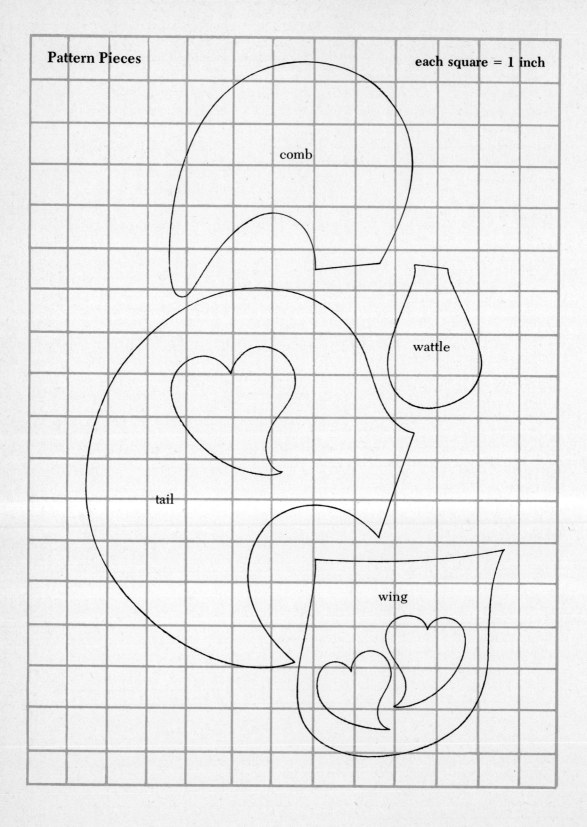

Pattern Pieces

each square = 1 inch

comb

wattle

tail

wing

6. On brown wrapping paper, draw 1-inch grid and enlarge pattern pieces (see "Helpful Hints"). Cut out pieces.

7. Place patterns on lightweight cardboard; for tail, wings, and comb, draw around each *twice* and cut out. For wattles, draw around pattern *four* times and cut out.

8. With masking tape, tape two tail pieces together around top and underneath sides, but leave front edges untaped. Pin front edges of tail to sides of body and then tape securely in place with masking tape (Figure 3).

9. Tape two wattle pieces together and then the other two. Tape one Popsicle stick to flat portion of each wattle, and attach one wattle to each side of head by pushing stick into Styrofoam (Figure 3).

10. Tape all edges of comb together. Cut slit in center of head, and push flat portion of comb into head just above beak (Figure 3).

11. Mix a batch of Sculptamold as directed on package, and apply over entire bird. Use spoon and blade of table knife to smooth.

12. Pin flat portions of wings to body; push one Popsicle stick into body under each wing, and tape stick to underside of wing. This gives support to wing and holds it away from body (Figure 4).

13. Coat wings with Sculptamold. Allow to dry, and add more Sculptamold if necessary. When figure is completely dry, sand all surfaces with fine sandpaper.

14. Apply two coats of gesso, allowing drying time between coats.

15. Paint rooster with acrylic paints. You may follow color scheme shown in color photograph or paint as you wish.

16. Spray with two coats plastic spray, allowing ample drying time between coats.

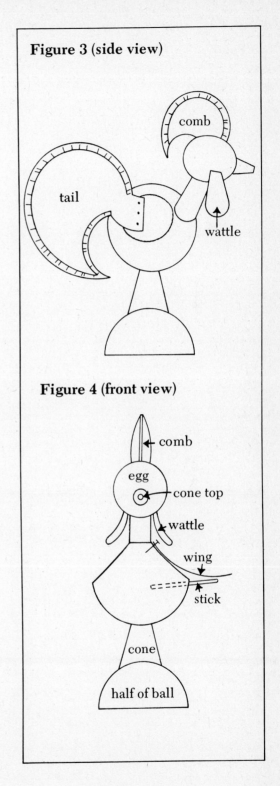

Figure 3 (side view)

Figure 4 (front view)

Chapter 3

Bedroom

Romania

Dowry Chest

Romania claims artistic traditions thousands of years old, and some ancient designs are visible even today in her folk art. Still popular with contemporary craftsmen is a primitive wood-decorating style called *Ritz-Technik*. This craft involves the scoring or incising of designs on a wood surface. While this simple technique is characteristic of all Romanian wood carving, the truly distinctive trademark of Romanian work lies in the geometric quality of their designs. Patterns are composed of circles, semicircles, spirals, and crosses that are inventively combined in a symmetrical fashion. We find these designs as vigorous and as eye-catching as they were when first carved into wood.

Every Romanian peasant girl kept a dowry chest that was carved in these traditional patterns. The following project is based on one of these patterns, but the geometric figures on this chest are curious. Although they are identical, the figure could be construed as being either a man in trousers or a woman in a long skirt and coat. Perhaps the two figures were meant to signify the happily married couple. The open areas on top of the chest provide a place in which to carve the names of the bride and groom and their wedding date. All the carving on this chest is done simply by turning a traced line into a carved line of very shallow depth. For this task, all you will need is a sharp carving knife.

Materials

clear-grade pine or clear shelving lumber
(free of knots):
  1 piece, ¾ × 17 × 31¾ inches, for lid
  2 pieces, each ¾ × 17 × 29½ inches,
    for front and back
  2 pieces, each ¾ × 17 × 15 inches, for
    sides
  4 pieces, each ¾ × 5 × 24 inches, for
    legs
  2 pieces, each ¾ × 3½ × 12¼ inches,
    for braces
plywood:
  1 piece, ¾ × 15 × 31 inches, for bottom
19 feet dowel, ¼ inch in diameter
white glue
8 flat-head wood screws, #8, each 1¼
  inches long
wood filler
2 lengths piano hinge, each 5 inches
  long, with screws
antiquing-finish kit, containing blue base
  coat and white antiquing glaze
low-gloss plastic varnish
lid support with screws, in size and style
  of your choice

Tools

brown wrapping paper
pencil
ruler
scissors
masking tape
jigsaw *or* coping saw
pattern file, half-round
sandpaper, medium and fine grades
carbon paper
carving chisel, craft knife, *or* pen knife
U-gouge, small
drill with assorted bits
wooden mallet
4 pipe clamps (pipes should measure at
  least 24 inches long)
8 pieces scrap wood, for cushion blocks

center punch
2 C-clamps
screwdriver
paintbrushes

Procedure

1. On brown wrapping paper, draw 1-inch grid and enlarge pattern for leg piece (see "Helpful Hints"). Cut out pattern, tape to leg piece, and mark around outline. Repeat procedure for remaining leg pieces, and use jigsaw or coping saw to cut out. Smooth sawed edges with file. Sand edges and surfaces of all wood pieces with medium and then fine sandpaper.

2. On brown wrapping paper, draw 1-inch grid, enlarge design patterns and cut out. To complete pattern for other half of chest, lay pattern over carbon paper, carbon side up, and trace over all lines, producing design in reverse on back.

3. Tape patterns to chest lid, front, sides, and legs. Using carbon paper and a sharp pencil, transfer designs. To complete design on each piece, flip pattern over. Note that pattern for lid is the same as for leg and front except for the omission of row of triangles under central figures. When you trace pattern on lid, omit this row of triangles and include the dotted line. When you have flipped pattern over to trace remaining half, you will have two dotted lines dividing this space into three sections. The center section is for the carving in of the wedding date, one side section is to carry the name of the bride, and the other is for the name of the groom.

4. Designs are worked in simple, incised carving, about ⅛ inch deep. Using carving chisel, craft knife, or sharp pen knife, make three cuts to form a V-shaped groove. The first cut is made straight down along design outline and should be

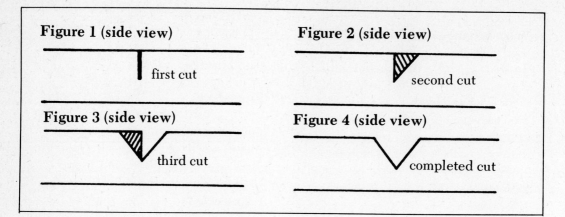

Figure 1 (side view) first cut

Figure 2 (side view) second cut

Figure 3 (side view) third cut

Figure 4 (side view) completed cut

of an even depth (Figure 1). The second and third cuts are made on either side of first cut by holding cutting blade at an angle (Figures 2 and 3) and are cut to same depth as first cut. (Figure 4 shows completed cut.) Where double horizontal lines appear on the pattern, make first cut between them and the second and third on the lines. All designs are incised in this manner except for the small circles. These are cut with a U-gouge that is held at right angles to wood. Complete all carving before assembling chest.

5. Cut dowel into forty 1½-inch lengths (for doweling legs to chest) and eighty-four 2-inch lengths.

6. To assemble chest, first refer to pattern to see where dowels are to be inserted. At these points, drill ¼-inch holes. Following doweling procedure given in woodworking section of "Helpful Hints," glue and, using wooden mallet, dowel together front, sides, and back. Lay bottom piece over the four assembled sides. Apply pipe clamps, placing cushion blocks between jaws, across width of bottom and tighten. Then drill all holes for dowels. Remove clamps and apply glue on edges of front, back, and sides. Reposition bottom piece over previously drilled holes and, with wooden

mallet, insert dowels. Clamp again, tighten, and allow drying time for glue. Remove clamps and then glue and dowel legs to chest.

7. Position and mark on lid placement for braces. Mark positions for four screws in each brace and center-punch each. Clamp one brace in position and drill four 3/32-inch holes, each about 1⅛ inches deep. With 5/16-inch bit, apply end to each hole only deep enough to countersink screwhead. Drive all screws just short of final depth. Then remove screws and clamps, apply glue to surface of brace, return to position, and drive all screws until they are about 1/16 inch below surface. Repeat for other brace. Fill screwhead depressions with wood filler and sand flush with surrounding surface. Screw top leaves of piano hinges to lower underside of lid, ¼ inch in from sides; screw bottom leaves of hinges to top edge of back piece.

8. Antique inside and outside of chest, following manufacturer's instructions. When dry, apply two coats of varnish, allowing drying time between coats.

9. When varnish has dried, screw lid support to inner side piece of chest and underside of lid, following manufacturer's instructions included with the package.

Assembly Diagrams

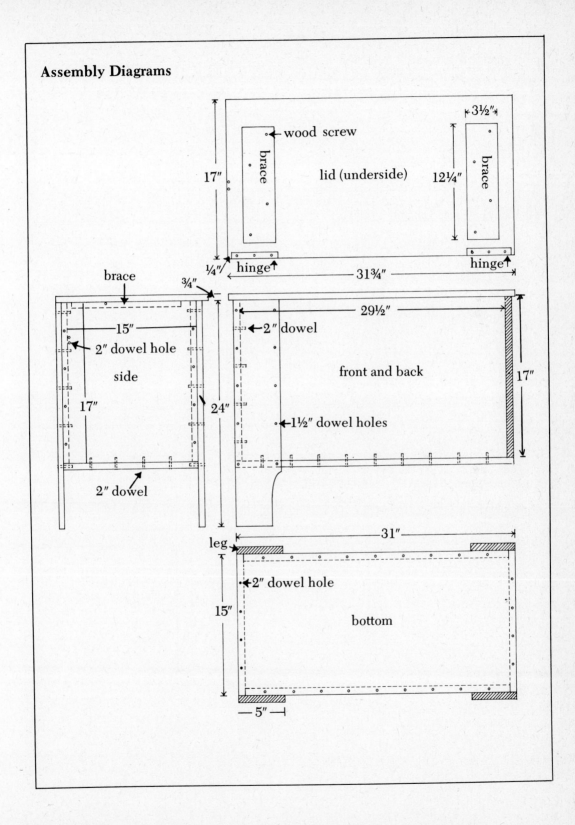

Design Patterns

each square = 1 inch

front, back, and lid

side

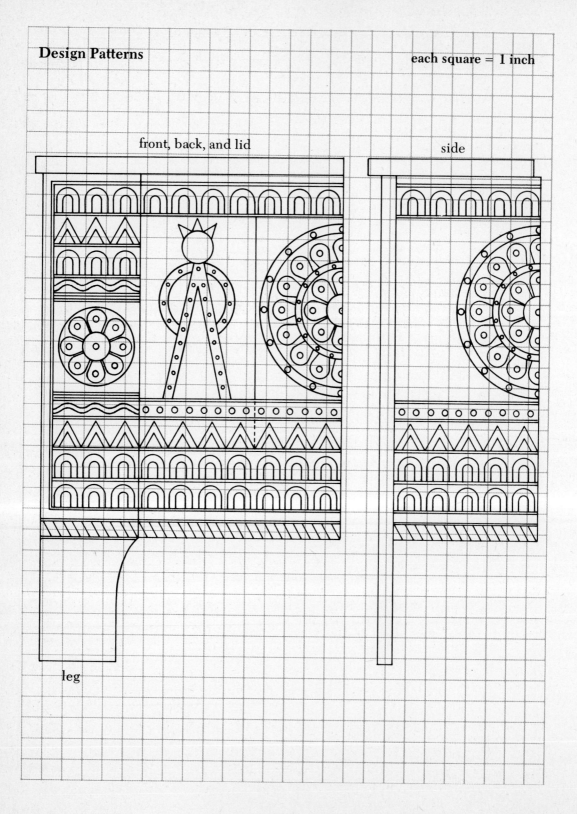

leg

Norway, Sweden, and Denmark

Rya Rug

Using a technique borrowed from the Scandinavians, who probably borrowed it from the Vikings, you can make a luxurious shag rug for your floor.

Today, the word *rya* refers to a handwoven rug, but, originally, the term described bedcovers that were made from knotted wool piles. Prior to this, furry animal skins had been used as bedcovers. Although warm enough, these skins became stiff and hard, and, what was worse, they couldn't be washed. Eventually, a way of making covers that were just as warm as skins but softer and washable was developed. This resulted in the rya. Closely resembling fur, the first rya covers were made of unspun wool knotted through fabric to form a high pile. Since the covers were used pile side down, design work on the back was needed. Usually geometric, these designs often included the owner's initials.

Over the years, the rya covers changed. Spun wool was used, the pile was cut shorter, and the backs were decorated with baroque floral patterns. During the day, these attractive covers were turned over and used as coverlets. Sometime later, it was discovered that the rya made an attractive floor covering, and, shortly thereafter, it became popular as a rug.

The rya knot, or stitch, is simple to learn and speedy to work. After you have mastered it, all you will need to weave a rya rug is backing material, yarn, and a needle.

Materials

1 piece backing fabric, 3 × 4 feet*
rya or rug yarn, 3-ply (approximate
  amounts):
  10 ounces, in red purple
  28 ounces, in purple
  32 ounces, in dark blue
  33 ounces, in white
  48 ounces, in light blue

Tools

brown wrapping paper
pencil
ruler
dressmakers' carbon, tracing wheel, and
  indelible felt-tipped pen; *or* **masking**
  tape and indelible felt-tipped pen; *or*
  hot-iron transfer pencil
scissors
tapestry needle, #13; *or* **rya needle**

*Remember that your choice of backing material
will greatly affect the durability of the rug. We used a
woven mesh fabric, made from hemp yarn, with 4
rows and 4 spaces per inch. If you wish, you can
convert any firmly woven, heavy-duty cloth, such as
burlap, to backing material by pulling out threads,
from selvage to selvage, every half-inch.

Procedure

1. On brown wrapping paper, draw 1-inch grid and enlarge design pattern (see "Helpful Hints").

2. Transfer pattern to backing fabric, using one of the methods described in "Helpful Hints."

3. For this project, use two strands of yarn to work each color section. (If you are working with skeined yarn, you can cut through one entire end of skein to form working lengths of yarn.)

4. With purple, begin stitching at left corner of bottom row on backing fabric. To start the stitch, insert needle from front into second hole from side edge. Bring needle out through first hole (Figure 1). As needle is pulled through, hold end of yarn at desired length of your pile. Bring needle down through third hole and out again through second hole. This completes a knot (Figure 2).

5. Continue across row in this manner (Figure 3), keeping loops at same length as beginning tail by holding yarn with fingers or by looping it around a ruler. Lengths can be uniform (Figure 4), or they can be varied for a shaggier look. The design may be worked by color-desig-

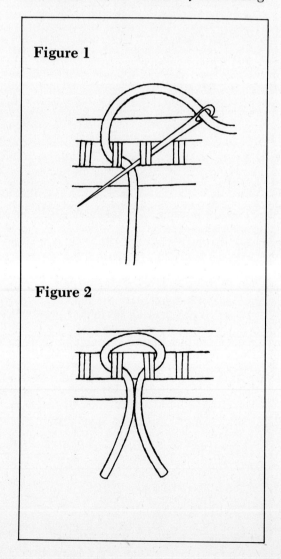

Figure 1

Figure 2

Design Pattern

each square = 1 inch

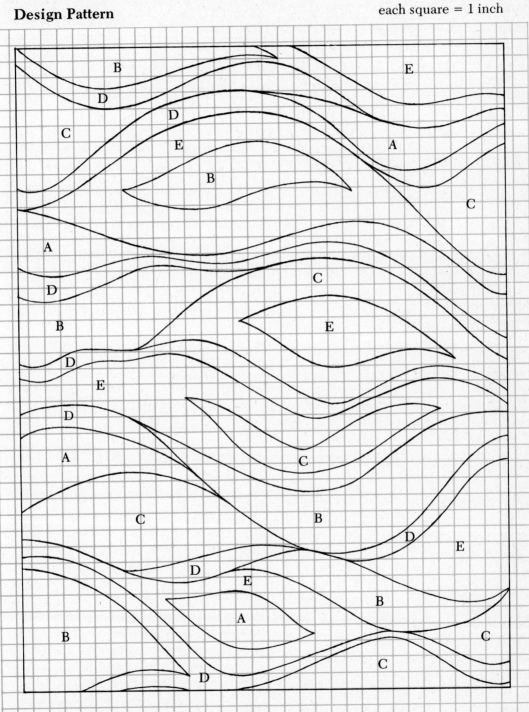

Color Code: A = red purple B = purple C = dark blue D = white E = light blue

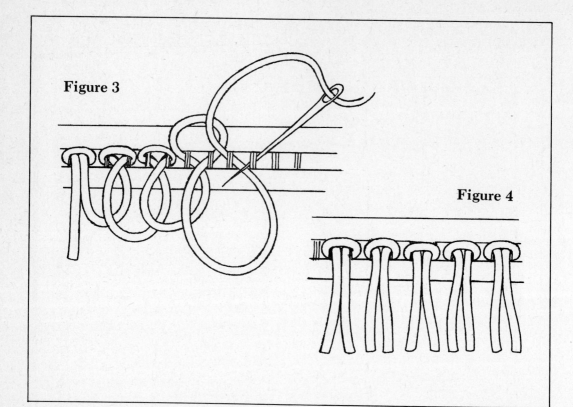

Figure 3

Figure 4

nated areas or row by row. To begin a new color or row, cut the yarn, leaving a tail the same length as the loops. After you have completed a few rows, cut the loops. These loops may range in length from 1½ to 3 inches, depending on the effect you wish.

6. Continue in this manner until entire rug has been completed. If necessary, whip down raw ends of backing fabric to the back. Latex backing will not be needed, since rya rugs are heavy and thick enough to be skidproof.

If you wish to make a rya rug from an original design pattern, remember that rya rug designs should be free-flowing. The rya stitch is best suited for large, sweeping patterns rather than small, detailed designs. Subtle shadings can be achieved by combining various hues of the same color thread in the needle at one time. The number of strands to be used at one time will depend on the weight of the yarn, the density of the fabric, and the proximity of the stitches. Rya yarn is sold by the skein or by the ounce and is available in two weights. To compute the total amount of yarn needed, work a 1-inch-square sample of the backing fabric, remove the yarn, measure how much was used, and multiply this figure by the total area of the backing fabric. This may be time-consuming, but general estimates tend to be unreliable. If you have overestimated the amount of yarn needed, many yarn dealers will buy back or exchange yarns. Or, you can make use of leftover yarn by trying your hand at making a rya pillow to match your rug.

Japan

Flower-stenciled Fabric

The Japanese have been famous for making stencils since the latter part of the seventeenth century. Using the traditional colors of indigo blue and white, these stencils were most popular in the production of textiles for kimonos. The original hand-stenciling process was very complicated. To begin, the artist had to gather half a dozen sheets of tough mulberry paper, prepare them with persimmon juice, and waterproof them with a hard-drying oil. These were then stacked and the design cut through with a knife and fine punch. One sheet was then covered with adhesive and strengthened with silk threads laid on side by side. A second stencil was then glued over the first, and the process repeated until all six layers were glued together. The most popular stencil patterns included dragons, carp, maple leaves, umbrellas, and abstractions of Arabic numbers and Roman letters, which were introduced by the Portuguese and Dutch traders.

Our pattern features chrysanthemums, which are symbolic of autumn—the season of joviality and easy living. The project is done with a silk screen instead of the paper stencil, silk, and persimmon juice, but the colors used are still indigo blue and white. Although silk screening is not difficult, it requires patience in preparation. For your first attempt, it might be wise to print a small piece of fabric, such as a pillow top or border design. Remember that hand-printing will not be perfect simply because it is hand-done.

Materials

smooth-weave fabric, white, preferably
    free of dressing*
1 can fabric ink, in indigo blue

Tools

board, 1 inch thick, 3 inches wide, as long
    as fabric width plus 6 inches
2 C-clamps
4 screw eyes, large enough to
    accommodate curtain rod
silk-screen kit, containing squeegee;
    stencil knife; water-soluble stencil
    film, 7 × 10 inches; silk-screen frame,
    10½ × 14 inches**
1 solid-metal curtain rod, same length as
    board
1 screw, small
screwdriver
small, flat stick (such as Popsicle stick)
brown wrapping paper
pencil
ruler
tracing paper
drawing board *or* heavy cardboard
masking tape
clean cloths
silk-screen glue
cardboard, small pieces
gummed paper tape
scrap fabric (optional)

tapestry needle and headless pins
    (optional)
thumbtacks (optional)
small mixing stick
yardstick
newspapers
paint thinner
scrub brush

*If fabric contains dressing, wash in hot, soapy
water or warm soda water (1 teaspoon soda to a
quart of water).

**The silk screen used here is a good size for a be-
ginner's first stenciling project, but it is impractical
if you wish to print yards of fabric. For more exten-
sive printing, use a larger screen and squeegee so
that you may print faster and with fewer repeats.

Procedure

1. Following Figure 1, set up printing
unit. Secure board to hard, smooth work
surface with C-clamps. Center one screw
eye at each end of board's front edge and
at each top corner of silk-screen frame, so
that when frame is lying flat on printing
surface, all four screw eyes align. Slide
curtain rod through screw eyes. With a
single screw, attach small, flat stick to
side of frame. This stick will be rotated to
raise and support frame.
2. On brown wrapping paper, draw 1-
inch grid and enlarge design pattern (see

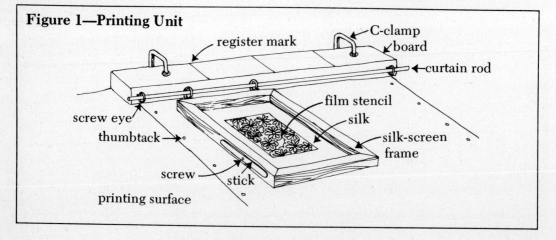

Figure 1—Printing Unit

register mark — C-clamp — board — curtain rod — film stencil — silk — silk-screen frame — screw eye — thumbtack — screw — stick — printing surface

Design Pattern   **each square = 1 inch**

"Helpful Hints"). Mark shaded areas. (Note that partial flower designs on right edge of pattern match partial flowers on left edge to complete flower shape. The same is true of top and bottom partial flowers. You must draw your pattern accurately so that each time you move the pattern over to make another print, the partial flowers become whole. To check your pattern, outline edges and be sure that lines are straight and parallel.) Lay a piece of tracing paper over right edge of pattern, and trace outline of partial design areas. Move tracing of right side to left side and bottom edge to top edge to make sure that areas match. Adjust if necessary.

3. Silk-screen stencils can be prepared a number of different ways. This project uses the film-stencil method. The film is composed of two layers: The bottom layer of film is a plastic backing sheet and the top layer is a water-soluble emulsion.

To cut the stencil:

a. Place pattern on drawing board or heavy cardboard. With masking tape, tape film over pattern with emulsion side up.

b. With stencil knife, cut film around shaded design areas, but do not cut through backing sheet. Peel cutout film areas from backing sheet to allow for open printing areas. Untape paper pattern and set aside.

4. To adhere film to silk screen:

a. Center film stencil under frame on printing surface. Lift frame and use ¼-inch tape strip to tape each corner of film to surface.

b. Dampen silk screen with clean wet cloth.

c. Lower silk screen over stencil, making sure that perfect contact is achieved over the entire film area.

d. To adhere film to silk screen, wipe screen with clean wet cloth. Stencil film should darken when wet. Areas that are lighter in color than others indicate poor adhesion; to remedy this, dampen again.

e. Remove excess moisture with dry cloth, using a firm, rubbing motion.

f. Allow 15 to 20 minutes for drying time. Stencil film will feel cool to the hand if still drying; it will be warm when dry. Once adhesion has taken place, lift screen and remove plastic backing sheet by picking up a corner of backing and peeling off slowly.

g. It is now necessary to block out silk areas between film and frame. This will prevent ink from running into areas not part of design pattern. Remove frame from printing unit. Turn frame so that silk side is up, and pour a small amount of silk-screen glue on one end of screen. With small piece of cardboard, scrape glue across screen, to block out all four open areas between edges of design and edges of frame. Be very careful to keep glue out of design areas.

h. After glue has dried, adhere gummed paper tape to tacked side of frame so that tape is half on wood and half on silk. Turn frame over and repeat, sealing all inside edges. This will prevent ink from seeping under frame during printing.

5. You will now need to make register marks on board for frame placement so that patterns will be printed continuously, without gaps or overlaps. To mark registers, reattach silk-screen frame, with silk side down, to printing unit. Measure width of stencil, and mark on board. Then, measure distance from left edge of stencil frame to stencil. This measure-

ment is the overlap of frame onto print. Subtract this distance from first mark, and make a second mark on board. This second mark will be aligned with left edge of frame for second print. Continue to make register marks on board for all prints. If you wish to experiment by printing a scrap fabric first, tape test piece to printing surface and make register marks. Read the following printing instructions (step 6) and print a row of designs. Adjust marks if necessary before printing on project fabric.

Another way in which to make register marks is to pierce silk with a tapestry needle as closely as possible to corners of screen. When printed, these holes will appear as tiny dots on cloth. Put headless pins in these dots and slide frame over for next print. Lower screen and slip holes over pins to evenly align print.

6. To print:

a. On printing surface, tape or tack fabric to be printed onto piece of heavy cardboard or drawing board.

b. Rest screen on support stick.

c. With mixing stick, spread generous supply of fabric ink as wide as design area across top of silk screen.

d. Align frame with register mark, and lower over fabric to be printed. Put squeegee behind ink supply at 45-degree angle, so that sharp edge rests on screen. Pull squeegee toward you with smooth, even pressure until it has passed well over design. Apply just enough pressure to clean silk behind squeegee.

e. Return squeegee to back of frame, lift frame, and stand it on support stick.

f. Move screen over, skip next repeat, line up register marks for third print, and repeat printing process. By printing every *other* repeat across the row, you allow time for ink to dry. When every other print is finished, move screen back and fill in patterns. Be sure to add ink from time to time. After completing an entire row of printing, allow 20 to 40 minutes for drying time.

7. Before repositioning fabric to print second row, use a strip of masking tape to mark on printing surface the position of each side of fabric and of each end of board. Measure and record distance from bottom edge of silk-screen frame to point where stencil begins. Loosen C-clamps and remove tacks or tape holding fabric. Pull fabric forward and align bottom edge of frame with top edge of printed row on fabric. Now move frame down over printed fabric the same distance as the previously recorded measurement. Position sides of fabric on vertical tape strips. Hold a yardstick straight across fabric and adjust fabric so that all printed edges align with yardstick edge. Secure fabric in place again. Check to make sure that board is on tape marks, tighten C-clamps, and print second row.

8. When printing is finished, remove the frame and place, silk side down, on layers of newspaper. Using piece of cardboard, scrape out remaining ink and replace in can for future use. Saturate screen with paint thinner, and use clean, soft cloth to wipe over screen area. Repeat wiping with clean cloths until both sides of silk are thoroughly clean. Wipe dry with a new cloth. To remove stencil from silk, soak both sides of silk with hot tap water. Loosen stencil with a scrub brush, and let stand for 5 to 10 minutes. Then hold side of silk on which stencil is *not* mounted under hot water to flush it off. Dry the silk, and screen will be ready for use again.

Italy

Trapunto Bedspread

During the time that Queen Anne was ruling in England, the ladies of the court occupied themselves with a new style of needlework just brought over from Italy. Called trapunto, this subtle needle art had a sculptural quality about it that depended on light and shadow for its effect. To work it, delicate designs of small flowers and leaves were first drawn on white linen and then outline-quilted to a lining of coarsely woven fabric. After all the designs were stitched, the linen was turned over and the larger designs were raised with bits of cotton stuffed through the meshes of the backing. To pad the stems, a tiny bodkin was used to draw cord between the linen and the lining.

Stumpwork, which is closely related to trapunto, was another popular pastime of the court ladies. Usually featuring stylized figures and animals, stumpwork designs were realized by embroidering, instead of quilting, them onto fabric and then stuffing them.

Although the process of decoration is the same as was used in Queen Anne's court, our trapunto spread is made with permanent-press sheets instead of linen. You may make it up in the soft blues shown in the photograph, or you may choose your own color scheme. You'll need a quilting frame, which you may either buy commercially or make yourself according to the instructions given in step 9. If you would like to try this technique on a smaller scale, trapunto is an attractive way to embellish pillows and clothing.

Materials

2 permanent-press queen-sized sheets, each 90 × 115 inches, for double bedspread*

3 yards nylon net, 72 inches wide

8 ounces cotton or acrylic rug yarn, 3-ply, in white or color to match sheet

1 bag Dacron stuffing, 1-pound size

17 spools #5 DMC cotton embroidery thread, in blue or color of your choice

5 yards cording, ⅜ inch in diameter

Tools

brown wrapping paper

pencil

ruler

seam ripper

straight pins

thread, for basting

dressmakers' carbon

tracing wheel

sewing-machine quilting foot with guide removed *or* regular foot

tapestry needle, #13

scissors

smooth, pointed tool, for positioning stuffing

quilting frame *or* 4 low-backed chairs of even height; 2 pieces plywood, each 1 × 2 × 102 inches; 2 pieces plywood, each 1 × 2 × 48 inches; 4 C-clamps; and muslin (see step 9)

crewel embroidery needle

sewing-machine cording foot

*If you wish your spread to fit a queen-sized bed, add a dust ruffle; for a king-sized bed, repeat the circles around entire pattern or simply move pattern units farther apart.

Procedure

1. On brown wrapping paper, draw 1-inch grid and enlarge pattern (see "Helpful Hints").

2. Using seam ripper, open top and bottom hems of both sheets and press.

3. Lay top sheet flat on floor with right side facing down. Run basting stitches lengthwise down center. Pattern is only one-quarter of complete design pattern, so that it must be traced onto bedsheet four times. First, measure 12 inches up from the bottom edge of sheet and mark off. Then pin pattern, right side up, to lower right corner of sheet, placing bottom of pattern on your marks. Be sure to line up left margin of pattern with center line of stitching. Slip dressmakers' carbon under pattern and, using tracing wheel, transfer design to fabric. Flip pattern sheet over to 12 inches above lower left corner and, again, pin pattern sheet to center line. Be sure to match left side of design to right side. Slip carbon under pattern and trace. Follow the same procedure for tracing on top half of sheet, beginning at upper left corner and matching top half of design to bottom.

4. Starting at the center and working toward the outer edges, baste nylon net to back of sheet in 6-inch grid pattern.

5. With quilting foot or regular foot, machine-baste all pattern outlines.

6. Trapunto is worked from the back, between the two fabric layers. Thread tapestry needle with doubled rug yarn. Insert needle through net and into casing formed by double line of machine-basting. Draw yarn through casing, keeping it relaxed. Figures 1 and 2 show how to fill point and stem motifs and chevron motifs. Begin at point A. Bring needle out at corner, reinsert needle, and bring out at point B, leaving an extra yarn loop at corner. Cut yarn. (Figure 3 shows detailed view of how to turn corners.) Reinsert needle at point C and bring out at point D. For point and stem motifs, reinsert needle at point E, bring out at point F, and start again at A. For star

shapes in chevron motif, turn corners as before, using one continuous piece of yarn. When you eventually run out of yarn, end off and start again only at corners. Once a section has been completed, smooth with finger along filled casing so that yarn loops work into corners. After filling a section of design pattern, pull fabric back and forth and smooth with finger along padded lines. Clip ends of yarn closely.

7. The design circles are lightly filled with Dacron. Spread apart net at the center of each circle and insert a small piece of stuffing. Use a pointed tool, such as a barbecue skewer or a paintbrush handle, to position padding.

8. When entire pattern is stuffed, smooth spread out on floor with net side facing up. Lay second sheet, right side up, on net. Match up edges and baste all layers together in a 6-inch grid pattern.

9. If you wish to make your own quilting frame, follow Figure 4 and assemble

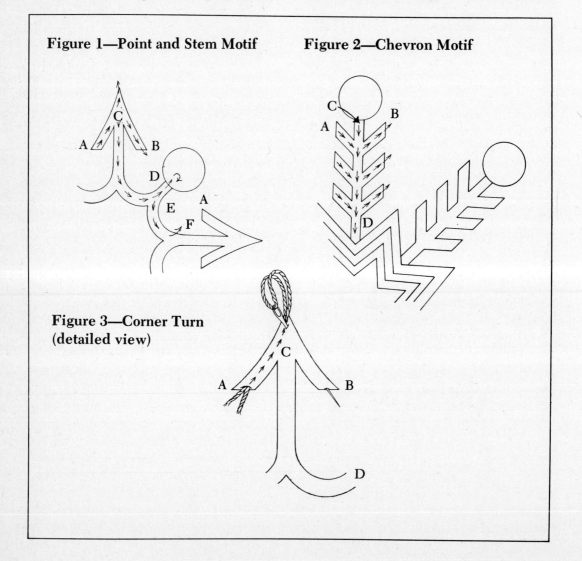

Figure 1—Point and Stem Motif

Figure 2—Chevron Motif

Figure 3—Corner Turn (detailed view)

Design Pattern (Quarter)   center line   **each square = 1 inch**

Figure 4—Do-it-Yourself Quilting Frame

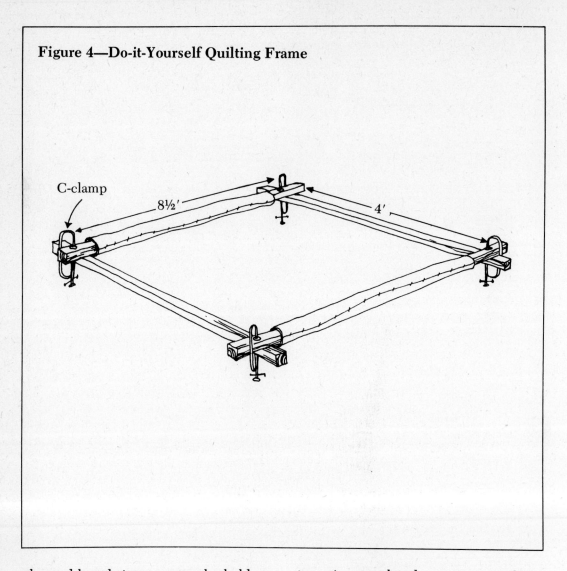

C-clamp

8½'

4'

plywood boards into a rectangle; hold at corners with C-clamps. Next, cover long wood pieces with muslin by basting it on. Then baste spread to these covered strips, pulling fabric as tautly as possible. Finally, rest the entire unit on four low-backed chairs, and you are ready to work.

10. Thread crewel needle with embroidery thread and, going through all layers of fabric, work all outlines with stem stitch or running stitch (see embroidery stitches in "Helpful Hints"). When a pattern is completed, remove machine-basting. When embroidery is completed, remove spread from frame.

11. Turn side and bottom edges of spread over cording and baste. Using a cording foot, machine-stitch as closely as possible to cording. To cover stitching, work stem stitch around spread above cording. Turn down narrow hem on top edge of spread, and sew by hand.

12. Remove all basting threads, and press completed spread lightly on wrong side.

Northwestern United States and Western Canada

Totem Pole Clothes Rack

Since the beginning of time, every one of the world's peoples has desired to give graphic expression to its legends and myths, and what a spectacular way the Indians of the Northwest chose! The creatures of their particular legends—the eagle, the raven, the fox, the frog, the shark, the mountain goat, the owl—all were remembered in the totem pole.

As an art form, the totem pole reached its peak of expression around 1875. By that time, wood and stone carving had been fully developed by a number of northern tribes located above the Frazier River in British Columbia.

Contrary to popular notion, totem poles had no spiritual significance to the Indians—they were merely extravaganzas—and the carvers were allowed a great deal of latitude in choosing designs and colors that appealed to them. The subject matter was usually traditional, however. For instance, some carvers chose to display their family history by carving in the aspect of each bird or animal from which his ancestors had descended. To ensure a happy homelife, he would also add the aspects of his wife's ancestors. After the death of a tribal member, a totem pole would sometimes be moved to the gravesite to serve as a memorial to the deceased.

Our brightly painted tin totem pole features the eagle, the owl, and the beaver.

Materials

6 coffee cans, 3-pound size

enamel spray paint for metal, in black

corrugated cardboard

contact cement

model airplane paint *or* hobby paint, in yellow, black, red, and blue

1 piece pine *or* scrap wood, 1 × 6 × 30 inches

wood primer

nails, each 2 inches long

1 plywood circle, 1 inch thick (or heaviest wood available), 12 inches in diameter

1 plywood circle, 1 inch thick, 6 inches in diameter

6 screws, about #6, each 1½ inches long

1 continuously threaded metal rod, ¼ in diameter, 3 feet long

7 washers, to fit rod

1 cap nut, to fit rod

6 hex nuts, to fit rod

3 sheet-metal screws, each ¾ inch long

Tools

drill with assorted bits

scissors

ice pick

brown wrapping paper

ruler

pencil

carbon paper

masking tape

watercolor brushes, medium

jigsaw *or* coping saw

paintbrush

hammer

screwdriver

pattern file, half-round

sandpaper, medium and fine grades

Procedure

1. In center of bottom of each can, drill hole large enough to accommodate threaded rod.

2. Spray all six cans with black paint.

3. From corrugated cardboard, cut circles to fit inside outer lip of solid ends of cans. Assemble enough circles to form a plug that will fit into open end of another can, and cement together. Make a total of five such plugs, and cement one to closed end of each of five cans. With ice pick, punch a hole through center of each plug large enough to accommodate rod.

4. On brown wrapping paper, draw 1-inch grid and enlarge design patterns (see "Helpful Hints"). Cut out patterns.

5. Turn seams of cans to center back. Blacken back side of pattern with pencil and, making sure that front of design is on front of cans, tape pattern to cans (penciled side against can); trace over all lines.

6. Following color arrangement shown in color photograph, paint designs on cans with model airplane paint.

7. On brown wrapping paper, draw 1-inch grid, enlarge patterns for beak and wings, and cut out. With masking tape, tape patterns to pine and draw around outlines. Saw out and smooth edges with file and then both grades of sandpaper.

8. Prime wings, beak, and 12-inch circle.

9. Paint wings and beak yellow and 12-inch circle black.

10. Checking first to make sure 6-inch circle will fit properly into open end of can #6, nail 6-inch circle securely to center of 12-inch circle.

11. Following pattern for placement, drill two holes through front of first can for beak. Through each side of can #2, drill two holes for each wing. Mark and drill corresponding but smaller holes into wings and beak. Holding screwdriver within appropriate cans, attach each piece with two 1½-inch screws.

12. To assemble totem pole, screw one washer and one cap nut on end of rod; pass other end of rod downward through

closed end of top can (having no plug). Through open end of bottom of same can, add one washer and one hex nut and tighten against underside of can's closed end. Thread other end of rod through closed end of can without cardboard plug. Through open end of same can, add one washer and one hex nut and tighten. Making sure that design patterns are in line, thread can #2 on rod, with closed end up. Push open end of can #1 over cardboard plug of can #2 and secure #2

on rod with another washer and hex nut. In same manner, thread remaining cans on rod, closed ends up, securing each with a washer and a nut.

13. Fit open end of bottom can over 6-inch wood circle (attached to 12-inch base). Around bottom edge of can, drill three small and evenly spaced holes through sides and into edge of wood circle inside can. Using these holes, secure pole to base with sheet-metal screws. Paint screwheads and cap nut with black paint.

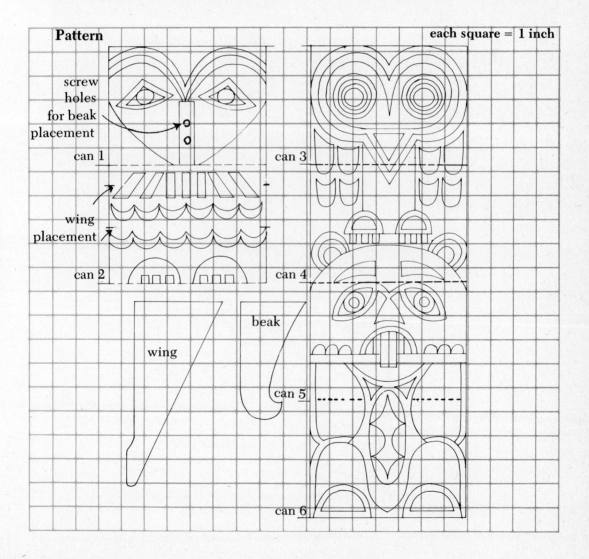

Pattern   each square = 1 inch

screw holes for beak placement

can 1

can 3

wing placement

can 2

can 4

wing

beak

can 5

can 6

Wax-Intarsia Hand Mirror

Today, raising sheep and horses is big business on the plains of Hungary, and the men responsible for the animals' health and safety occupy a vital position in the community.

Like other Hungarian peasants, the herdsman of the past delighted in colorful dress and accessories. Although he was required to spend much of his time with the animals, the herdsman was creative in his love of decoration, carving bone, horn, wood, and spoonbilled duck beaks into boxes, drinking horns, scythe-stone holders, wooden mirror frames, paprika pots, and salt cellars. These items were then decorated by a process known as *Spanyolozás*, or wax intarsia. This technique called for carving out a design in wood and then using a knife blade to pack the hollowed-out areas with different colors of softened wax. The Hungarian word *Spanyolozás* means "Spanish wax," and it refers to the red Spanish sealing wax first used by the herdsmen.

Popular *Spanyolozás* designs included stylized flower-and-leaf motifs as well as scenes from Hungarian history. The most common subject was probably Milfait Ferko, a legendary romantic bandit who lived in the Bakony Forest. He is usually shown dancing with the pretty, young wife of an innkeeper, as gypsies play music in the background.

For our mirror back, we used white glue instead of wax. Its design has been adapted from a box lid made of bentwood and worked in the original wax-intarsia technique.

Materials

breadboard with handle, 7 × 14 inches;
or other wood piece, in shape of
your choice, for mirror back

2 pieces plywood or hardboard, each ⅛
inch thick, same dimensions as
breadboard, for mirror holder

mirror, 1 inch smaller on all sides than
square portion of breadboard

white glue in applicator bottle

acrylic paint, in color of your choice, for
base coat

acrylic tube paints, in black, red, green,
and aqua

low-gloss plastic varnish

Tools

pencil

jigsaw or coping saw

ruler

sandpaper, medium, fine, and finishing
grades

watercolor brushes, small and medium

brown wrapping paper

scissors

masking tape

chisel and U-gouge, small*

varnish brush

lint-free cloth

*Available in set for beginners at art-supply stores.

Procedure

1. To make mirror holder, outline bread-board on one of plywood or hardboard pieces. Center mirror within square portion of outline, draw around it, and saw out wood on outline. Also saw around outline of handle. On second piece of plywood, draw around mirror holder and center cutout. Draw a second line ¼ inch inside center-cutout outline. Saw out neatly on inner line and around handle. This will serve as outer frame for mirror. Glue outer frame over mirror holder, matching edges of both pieces. From the back, set mirror into mirror holder (now attached to outer frame) and glue back of entire unit to breadboard. Weight it overnight to ensure a good glue bond. When glue is dry, sand frame edges with medium and then fine sandpaper.

2. With medium-sized brush, paint both sides of assembled hand mirror with base color; when dry, paint outside edges with black acrylic paint.

3. On brown wrapping paper, draw 1-inch grid and enlarge design pattern (see "Helpful Hints").

4. Cut out design pattern and tape to mirror back. Trace on design outlines with a sharp, hard pencil, using enough pressure to dent pattern into wood.

5. With chisel, make shallow cuts, about 1/16 to ⅛ inch deep, around outlines of areas to be cut out (shaded areas on pattern). Use U-gouge to remove center portions of areas.

6. Following color scheme shown in color photograph, paint cutout areas. When paint is dry, fill cutouts with white glue. (Glue is white when first applied but will dry clear.) Let glue dry completely, and then fill depressions a second time, allowing glue to mound.

7. When glue is completely dry, use small brush to paint black outlines around design areas and pattern lines that were not cut out.

8. With varnish brush, apply first coat of clear varnish on mirror back, frame, and edges. When varnish is dry, sand lightly with finishing sandpaper, dust carefully with lint-free cloth, and then repeat procedure with a second coat of varnish.

Design Pattern

each square = 1 inch

Alternate Design Pattern

Chapter 4
Family Room

Russia

Owl Coat Hook

Wooden toys carved in Russia have always been fascinating. Jointed bears, paddles set with pecking chickens, lots of dolls, and miniature samovars are just a few of the endless types that the people delight in making. Most are made by peddler wood carvers called *Kustaris*. Many pieces are left natural, while others are brightly painted. Wood carving is also used to embellish homes, furniture, sleighs and wagons, and even looms. It is among the most popular of Russian crafts because it requires few tools.

Our coat hook might well have been carved by a *Kustari* for a mother who wanted to teach neatness to her child while, at the same time, offering a little fun, for as soon as a garment is hung up on the hook, the owl responds by spreading open his wings.

Materials
redwood*:
1 piece, 2 × 5½ × 13½ inches, for body
1 piece, ¾ × 5½ × 3¼ inches, for back-of-head block
1 piece, 1½ × 4 × 7½ inches, for hook
1 piece, ¾ × 2¾ × 2½ inches, for back-of-hook block
2 pieces, each ¾ × 3 × 6¾ inches, for wings
white glue
wood stain (optional)
low-gloss plastic varnish
string
2 wood screws, #6, each 1¼ inches long
1 inch dowel, ¼ inch in diameter
2 tacks
4 inches lightweight wire

Tools
brown wrapping paper
pencil *or* ballpoint pen
ruler
carbon paper
scissors
2 C-clamps
masking tape
jigsaw *or* coping saw
wood chisel
small set of carving tools
old breadboard and 1 piece 2 × 4
nails
hammer
drill with assorted bits
varnish brush
screwdriver

*Any other wood with a smooth, even grain may also be used. If this is your first attempt at wood carving, choose a medium-hard wood.

Procedure
1. On brown wrapping paper, draw 1-inch grid and enlarge pattern for body, hook, and right wing (see "Helpful Hints"). When making wing pattern, place carbon paper, carbon side up, under wrapping paper to produce reverse pattern on back of sheet. Cut out patterns.

2. Glue and clamp back-of-head block to body piece. When glue is dry, remove clamps. Tape patterns to appropriate wood pieces; outline and trace over all design lines, pressing hard enough to indent the wood. Flip wing pattern over to transfer design for other wing. Saw out owl shape.

3. With wood chisel, cut slot ½ × 1½ × 7½ inches on back of body for hook (Figure 1).

4. Cut out wing piece and hook piece with saw. Carve hook as shown in photograph. Insert in slot to check for fit and remove. Sliding areas must be smooth.

5. Glue and clamp back-of-hook block to side blocks. After glue has dried, remove clamps.

6. Nail a piece of 2 × 4 to one end of an old breadboard, and then fasten breadboard to worktable with C-clamps. Push owl piece against the 2 × 4. This will act as a backstop and will allow you to use pressure on the wood-carving tools. Begin carving owl by roughly cutting away wood to body contours. Then complete fine carving. Do not attempt to complete one area at a time but keep entire design developing at same rate.

7. Place hook stem and wings in appropriate positions but do not attach. Drill hole through hook stem for ¼-inch dowel and another (about ⅛ inch in diameter) for string (Figure 1). Drill two corresponding holes through each wing for screw and string.

8. If you wish, stain completed piece and finish with plastic varnish, or apply varnish to natural wood. Allow drying time.

9. Set up string arrangement as shown in Figure 1. Thread string through all three

holes, but don't tie knot yet. Screw wings in place, pull slack out of string, and knot. Glue dowel in hook stem. Dowel should project ½ inch. Add tacks and wrap one end of wire around each, as shown in figure, to keep hook stem in place. Side view of assembled coat hook should resemble Figure 2. Fly-test wings to see whether they will fly up when weight is placed on hook. If they stick or are slow, back off screws slightly. Drill small hole in the center back of head, for hanging.

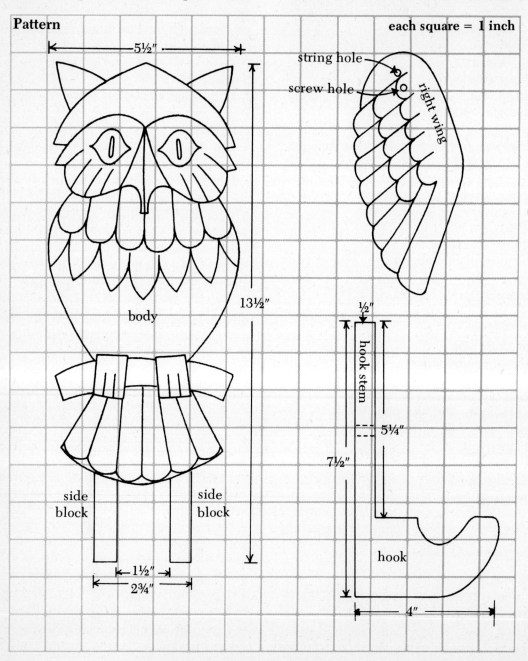

Pattern

each square = 1 inch

5½"

string hole

screw hole

right wing

13½"

body

side block

side block

½"

hook stem

5¼"

7½"

hook

1½"

2¾"

4"

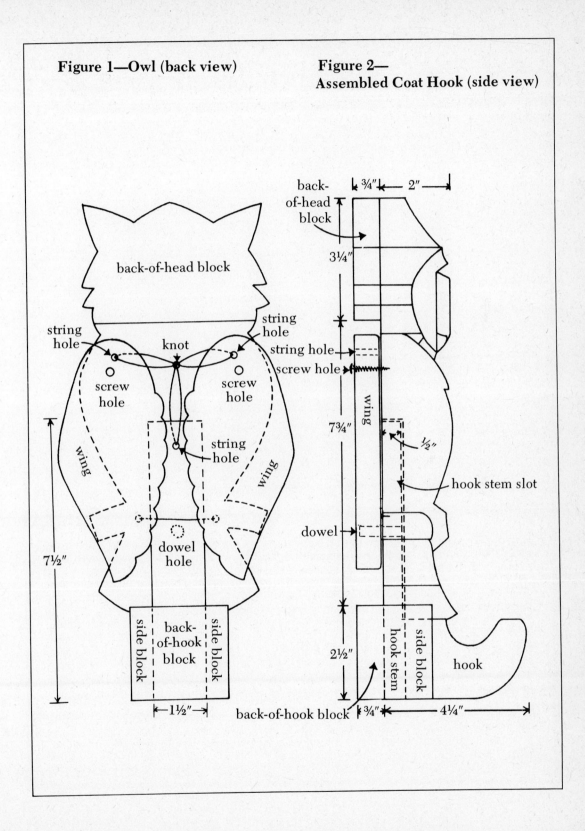

Figure 1—Owl (back view)

Figure 2—Assembled Coat Hook (side view)

Peasant Embroidered Robe

Embroidery is an important art form the world round. Distinctive patterns and stitches on church appointments, curtains, linens, bedding, rugs, and, of course, peasant costumes often tell the country of origin and sometimes even the specific area of the country. For the historian, embroidered costumes in particular can provide valuable insight into bygone eras. Traditional folk costumes are handed down from generation to generation, treasured, and regarded as integral parts of national heritage and culture.

The design in this project is European in origin. Although the overall design seems complex, the patterns are actually very simple once they have been broken down into sections. The robe, which is made from an open-weave wool, will measure about 59 by 71 inches, not including fringe, when completed. Since you will need only small amounts of each color yarn for the embroidery, amounts have been designated in yards rather than ounces. If you wish, other kinds of yarns, such as Persian, needlepoint, crewel, DMC tapestry, and embroidery, can be used. If you wish to embroider the pattern on all four corners of the robe rather than on just one, remember to increase the amount of yarns accordingly.

Our all-purpose robe may be used as a decorative draping for a chair or couch, or it may be worn as a wrap during cool weather. It might also be used as a bed throw.

Materials

2 yards wool or synthetic fabric, 60
   inches wide, in color of your choice
thread, in color to match fabric
knitting worsted, 4-ply (approximate
   amounts):
   35 yards, in green
   6 yards, in yellow
   10 yards, in yellow orange
   14 yards, in orange
   21 yards, in red
   12 yards, in magenta
   12 ounces, in color of your choice,
   for fringe

Tools

brown wrapping paper
pencil
ruler
straight pins
dressmakers' carbon
tracing wheel
embroidery hoop, large
yarn needle
1 piece cardboard, 5 inches wide (length
   is unimportant)
crochet hook, medium

Procedure

1. Turn a rolled hem, approximately ⅜
inch, on edges of fabric.
2. On brown wrapping paper, draw 1-
inch grid and enlarge pattern (see
"Helpful Hints"). Place carbon on one
corner of fabric, pin pattern over it, and
trace.
3. Place fabric in large embroidery hoop
and embroider design, following photograph for color scheme. Stems are done
in chain stitch; remainder of design is
done in satin stitch (see embroidery-
stitch section in "Helpful Hints").
4. For fringe, wrap a quantity of yarn
around 5-inch dimension of cardboard
and cut across one end to make 10-inch-
long strands. Fold two strands of

yarn in half. Inserting crochet hook
through right side of fabric, draw folds
through fabric, just above the hem, from
the wrong side to the right side. Pull ends
through loop and tighten (Figure 1). Continue to attach fringe completely around
the robe, leaving ⅜- to ½-inch spaces.

Figure 1

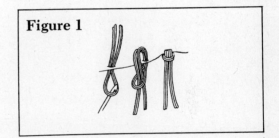

Design Pattern

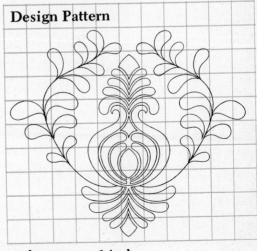

each square = 1 inch

New Guinea

Sepik Coat Hook

If you were to live along the Sepik River in New Guinea, your home would be constructed of palm fronds and tree trunks. Furniture would be minimal because of a steaming climate that causes wood to rot quickly and a plethora of wood-eating insects.

To cope with this environment, the people of the area devised a rather unique method of protecting valuables and foodstuffs. From forked tree branches, they fashioned hooks to hold net bags or baskets and hung them from the rafters. Items to be stored were placed in bags or baskets and thus placed out of the reach of insects, rats, and thieves.

This common Sepik furnishing has been adapted here to serve as a coat or hat hook.

Materials

pine:
    1 piece, 1 × 10 × 26¼ inches, for body
    1 piece, 1 × 5 × 6 inches, for front hook
balsa:
    1 piece, 1½ × 2 × 12 inches, for nose,
      brow, and mouth
    1 piece, ⅛ × 2 × 36 inches, for eyes
3 inches dowel stock, 3/16 inch in
    diameter
white glue
straight pin
acrylic tube paints, in red oxide, white,
    and black or in colors of your choice
low-gloss plastic varnish

Tools

brown wrapping paper
ballpoint pen *or* pencil
ruler
masking tape
carbon paper (optional)
jigsaw *or* coping saw
sandpaper, medium and fine grades
drill, with 3/16- and ⅜-inch bits
U-gouge, small
craft knife
varnish brush

Procedure

1. On brown wrapping paper, draw 1-inch grid and enlarge all patterns, including design lines (see "Helpful Hints").

2. Tape patterns for body piece and front hook piece to pine and, by indenting wood with pencil or pen, transfer outlines and design lines. To complete design for body piece, transfer design lines also. To obtain design pattern for right side of face, place pattern over carbon paper, carbon side up, and draw over design lines made for left side of face.

3. Remove patterns and saw out pieces on outlines. With craft knife, carve hook (see photograph), tapering it to a point. Then tape pattern to hook and transfer design lines to both sides. Sand all body edges with medium and then fine sandpaper.

4. Following pattern for proper placement and using ⅜-inch bit, drill hole through top of head.

5. With U-gouge, incise all areas shown as white in photograph to a depth of approximately 1/16 inch.

6. Cut dowel into two 1½-inch lengths. With 3/16-inch bit, drill holes for dowels in body piece and front hook piece, following pattern for proper placement.

7. To make eyes, outline pattern for largest part four times on balsa; outline remaining patterns twice. Saw out all parts. Glue two of the large pieces together to form a piece ¼ inch thick; repeat with other two large pieces. Sand edges of all parts with fine sandpaper. To assemble left eye, place one large piece on the bottom and glue remaining pieces on top, going in order of size. Note that pieces are not centered over each other as they are assembled; follow pattern for proper positioning. Assemble right eye in same manner but work with balsa pieces turned over so that direction of completed eye will be reversed. Then, following right side of pattern for proper positioning, glue eyes in place on face.

8. To make nose, balsa will have to be pieced. To do this, outline pattern on balsa for portion of nose above dotted line and saw out. Repeat for lower portion of nose. Glue two sections together, holding in place with a straight pin inserted at an angle, as shown. When glue is dry, carve nose to shape with craft knife, following shape indicated by end view of nose. Then carve out nostrils (shaded portions on end view). Following pattern for proper positioning,

glue nose in place on face. When glue is dry, sand nose with fine sandpaper.

9. Outline eyebrow pattern on balsa block and saw out. Carve to shape, following shape indicated by end view, and glue in place on face. Repeat procedure for mouth. When glue is dry, sand pieces with fine sandpaper to smooth surfaces.

10. Paint white and red oxide areas of assembled piece and allow to dry. Then, with black, outline all white areas and paint outer edges and back of piece.

11. When paint is thoroughly dry, apply a coat of varnish over the entire piece.

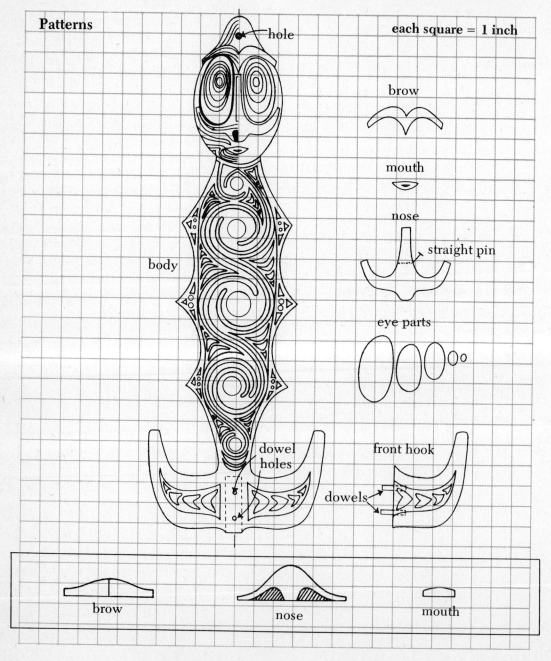

Patterns

each square = 1 inch

hole

brow

mouth

nose

straight pin

body

eye parts

dowel holes

front hook

dowels

brow

nose

mouth

Peru

Decorated Gourds

In many cultures of the world, gourds function as containers for all types of things. They are relatively unbreakable and are free for the growing. For centuries, the Indians of Peru utilized gourds in just this manner, sometimes decorating them with horizontal bands of geometric motifs and sometimes fancifully interpreting the gourd shapes as men and women or fish, bird, and other animal figures, so that in addition to being functional, these pieces were also beautiful.

With the introduction of cheaply made, mass-produced ceramics, these gourds became purely decorative.

Gourd designs can be burned into the gourd, or the entire gourd can be stained with wood stain and then shallowly carved with a small veining gouge and craft knife.

Materials
gourd

wood stain, in mahogany or other shade of your choice

1 wood block, size of your choice, for base

1 dowel, diameter and length of your choice

paint, in black, for base (optional)

low-gloss plastic varnish

Tools
pot cleaner (optional)

pencil

paintbrush

veining gouge, small

craft knife

drill

white glue

varnish brush

Procedure
1. Select gourd whose shape suggests a bird or fish to you. If you want to start from scratch, grow your own gourds, following directions on seed package. When gourds have matured, remove from vine and place in warm, dry place to dry. Turn from time to time to avoid mildew. It may take a number of weeks for gourd to dry completely, but, whether you have purchased a gourd or grown your own, it is essential that it be thoroughly dried before you start the project. Once it has dried, submerge in water for 1 hour. If there are blemishes or stains on surface, detergent should be added to water. Rub off outer skin with pot cleaner, making sure to remove it all.

2. With pencil, draw design on gourd. It is better to draw directly onto gourd than to trace a prepared design, since each gourd will add its own unique character to the figure. Also, tracing a design onto a rounded surface is no easy task and results are often unsatisfactory.

3. Choose areas of design you wish to darken. Following manufacturer's instructions, apply stain, using paintbrush. A second coat may be necessary.

4. When stain is completely dry, use a small veining gouge to cut out all outlines. These cuts will reveal the inner part of the gourd, which is much lighter in color than the natural surface and contrasts well with both the natural and stained areas. If you wish to cut out a large area, such as the inside of the beak of the bird, outline area with veining gouge and then remove remaining gourd skin with craft knife.

5. To make a stand for your carved gourd, drill hole large enough to accommodate the dowel in the block of wood and in the bottom of gourd. Glue dowel into block and paint both, if you wish. Put glue on end of dowel and around hole in gourd. Insert dowel in hole. Let glue dry.

6. Apply two coats of varnish to the finished gourd. Allow to dry between coats.

Alternate Design Pattern

Alternate Design Patterns

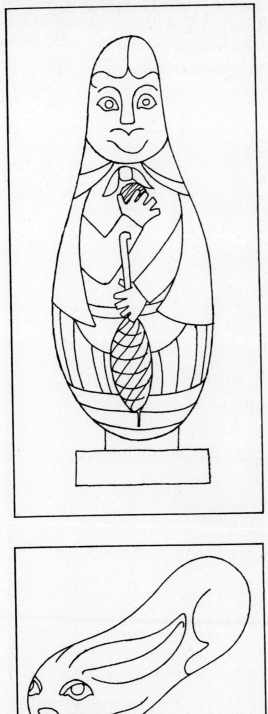

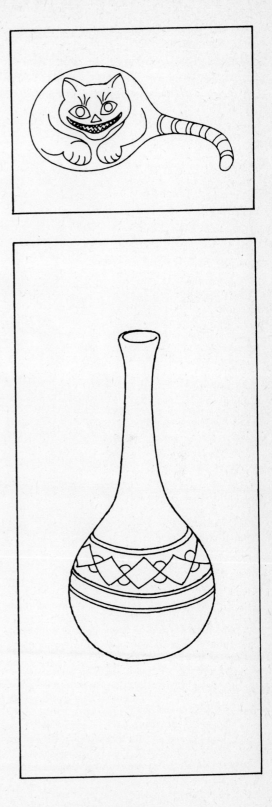

Haiti

Metal Cutouts

The subjects of Haiti and voodoo seem to go hand in hand, since voodoo is an integral part of Haitian culture. In fact, up in the hills, metal voodoo plaques are made in secret and transported to Port-au-Prince, where they are sold to tourists and voodoo practitioners. These cutouts, made today from tops of discarded oil drums, were originally used to mark graves so that the spirits would know where the dead had been placed. Although these designs combined Christian symbolism with voodoo, designs purely voodoo in origin and featuring Loa, the voodoo spirit, were also prevalent.

The two designs in this project feature the double-headed cow, which is analogous to the good-luck dragon in Chinese mythology, and a biblical scene, depicting what seems to be Adam and Eve in the Garden of Eden. Both designs can be made from a single piece of 36- by 36-inch aluminum sheeting and flat black spray paint for metal.

Materials

For *Adam and Eve:*
- 1 piece aluminum sheeting, 22¼ × 23¼ inches
- 1 piece wood, 1 × 1 × 2½ inches, for brace
- 1 screw eye, small

For *Two-Headed Cow:*
- 1 piece aluminum sheeting, 12 × 23½ inches
- 1 piece wood, 1 × 1 × 5 inches, and 2 pieces wood, each 1 × 1 × 3 inches, for braces; *or* 1 piece wood, 1 × 1 × 12 inches, for standing base
- 2 screw eyes, small

metal glue
flat spray paint for metal, in black
floral wire, for hanging

Tools
brown wrapping paper
ruler
scissors
pencil
masking tape
ballpoint pen or felt-tipped pen
coping saw
scrap wood, for work surface
hammer
cold chisel
center punch
small files: half-round, round, and triangular
newspaper pad
ball-peen hammer
metal hole punch, 5/32 inch in diameter
glass cutter, having ball on one end
screwdriver
drill

Procedure
1. On brown wrapping paper, draw 1-inch grid and enlarge pattern (see "Helpful Hints"). Cut out pattern, tape to aluminum, and draw around it with ballpoint or felt-tipped pen. Remove pattern.

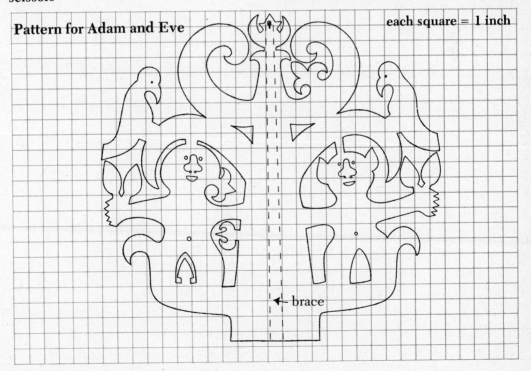

Pattern for Adam and Eve   **each square = 1 inch**

← brace

2. Start cutting aluminum on the peripheral outline, using sharp scissors or a coping saw. To work around problematic curves, bend aluminum slightly with your fingers—it can be flattened later.

3. To cut out inside areas, place aluminum on a scrap-wood surface. With a cold chisel and hammer, tap a hole in the centers of large inner areas to make a space for insertion of scissor blades. Then cut out. Cut out small inner areas by making a series of overlapping holes with center punch. If an area is close enough to the edge to use a coping saw, use center punch to make a hole large enough to insert blade. Then disassemble saw, insert blade, reassemble saw around blade, and saw out area on outline.

4. File all edges smooth. Place aluminum on thin newspaper pad and pound lightly on both sides with round end of ball-peen hammer. This slight denting will add texture and strength to the aluminum.

5. Place aluminum on scrap-wood work surface and, using metal hole punch, make holes and indentations for eyes, nostrils, and navels. To shape three-dimensional noses on Adam and Eve piece, turn aluminum face down on newspaper pad and place metal ball of glass cutter at center of nose. Strike ball with hammer, denting metal forward. Repeat for right and left sides of nose. Turn metal over, and, gently applying hammer to screwdriver, tap around outline of nose.

6. To hang cutouts, glue wood braces to back of piece. Placement is indicated by dotted lines on pattern. If you wish, you can make a standing base for the Two-Headed Cow by gluing wood base piece to back side of metal in position indicated by heavy dotted line on pattern.

7. Spray-paint entire piece. To hang, twist in screw eye or eyes and add wire.

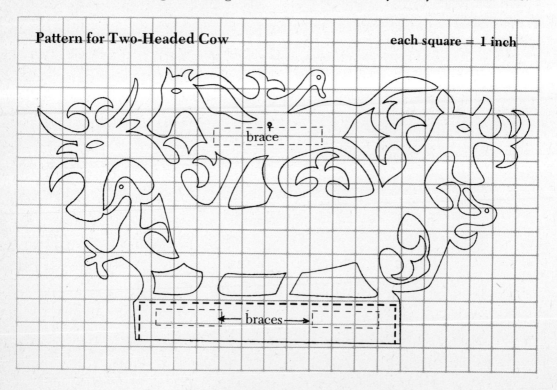

Pattern for Two-Headed Cow   each square = 1 inch

brace

braces

Alternate Pattern

Africa

Bakota Ancestor Figure

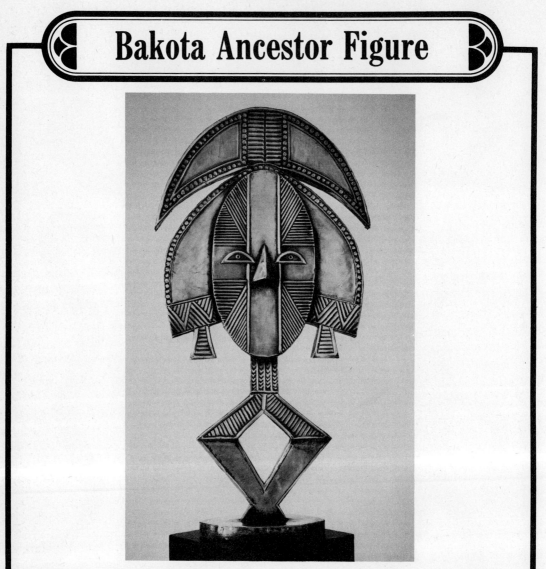

If you always wanted a *Mbula-Ngula* but couldn't find one, now you can make one yourself. A *Mbula-Ngula* is an abstract, copper-clad figure made by the Bakota tribesmen of Gabon, Africa. Although the Bakota share the area of the Ogowe River with similar tribes, the art of the Bakota is in marked contrast to theirs. In fact, it is easy to believe that it might have been a profound influence on Picasso in his early cubist period.

Originally, *Mbulu-Ngulu* were made to protect tribal ancestors from the effects of evil. Kept atop the baskets or boxes that held the skulls of deceased chieftains, these distinctive figures were made from a wooden armature covered with sheets of beaten copper or brass and featured a stylized oval face with a crescent-shaped coiffure, a cylindrical neck, and an open, diamond-shaped body. Ours is constructed with four pieces of wood and has been covered with a piece of tooling copper to which an antique finish has been given.

Materials
plywood:
   1 piece, ¾ × 13 × 25 inches, for body
   1 piece, ¾ × 6½ × 11 inches, for face
   1 piece, ¾ × 5 × 8 inches, for base
1 piece pine, 2 × 2 × 2¼ inches, for nose
3 inches dowel, ¼ inch in diameter
1 piece tooling copper, 1 × 3½ feet
contact cement
liver of sulfur
lacquer spray
1 piece felt, 13 × 25 inches, in black; *or*
   acrylic paint, in black, for back of figure
1 piece felt, 5 × 8 inches, in black, for
   base

Tools
brown wrapping paper
ruler
pencil
scissors
masking tape
jigsaw *or* coping saw
sandpaper, medium and fine grades
drill with ¼-inch bit
ballpoint pen
steel wool, extra-fine
newspaper pad
wooden modeling tool
craft knife

Procedure
1. On brown wrapping paper, draw 1-inch grid and enlarge patterns for wood parts (see "Helpful Hints"). Cut out each enlarged pattern part and tape to wood. Draw around each part and saw out. Make three-dimensional nose by sawing to the shapes indicated in views given within box on pattern. Saw out slot in base and check fit of figure to base. Remove patterns. Sand all edges smooth.

2. Position face part over body. Drill ¼-inch-diameter holes at center forehead and center chin, through both pieces of wood. Cut dowel into two 1½-inch pieces. Dowels will be used to join face to body. Glue ends of dowels into face portion of body. Fit face part on protruding ends of dowels, but do not glue. Sand dowel ends flush with face. Remove face.

3. On brown wrapping paper, draw 1-inch grid, enlarge patterns for copper, and cut out. Tape patterns to copper, in same arrangement shown on pattern, leaving about ½-inch space between each. Trace over design patterns with ballpoint pen. Check reverse side of copper to make sure indentations have come through.

4. Cut out copper parts with scissors, leaving a ¼-inch margin on edges of parts A through F. Remove patterns and clean copper with steel wool.

5. Tool designs, following directions given for metal tooling in "Helpful Hints." Work on a newspaper pad over a smooth, hard surface. A ruler can be used as a guide for tooling straight lines.

6. Following manufacturer's directions, apply contact cement to one piece of copper and its corresponding wood part. Leave edges until last. Place metal on wood. Press metal to wood by going over depressed lines with modeling tool. This will ensure a good bond. For rounded edges of face and base, cement metal to surface and cut out tiny V shapes from edge of metal to edge of wood, all the way around. Apply cement and burnish metal to edges with modeling tool. Use enough pressure to flatten metal. With craft knife, cut out center slot in base. Fold copper covering for nose on lines and glue to nose piece.

7. Glue remaining strips to wood edges, following designations given on pattern. Since the figure is sectioned off, strips do

Cutting Patterns for Wood

each square = 1 inch

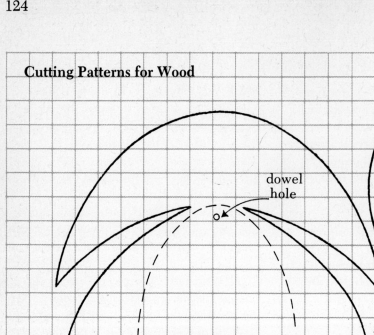

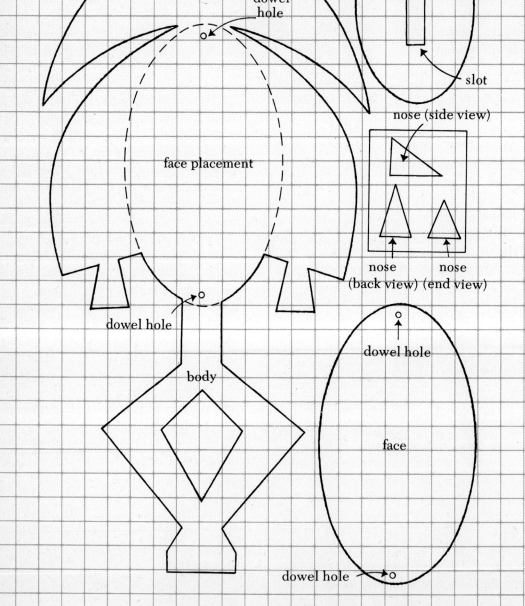

base

slot

dowel
hole

nose (side view)

nose   nose
(back view) (end view)

face placement

dowel hole

dowel hole

body

face

dowel hole

Cutting Patterns for Copper

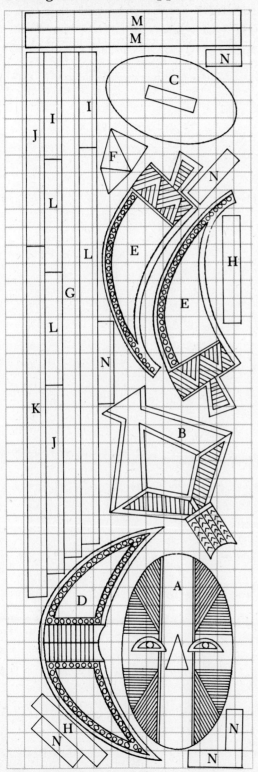

each square = 1 inch

not have to be continuous. Fit strips to the required length, cut, and cement, allowing approximately ⅛ inch from front edge. Burnish margins over back edges.

8. Apply cement to projecting dowel ends and to back of face piece; dowel face piece in position on body. Cement body to base. Then cement nose to face. Allow glue to dry overnight.

9. Rub entire piece with steel wool. To antique copper, apply liver of sulfur (see metal-tooling instructions in "Helpful Hints"). When dry, rub highlights with steel wool. Dust well; spray two coats of lacquer over entire piece.

10. Once lacquer has completely dried, paint back of figure black or cover with black felt. Cover bottom of base with felt to prevent scratching of finished surfaces.

Assembling Code:

A = face
B = body
C = base
D = top hair
E = side hair and earring
F = nose
G = face edging
H = neck and face edging
I = inner leg edging
J = outer leg edging
K = base edging
L = top hair edging
M = side hair edging
N = hair and earring edging

Rooftop Church

In Ayacucho, a town in the heartland of Peru, folk artisans make little clay churches that they fasten to the tile roofs of their homes. It is believed that such a clay church will bring blessings to the house it adorns. The town itself, some 8,500 feet above sea level, features many churches, all of which show strong Spanish influence.

Our little church can be made of self-hardening clay, using the slab method of rolling the clay out, cutting the walls, and assembling. Since many of us live in places where having a church perched on our rooftop wouldn't be too practical, ours has been made into a plant holder. The church is wobbly and uneven, but that's part of its charm. Notice the clock. Its numerals show thirteen hours—a number of which are backwards.

Materials
5 pounds air-dry clay
acrylic tube paints, in red oxide and
    burnt umber
floral wire *or* spool wire, 8 inches long
plant container

Tools
cardboard
pencil
ruler
scissors
plastic-covered work surface
rolling pin *or* round bottle
table knife
bowl of water
damp cloth
darning needle, large
watercolor brushes, small and medium

Procedure
1. On cardboard, draw 1-inch grid and enlarge pattern for front (see "Helpful Hints"). Cut around outline and cut out all areas that are marked with slanted lines.
2. On plastic-covered work surface, roll out clay to about ¼-inch thickness, using rolling pin or round bottle. With table knife, cut out piece of clay about 6 × 7½ inches for floor of church. As you cut the slabs specified in the following steps, keep in mind that the slab method of clay working is an open process and that dimensions will not be exact.
3. Roll out more clay, place pattern over it, and cut around outline. With a table knife, cut out openings for doors and windows. Measure and cut two strips about 1¾ × 7 inches for side returns on front of church. Dip fingers in water and run along edges to be joined. Join side returns to front, pushing edges together firmly and smoothing clay. Dampen

bottom edges of church front and side returns, and join to floor about 1 inch from front edge. The side returns become inner walls of bell tower (Figure 1). Clay will be a little wobbly at first, so prop walls with clay box or anything handy.
4. Make one bell tower at a time: Cut two strips of clay, each about 1 × 7 inches, to serve as front and back walls of tower. Cut out hole for window, following photograph for position. Dampen one edge of front and back tower walls and join to side return wall, forming three sides of tower. At base of inner wall of tower, cut a small door to allow air to circulate and hasten drying time. Repeat process to make tower for other side of church.
5. Roll out clay and cut 7½ × 3¼-inch slab of clay for back of church, dampen one 7½-inch edge, and join to floor slab. Then cut two pieces for side walls, each 4½ × 7 inches. Curve back portions of side walls, as shown in Figure 2, so that height at back edge is only 3¼ inches. Join side walls to edges of tower walls, floor, and back wall to resemble top view of church shown in Figure 3. Cover church with damp cloth and allow to stand overnight. The clay will stiffen some so that adding the tops of the bell towers and trim will be easier.
6. Cut two pieces of clay, each 1½ × 1½ inches, for platforms of bell towers. Dampen top edges of tower walls and attach platform to each tower. The platform edges overhang the tower walls (Figure 4).
7. For front and back walls of top bell tower, cut clay slabs about 1½ × 2¼ inches. Cut out arches in front and back. For side walls of top bell tower, cut two pieces, each about ½ × 2¼ inches. Dampen edges and attach front, back,

and sides of both top bell towers. Do not mount on platform yet.

8. Cut two dome platforms, each about 1½ × 1½ inches. Cut two 2½-inch-diameter clay circles for domes. Push up clay in center of circles to form a rounded top and flatten bottom edges. Dampen dome edges and attach to dome platforms. Cut out small arch in front of each dome and use pencil point to make hole above arch. Dampen edges of bell tower top and position dome platform on it. Then join each dome to platform.

9. Mold clay into figures, cross, and other

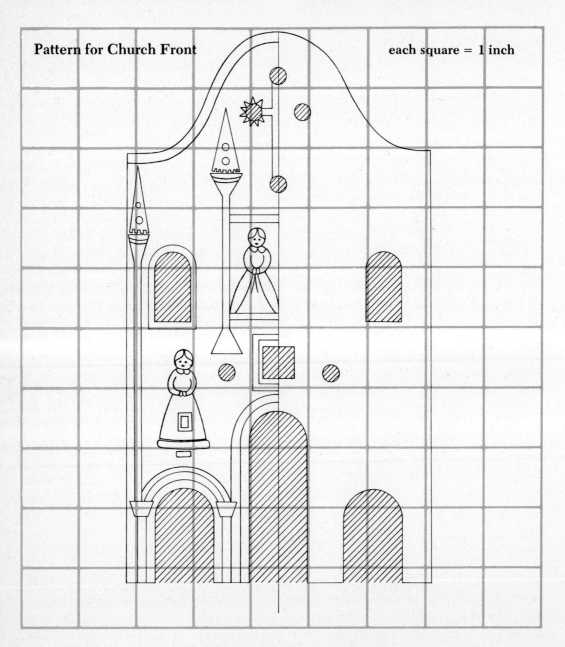

Pattern for Church Front   each square = 1 inch

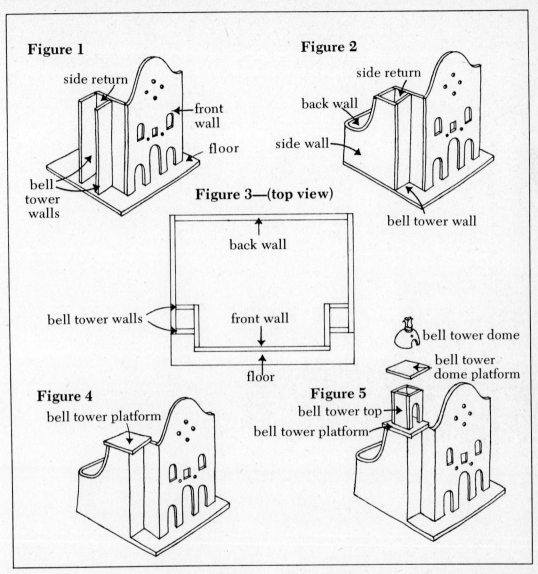

Figure 1

side return

front wall

floor

bell tower walls

Figure 2

side return

back wall

side wall

bell tower wall

Figure 3—(top view)

back wall

bell tower walls

front wall

floor

Figure 4

bell tower platform

Figure 5

bell tower dome

bell tower dome platform

bell tower top

bell tower platform

decorative shapes, as shown in photograph. Dampen clay pieces and add to church. Shape two small bells and, with darning needle, poke a hole through top of each for hanging. Set aside to dry. Make hole in center of each dome platform.

10. Let finished building air-dry.

11. When church is dry, paint all details. Cut two 4-inch lengths of wire. Loop end of one 4-inch wire and, through arch, run other end down through hole in dome plat-

form. Thread bell on end and draw up into tower; twist end into loop and cut off any extra. Repeat bell-attaching process in other bell tower.

12. Add plant container in back. Remember that this clay is not waterproofed. It will not melt but it will absorb water, so either use a watertight container for your plant material or waterproof the clay according to the manufacturer's instructions given on the package.

Chapter 5
Cozy Corner

Peru

Knitted Pillow

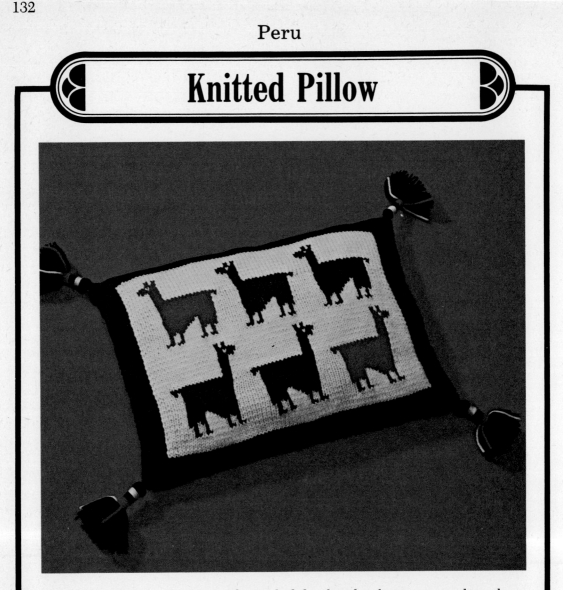

As early as 2500 B.C., Peruvian craftsmen had developed techniques to produce almost every known fabric. Both wool and cotton were handwoven into various textiles, including tapestry and lacelike gauze. Many fabrics were then decorated with embroidery.

Today, in the mountains of Peru, women continue to spin wool, a good portion of which is supplied by the vicuña and the alpaca. Because the wool from the vicuña amounts to only one-quarter to one-half pound every two years, it has always been highly prized. In the past, the Incas had allowed only royalty to wear it and severely punished any violators of this tradition. The alpaca, on the other hand, yields from four to six pounds of wool every two years. At the present time, experimental crossbreeding has produced the hybrid paco-vicuña, along with the hope of increasing the wool yield while retaining the qualities native to each.

The pattern for this pillow was designed by the Incas who lived high in the Andes. The alternate design patterns are other motifs from Incan textiles, woven about A.D. 700 to 1100. You might wish to adapt them for your own knitting or needlepoint designs.

Materials
knitting worsted, 4-ply (approximate amounts):
 6 ounces, in black
 2 ounces, in eggshell
 ½ ounce, in orange
 ½ ounce, in brown
2 pieces fabric, each 14 × 19 inches, for inner lining
Dacron stuffing

Tools
knitting needles, size 7
scissors
crochet hook, size G
ruler
cardboard

Gauge: 5 stitches to an inch, 8 rows to an inch

Procedure
1. With black yarn, cast on 86 stitches; work in seed stitch (k 1, p 1) for 10 rows, or 1¼ inches (cast-on row is included). Alternate stitch for each row, working k 1, p 1 across first row and p 1, k 1 across second row.
2. With black, begin row 11 in seed stitch, working 7 stitches; then attach eggshell and k 72; to finish row, k 7 in black. Continue with black in seed stitch (k 1, p 1) and eggshell in stockinette stitch (k 1 row, p 1 row) for a total of 6 rows.
3. Continuing to begin and end each row with 7 black seed stitches, set in design block, using stockinette stitch and working one stitch for each square on pattern. Use colors shown in photograph. When changing colors, avoid leaving holes by twisting color no longer in use once around color in use. Carry unused strands loosely along back side of the work, and twist with color in use every fourth or fifth stitch. When last row of eggshell design block is completed, add top border as follows: Work 7 seed stitches in black, k 72 in black, and end with 7 more seed stitches in black. To complete border, work 9 more rows, or until border is same width as bottom border, in black seed stitch.
4. With black yarn, cast on 86 stitches for back of pillow and work in seed stitch to same length as pillow front.
5. With right sides together, machine-stitch around three sides of inner pillow lining pieces, turn right side out, stuff, and hand-stitch fourth side closed.
6. With right sides of knitted pieces facing out, single crochet around three sides, inserting hook from top side. When three sides are joined, keep yarn attached and block pieces. After blocking, slip in liner pillow and finish crocheting edges together.
7. To make tassels, cut a piece of cardboard so that one of its dimensions is 4 inches. For each tassel, wrap 50 turns of black yarn around 4-inch dimension. Draw a 15-inch-long doubled strand of black yarn under strands at one end of the cardboard and tie a secure knot. Cut strands at opposite end of cardboard. Run a length of eggshell from bottom of tassel up to ½ inch below knot, and tightly wrap 10 rounds. Tie off and cut both ends to length of tassel. Repeat with brown and then orange. Trim tassels so that they are even, and sew ends of the black strands from original knot to corners of the pillow. With crochet hook, run these ends down through tassel tops into tassels so that they are hidden from view.

Design Pattern

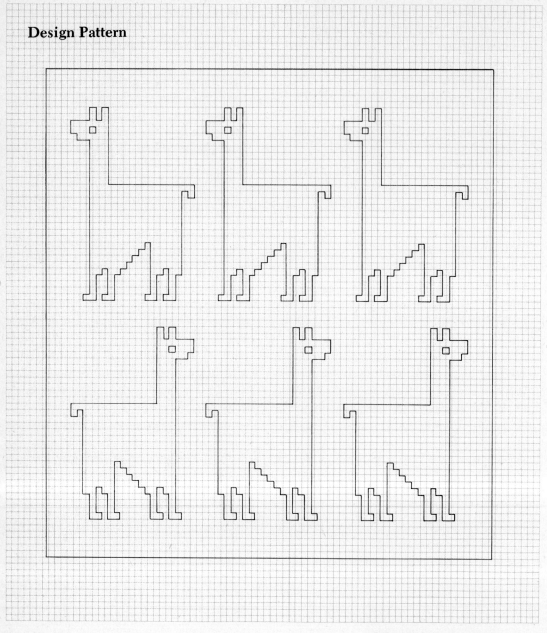

each square = 1 stitch

Alternate Design Patterns

Ainu-design Pillow

The Ainu people are an ancient Caucasianlike group who may, at one time, have occupied all of Japan. For the past seven thousand years, they have lived on the island of Hokkaido in the Japanese archipelago. Today, it is estimated that there are only three hundred full-blooded Ainus left.

The ceremonial robes of the Ainus are decorated in a distinctive manner. A chain stitch is embroidered, often over appliquéd areas, into mazelike designs. Scrolls, brackets, straight lines, and curves are combined in traditional ways completely from memory and without benefit of a pattern.

Originally, the Ainu garments were made of *attush*—a cloth that was woven from the inner bark of mountain elms. The bark was softened in water, split into long threads, colored with vegetable dye, woven, and then embroidered. Today, the embroidery and appliqué work is done on cotton. Traditionally, both Ainu men and women wear embroidered coats, while the women also wear embroidered headbands. Embroidery work is usually done in white, blue, yellow, or red, while background materials are usually colored dark blue, dark green, or black.

You can duplicate the Ainu design on this pillow by simply sewing on soutache braid, or make it authentic and work the pattern in two or three rows of chain stitches.

Materials
2 pieces felt, each 15½ × 18 inches, in black
white glue in applicator bottle
3 packages soutache braid, in white
thread, in white
Dacron stuffing

Tools
brown wrapping paper
pencil
ruler
dressmakers' carbon, in white
tracing wheel
straight pins

Procedure
1. On brown wrapping paper, draw 1-inch grid and enlarge design pattern (see "Helpful Hints"). Using dressmakers' carbon and tracing wheel, transfer pattern onto one piece of felt.

2. Apply a thin, even line of white glue onto a section of design outline. Position soutache braid on glued area, pinning in stubborn places.

3. Continue applying glue and braid to entire design. Allow glue to dry.

4. Machine-stitch braid in place.

5. With right sides of felt pieces facing, stitch together, ¼ inch in from outer edge, leaving a section open for stuffing.

6. Turn pillow right side out, stuff, and stitch the opening together by hand.

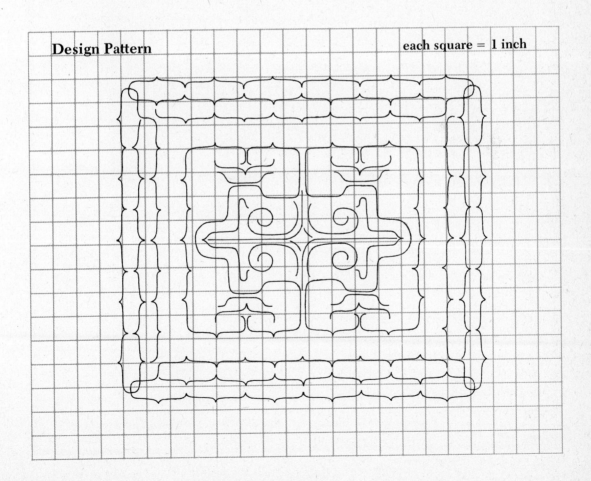

Design Pattern   each square = 1 inch

Kuwait

Embroidered Pillow

Until the discovery of vast oil deposits in 1945, the world knew little about a small stretch of remote desert land called Kuwait. Today, however, it is an independent, oil-rich sheikdom that has, almost overnight, earned a position of power and worldwide respect.

Our pillow design was adapted from a room-sized Kuwait rug, or *kilim*, made from three strips of embroidered handwoven wool sewn together. The embroidered pattern features the camel, which is the true measure of a Bedouin's wealth. This particular type of embroidery, called *tambour*, has long been used with great skill by the Asians. Basically, it is done by working the chain stitch with a hook rather than a needle. The material is first stretched over a round tambour frame. The working thread is held in the left hand below the hoop and is pulled through the cloth with a hook. With experience, an embroiderer can work rows of chain stitching very quickly, using a continuous thread. Very often, a whole family will work on a rug at the same time, sometimes using nothing more than a bent nail set into a handle for a hook and a tire rim for a frame.

These rugs are made for personal use, and they are a necessary part of a girl's dowry. When the rugs are hung on the tent walls or laid on the floor, they offer protection against both heat and cold, for, in Kuwait, temperatures range from an astonishing high of 165 degrees on hot days during the summer to a low of 50 degrees during the wintertime.

Materials

1 piece burlap, 16 × 20 inches
yarn, 4-ply (approximate amounts):
   1½ ounces, in red
   1 ounce, in green
   1½ ounces, in magenta
   ¼ ounce, in orange
   ½ ounce, in yellow
1 piece fabric, 18 × 36 inches, for backing
3⅓ yards cording, #200
Dacron stuffing

Tools

brown wrapping paper
pencil
ruler
dressmakers' carbon
tracing wheel
indelible felt-tipped pen
frame, large enough to accommodate at
   least 14 × 18 inches of burlap*
tack hammer and tacks *or* staple gun
crochet hook set in handle *or* plain
   crochet hook
scissors
sewing-machine zipper or cording foot

*This can be any wooden frame or canvas-stretcher bars, which are available at art-supply stores at a reasonable price.

Procedure

1. To prevent burlap from raveling, machine-stitch around edge of fabric. On brown wrapping paper, draw 1-inch grid and enlarge design pattern (see "Helpful Hints"). Center and trace pattern on burlap, using carbon and tracing wheel. Connect dots with indelible felt-tipped pen.

2. Place burlap over frame and tack or staple center of each side of fabric to frame. Keeping fabric straight and taut, continue tacking from centers to corners of each side.

3. Begin work anywhere on pattern and complete one color section at a time, following photograph on page 130 for color scheme. Holding yarn under frame, push hook down through fabric from top and draw up a yarn loop. Holding loop on hook, push hook down again through fabric and pull up a second loop. Draw second loop through first loop to make first stitch of chain. The loop left on hook will serve as first loop for next stitch. Stitch around a design outline first; then work toward its center following this outline. To outline central diamond shape, chain-stitch loops so that they resemble a row of script *e*'s.

For each design, establish stitch pattern and direction, and then follow same path for each repeat of that design. The trick is to maintain continuous stitching without breaking off yarn to begin another row. There are no set rules to follow for completing pattern; choose the best way for you. All thread ends are run through to back.

4. To assemble pillow, first refer to cutting diagram. From backing fabric, cut a piece to measure 13 × 17 inches. On front piece, trim excess burlap to ½ inch on each side of pattern to allow for seaming. Machine-stitch edges to prevent raveling. (Back and front pieces should be same size.) Then, from backing fabric, cut two 2½-inch-wide boxing strips, each 29¼ inches long. Use remaining backing fabric to cut 1½-inch-wide bias strips.

5. Join the two boxing strips to make one long strip. Stitch together bias strips to form one continuous strip. With bias strip right side out, cover cording, and, using zipper or cording foot, stitch as closely as possible to cording.

6. Sew cording to right side of pillow front and back as closely as possible to

edge. With right sides together, join boxing strip to cording on pillow front. Repeat process to join pillow back, leaving open a section through which to insert stuffing. Turn right side out, stuff, and then hand-stitch opening together.

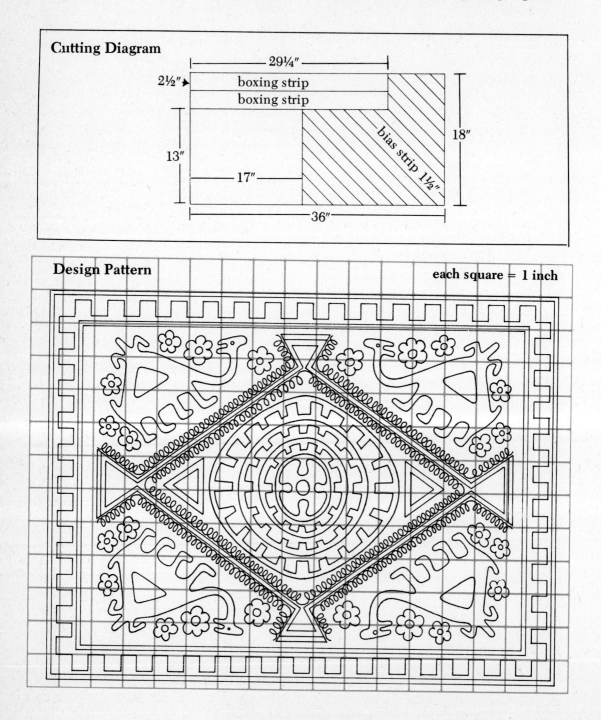

Cutting Diagram

29¼"

2½"

boxing strip
boxing strip

bias strip 1½"

18"

13"

17"

36"

Design Pattern each square = 1 inch

Alternate Design Patterns

Alternate Design Patterns

Alternate Design Patterns

Kashmir, India

Crewel Embroidery Pillow

From the fabled vale of Kashmir comes the *namda* rug—and the inspiration for this pillow. *Namda* is a coarse, pressed, nonwoven woolen cloth used in India for horse blankets and carpets. Articles of this material are usually decorated with tambour embroidery, which is a chain stitch worked with a hook. Our felt pillow is done with the same ancient stitch, but we will use a needle instead of a hook.

Our pillow is embroidered in just two stitches, the chain stitch and the outline or stem stitch. Both are very easy to work, and they truly enhance the eye-catching design.

Materials

felt:

    1 square, 18 × 18 inches, in white

    2 squares, each 24 × 24 inches, in orange

    1 strip, 1½ inches wide, 1⅔ yards long, in orange

Persian-type crewel yarn (approximate amounts):

    1½ ounces, in blue

    ¾ ounce, in orange

    ½ ounce, in black

    ½ ounce, in white

2⅔ yards cording, #200

Dacron stuffing.

Tools

brown wrapping paper

pencil

ruler

scissors

dressmakers' carbon

tracing wheel

crewel needle

sewing-machine zipper or cording foot

Procedure

1. On brown wrapping paper, draw 1-inch grid and enlarge design pattern (see "Helpful Hints"). Complete pattern for other half of pillow by laying pattern over carbon, carbon side up, and tracing over lines, producing design in reverse.

2. Cut out pattern, and use carbon and tracing wheel to transfer to white felt. Cut white felt on heavy black line (see pattern). Center white felt on one square of orange felt and machine-stitch around all edges. In the four cutout areas around the pattern and at the center, transfer small flower designs to orange felt.

3. Work design areas in colors that are shown in photograph. Because felt stretches, do not use hoop. Avoid puckering by keeping stitches loose and even.

Before you begin, refer to "Helpful Hints" for explanation of chain stitch, outline stitch, and stem stitch. To work small flowers and stems, chain-stitch all outlines first and then fill in with second color, still using chain stitch. Work an outline or stem stitch in black around edge of design.

For the large five-flower groups, first work narrow end of flower from outline to middle; then change colors and work rest of flower, finishing with chain-stitch border at wide edge. With black, outline flower groups, using stem stitch or outline stitch.

4. Cover cording with the strip of orange felt and, using zipper or cording foot, stitch as closely as possible to cording. Then, with right sides together, machine-stitch cording to pillow top.

5. With right sides together, machine-stitch front piece to back piece, leaving a section open for stuffing. Turn right side out, stuff, and stitch opening by hand.

Design Pattern (Half)

center

each square = 1 inch

Alternate Design Patterns

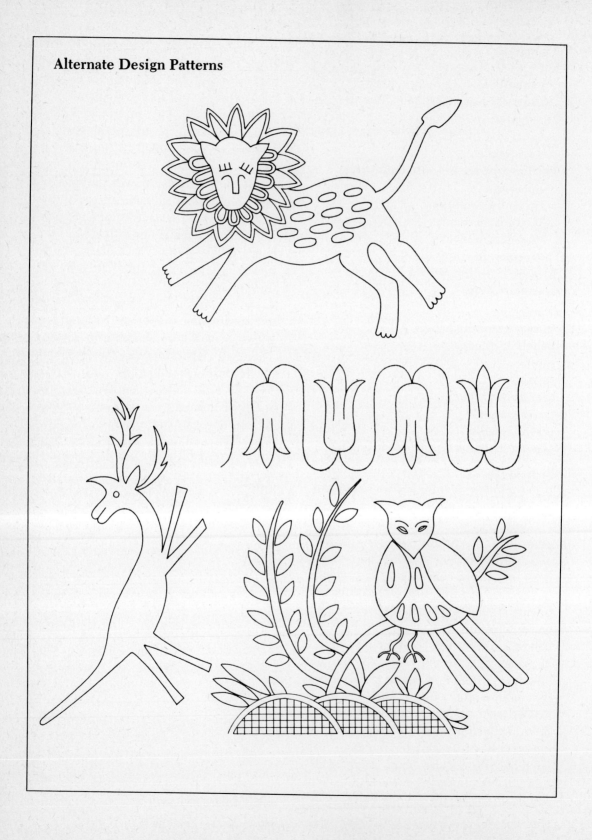

Alternate Design Patterns

San Blas Islands, Panama

Reverse Appliqué Pillow

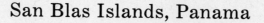

Molas are the unique handcraft of the Cuña Indian women of Panama's San Blas Islands. The *mola* consists of several rectangular layers of brightly colored cloth. The rectangles are basted together, and then small areas of one layer or of several are cut away. This technique can best be described as "reverse appliqué." These decorative panels are then used to form the fronts and backs of blouses.

Most Cuña women, who begin to sew at the age of seven or eight, have from five to thirty molas in their wardrobe. The working time required to make one panel may range anywhere from forty to seventy hours. The subject matter for the designs is endless—animals and birds, fish and mermaids, and human figures are all commonly used.

For anyone who enjoys needlework, reverse appliqué offers a fascinating challenge. You might like to try making a reverse appliqué piece to use as a wall hanging, or you can make it to serve as trim on an article of clothing, perhaps using it as a pocket.

Materials

cotton fabric rectangles, 18 × 21 inches,
   one each in black, orange, and yellow
   and two in red
thread, in colors to match above fabrics
scraps of cotton fabric, in light aqua, dark
   aqua, blue, lavender, purple, light pea
   green, and moss green
1 package piping, in red (optional)
Dacron stuffing

Tools

brown wrapping paper
pencil
ruler
scissors
dressmakers' carbon, in white
tracing wheel
needle

Design Pattern

Procedure

1. Stack fabric pieces with one piece of
red on the bottom, orange next, then yellow, and black on top. Baste all layers
together around outer edges.

2. On brown wrapping paper, draw 1-
inch grid and enlarge design pattern (see
"Helpful Hints"). Cut out pattern and
transfer to top layer, using dressmakers'
carbon and tracing wheel.

3. In color photograph, note yellow design lines on rooster figure. To reveal
yellow fabric, start first cut by carefully
pushing point of scissors through black
layer on outside yellow design line.
Begin cutting but do *not* cut out design—
as you cut, leave a small bridge of uncut
fabric every 2 or 3 inches. Turn edges
under to rooster outline and, with black

each square = 1 inch

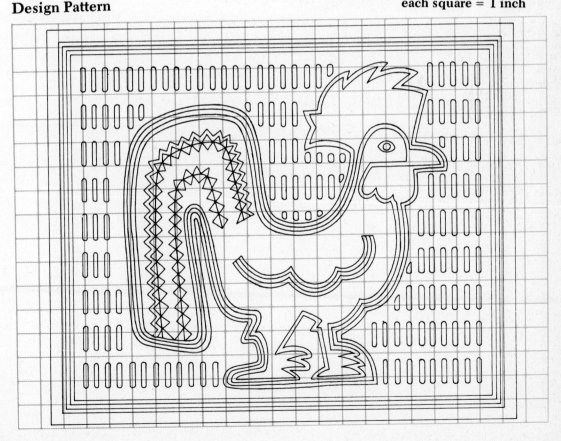

thread, whip down, stitching every ¼ inch and sewing through all layers. Cut bridges as you come to them, and clip corners and curves as necessary so that fabric will lie flat. Repeat this procedure to reveal all other yellow areas within rooster figure.

4. Cutting through top *two* layers, repeat process to reveal orange design areas (see photograph). To expose red fabric, cut through top three layers. Make no cuts on red fabric, since this is the background.

5. Cutting through top layer only, cut background slits to measure about 1½ inches. To add various colors, cut strips of fabric slightly wider than the slits and slip under. If you wish, you may baste scrap to top fabric to hold in place. Turn under edges of slit and stitch through all layers of fabric to the back.

6. After completing figure and background, add a border around the edges. Working one side and one color at a time, cut on color outline; turn under edges and sew down.

7. If you wish to add piping, stitch piping to edge of pillow top at seam allowance. With right sides facing, machine-stitch second piece of red fabric to front of pillow, leaving open a section for stuffing.

8. Turn pillow right side out, stuff with Dacron, and sew opening together by hand.

Alternate Design Pattern

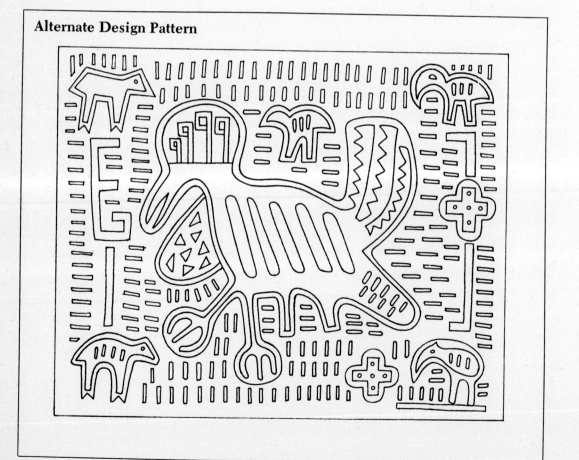

Alternate Design Patterns

Coptic Triptych

Ethiopia is the only country in Africa with over thirty centuries of recorded history, a history that has left a rich heritage of art. For centuries, Ethiopia remained a hidden empire, secluded from the world by natural barriers and traveled by few. However, with the vast expansion of Christianity around A.D. 300, local styles of art developed over the world. One of the most important of these is called Coptic, which was produced by Christians living in the Nile Valley from the fourth century until the seventh-century Arab invasion. At the same time, Christianity had come to Ethiopia, and close ties existed with the Coptic Patriarchate in Alexandria. So, while Coptic arts were on the decline in Egypt, they continued vigorously in Ethiopia. So far, some 15,000 churches are known to exist in Ethiopia, many of which contain great treasures of religious art from this period.

Materials

rough-cut redwood *or* any other type of
  weathered wood with a soft, even
  grain:

  1 piece, ¾ × 6½ × 11¾ inches, for
    facade

  1 piece, ¾ × 11¾ × 23¾ inches, for
    central panel

  2 pieces, each ¾ × 5⅞ × 15⅝ inches,
    for doors

  1 piece, 1¾ × 1¾ × 14 inches, for top
    of base

  1 piece, 1½ × 3 × 16⅝ inches, for
    bottom of base

  2 pieces, each ¾ × ¾ × 1¼ inches, for
    knobs

acrylic tube paints, in light blue, dark
  blue, yellow, red, and white or colors
  of your choice

white glue

brads, each 1¼ inches long

2 flat right-angle mending plates, 5
  inches

2 wood screws, each ½ inch long

6 wood screws, each 1¼ inches long

2 pairs hinges, small, with screws

Tools

brown wrapping paper
pencil
ruler
carbon paper
scissors
jigsaw *or* coping saw
sandpaper, finishing grade
masking tape
nailset
wood-burning tool
wood chisel
mallet
file
drill with ⅛-inch bit and ¼-inch bit
center punch
2 C-clamps

scrap wood, for cushion blocks
watercolor brushes, small and medium
hammer
screwdriver

Procedure

1. On brown wrapping paper, draw 1-inch grid and enlarge patterns, including all design lines. In making pattern for inside of door, place wrapping paper over carbon paper, carbon side up, to produce reverse pattern on back of sheet.

2. Cut slot in back of 14-inch base piece: Measure in 1⅛ inches from each end of length of piece, mark across width of wood at these points, and saw along marked lines to a depth of ¾ inch. Chisel out wood between saw cuts. With bottom edges aligned, place central panel in slot and check for fit, making adjustments if necessary.

3. Tape facade pattern to wood, mark outline of one half, flip pattern over to complete outline, and saw out. Matching outer edges of facade to top of central panel, glue and, with brads and nailset, nail together. File outer edges if necessary.

4. Lightly sand wood on design areas, especially in general areas of hands and faces. Tape design patterns to wood and transfer all design lines, either by indenting wood with a hard pencil or with carbon paper and a pencil. Flip pattern over to transfer lines for inner side of other door.

5. Heat wood-burning tool and burn design outlines into wood on all pieces. Be sure to include design lines for outside of doors, also. For background areas, place wedge-shaped side of tip of wood-burning tool against wood and overlap burns, thus darkening the areas.

6. With acrylic tube paints, paint design

areas as shown in photograph or in color scheme of your choice.

7. Center 14-inch base piece on 16⅜-inch base piece, lining up back edges (slot will be facing back edge, as shown on pattern). Glue and clamp bases together, using cushion blocks to protect wood (see woodworking section in "Helpful Hints"). Allow glue to dry completely and then remove blocks and clamps.

8. Glue and clamp central panel in slot, again using cushion blocks to protect wood. Allow glue to dry; remove clamps. Check to make sure panel stands firmly.

9. Place assembled base and central panel face down on workbench, propping up panel portion with scrap wood to make it level. Position mending plates on back of base, as shown on pattern. With center punch, mark positions for screw holes. Using ⅛-inch bit, drill holes; screw plates to base with 1¼-inch screws and to central panel with ½-inch screws.

10. Following knob-detail diagram, shape knobs for door fronts: For each knob, measure and mark line AB ⅜ inch in from each edge of wood piece. Saw on AB lines to a depth of ¼ inch. Mark ¼-inch squares (see bottom view) on op-

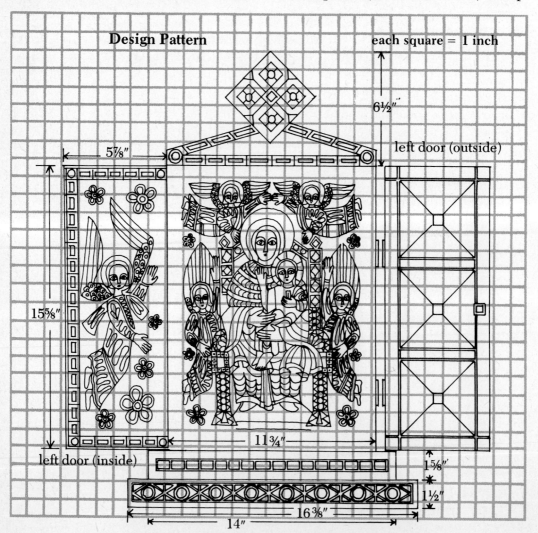

Design Pattern

each square = 1 inch

6½″

left door (outside)

5⅞″

15⅝″

left door (inside)

11¾″

1⅝″

1½″

16⅜″

14″

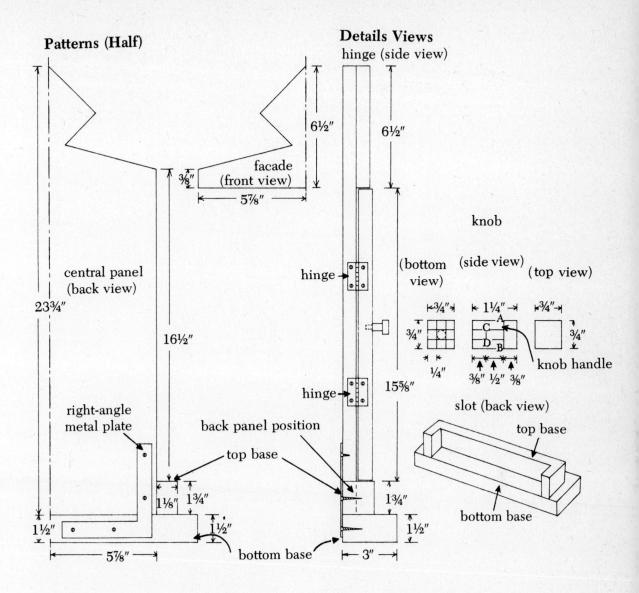

Patterns (Half)

central panel (back view)

23¾"

16½"

⅜"

facade (front view)

5⅞"

6½"

right-angle metal plate

top base

back panel position

1⅛" 1¾"

1½"

1½"

5⅞"

bottom base

Details Views

hinge (side view)

6½"

6½"

hinge

hinge

(bottom view)

knob

(side view) (top view)

knob handle

¾"

¾"

¼"

1¼"

A
C
D
B

¾"

¾"

⅜" ½" ⅜"

15⅝"

slot (back view)

top base

bottom base

1¾"

1½"

3"

posite edge of wood. Place chisel blade on these lines and tap with mallet, splitting off wood to form knob. Mark line CD on wood (see side view), ⅜ inch in from end. With file, round edges of this end to form a ¼-inch-diameter dowel (shown by dotted circle on bottom view).

11. Mark positions for knobs on door fronts and center-punch. With ¼-inch bit, drill ⅜-inch-deep hole. (Wrap masking tape around drill bit ⅜ inch up from bit point to act as a depth gauge.) Glue knob end into hole, using C-clamps with cushion blocks to apply light pressure. After glue has dried, remove clamps. Then mark design pattern on end of each knob and burn in.

12. Following hinge placements indicated on pattern, hinge side panels to center panel, center-punching holes.

Chapter 6

Sunny Corner

France

Crow Cats

If you were to hang your fruit tree full of cat faces, perhaps you would attract the fruit rather than the birds! At least that was the hope of the French gardener who designed these fierce bird watchers. The pattern for these cats came from a charming garden shop in Fécamp, on the coast of France.

Why not make several faces and decorate your sunny corner with a cat-face mobile? Or, if you wish, hang the crow cats from your fruit tree and watch them go to work.

Materials
1 piece aluminum sheeting, 6 × 6 inches
2 marbles, each 1 inch in diameter
enamel spray paint for metal, in black

Tools
brown wrapping paper
ballpoint pen *or* pencil
ruler
scissors
masking tape
tin snips (optional)
coping saw
small files: flat and half-round
drill with small bit

Procedure
1. On brown wrapping paper, draw 1-inch grid and enlarge design pattern (see "Helpful Hints").
2. Cut out pattern and tape to aluminum piece. Mark outline on aluminum with ballpoint pen or pencil, draw in details, and cut out shape with tin snips or coping saw. With files, smooth all edges.
3. In nose, mouth, and whiskers, drill holes large enough to accommodate saw blade. Also drill hole at center of each eye and in hanger at top of head.
4. To saw out whiskers, nose, and mouth, disassemble coping saw, insert blade in drilled hole, and then reassemble saw around blade. Smooth all edges with files. Saw on lines in each eye.
5. Bend prongs in eyes, alternating one forward and one backward, at right angles to face. Smooth edges with files. Hold each marble in eye hole and bend prongs on front side of face to fit around marbles. Remove marbles from back side.
6. Following manufacturer's directions, spray-paint both sides of face.
7. When paint is dry, reinsert marbles and bend back prongs to hold marbles in.

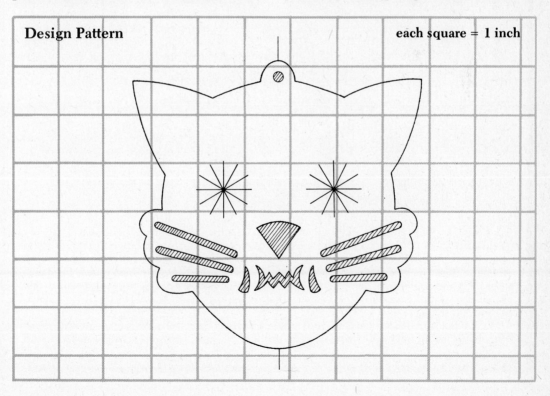

Design Pattern   each square = 1 inch

Scarecrow

Our smiling, self-satisfied little bird is from Guatemala, where he is a hard-working fieldhand on duty to protect the crops from other birds. A close relative of our bird was purchased in Antigua, in a store that stocked flocks of them, all in different sizes and all hanging from the ceiling. Some of the larger birds boasted twenty-four-inch wingspans. These figures are carved by the Indians in the area, and they are not made or sold in any other part of the country. It's our guess that their function is to guard the coffee plantations of Antigua.

A flock of these marble-eyed crows hanging from your ceiling or garden trees would be fun to have. This project provides a good introduction to carving-in-the-round.

Materials

clear-grade redwood*:

 1 piece, 4 × 4 × 9½ inches, for body

 2 pieces, each ⅜ × 4½ × 9 inches, for wings

 2 pieces, each 1¾ × 1¾ × 3 inches, for legs and feet

2 black marbles, each approximately ½ inch in diameter

Duco cement

Tools

brown wrapping paper

pencil

ruler

scissors

masking tape

jigsaw *or* coping saw

vise

carving chisel

carving knife

U-gouge, small

drill

sandpaper, coarse grade (optional)

Procedure

1. On brown wrapping paper, draw 1-inch grid and enlarge patterns for side and top views of body, leg, foot, and wing (see "Helpful Hints"). Cut out patterns.

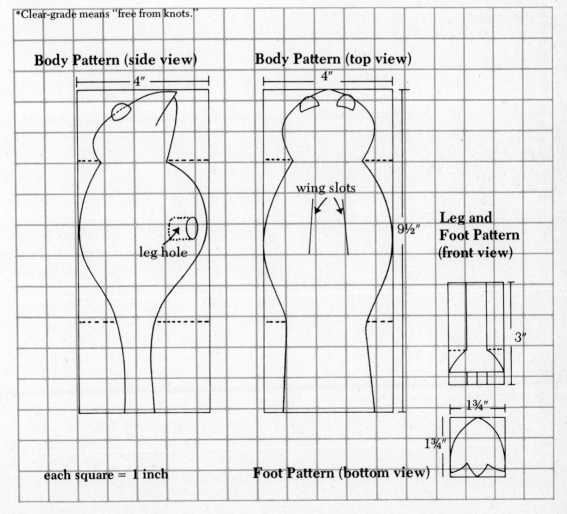

*Clear-grade means "free from knots."

Body Pattern (side view)

4"

leg hole

Body Pattern (top view)

4"

wing slots

9½"

Leg and Foot Pattern (front view)

3"

1¾"

1¾"

Foot Pattern (bottom view)

each square = 1 inch

2. Tape body patterns to appropriate wood piece and draw around outlines with pencil. Draw in pattern details and dotted lines, as shown on pattern. Remove patterns. With saw, make straight cuts on dotted lines. Secure body in vise and roughly chisel out a V-shaped cut between neck and head. Roughly chisel tail area to shape.

3. Using carving knife, begin carving wood to bird shape, and continue until desired body and head shape is finished.

4. Tape leg and foot patterns to wood pieces and draw outlines. Draw in dotted line at ankle area and remove pattern. With saw, make straight cuts on dotted lines. Roughly chisel off excess wood at sides and then carve legs to rounded shape.

5. Saw bottom of foot to shape and then carve foot. Repeat for second leg and foot.

6. Tape wing pattern to appropriate wood piece, draw around outline, and saw out wing. Repeat for second wing. Use U-gouge to work in feather design (see photograph).

7. Make holes for eyes with U-gouge. As you work, fit marbles in sockets to ensure a good fit. Glue marbles in place with Duco cement.

8. Drill two holes in body for legs, making sure that holes are parallel to each other. Shape top ends of legs to fit holes. Before gluing legs, fit into body and check to make sure that bird will stand up well. Adjust tops of legs as necessary; then glue in. After glue has dried, check bird again for its ability to stand well. If further adjustment is needed, place a sheet of coarse sandpaper on a flat surface and, holding bird firmly in an upright position, rotate feet over sandpaper.

9. Following lines marked on top of body for wing slots and referring to woodworking section in "Helpful Hints," chisel out a slot for each wing (slots are angled so that wing tips will flare). Fit wing tabs in slots and then glue in place.

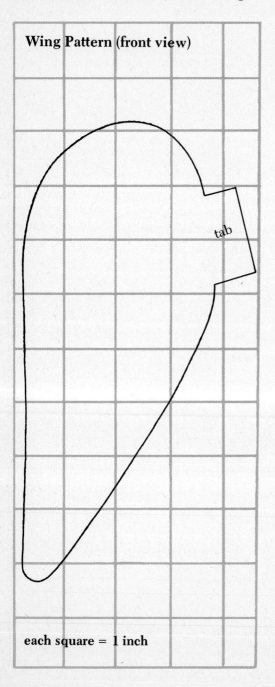

Wing Pattern (front view)

tab

each square = 1 inch

Italy

Vegetable String

For years, people in this country have coveted the brightly colored vegetable strings often seen in gourmet and gift shops. Crammed with garlic bulbs, red and white onions, carrots, and tomatoes, most of these decorated strings originate from a shop in Florence, Italy. There, each vegetable is made from a rough core shaped from excelsior and then wrapped with raffia. The brilliance of the colors is accounted for by the fact that the raffia is dyed right there in the shop. The same results can be achieved by combining Styrofoam with a colored straw made of cellulose fibers, which comes from Switzerland.

The vegetable string in this project is laden with carrots and onions. If you wish to add additional shapes, increase materials accordingly. Then hang a string full of vegetables in any corner of your home, or offer your bounty as a shower or housewarming gift.

Materials

Styrofoam:

    8 balls, each 3 inches in diameter, for large onions

    6 balls, each 2 inches in diameter, for small onions

    7 to 12 feet of pole, 2 inches in diameter, *or* enough 2-inch-wide block scraps to make sixteen 5- to 8-inch-long carrots

5 skeins Swistraw, in orange, for carrots

3 skeins Swistraw, in matte white, for onions

11 chenille stems, cut into 2-inch lengths, in white

white glue

unraveled binders' twine, for roots

approximately 150 feet binders' twine, for braid

wire, lightweight

Tools

carrot and onion (to serve as models)

serrated-edge paring knife

ruler

scissors

darning needle

Procedure

1. To cut vegetable shapes from Styrofoam, use a carrot and an onion to serve as models. For onion shapes, simply press balls on hard surface to flatten tops and bottoms slightly. To make carrots, use serrated-edge knife to cut shapes from Styrofoam pole or glue scrap blocks together and then cut to shape. Lengths may vary from 5 to 8 inches or be as long as you desire. Then roll shapes on table, molding them with fingers.

2. To prepare straw to wrap vegetables, leave straw tied in skeins and saturate in water. (Keep straw wet all the time that you are working with it.) Then locate end of straw in center of skein and pull out, for wrapping.

3. Make hangers next. Use one 2-inch length of chenille stem for each vegetable. With a drop of glue, attach end of straw to one end of stem. Stretching straw, wrap around stem; cut straw and glue to end. Bend stem into a loop and twist ends together. With darning needle, make a hole in top of each vegetable. Put glue on twisted end of loop and push down into hole. This loop will hang vegetable on string (Figure 1).

4. To make roots, use darning needle to make a hole in bottom of each vegetable. Bend a chenille stem into a U shape. Then cut unraveled binders' twine into various lengths. Lay twine over chenille loop, allowing it to hang down, twist ends of loop, and then push ends all the way into vegetable (Figure 1).

5. To wrap onions, glue one end of saturated white straw to top of onion. Holding end in place with index finger, wrap around onion, going from top to bottom; wrap around bottom chenille stem and back up to top. Stretching straw in width and length with ball of thumb, pull enough straw out to wrap onion from top to bottom. Wrap, overlapping each previously wrapped strand halfway. If straw should break, glue end to top or bottom of onion, and start again. When wrapping is completed, glue at bottom.

6. To wrap carrots, pull end of orange straw from skein and spread open with thumb, as described above. Glue end of straw to top of vegetable, and, working from top to bottom, wrap straw in figure-8 pattern (Figure 2) until top is covered. Cut straw and glue end. Finish covering by wrapping straw around carrot, going

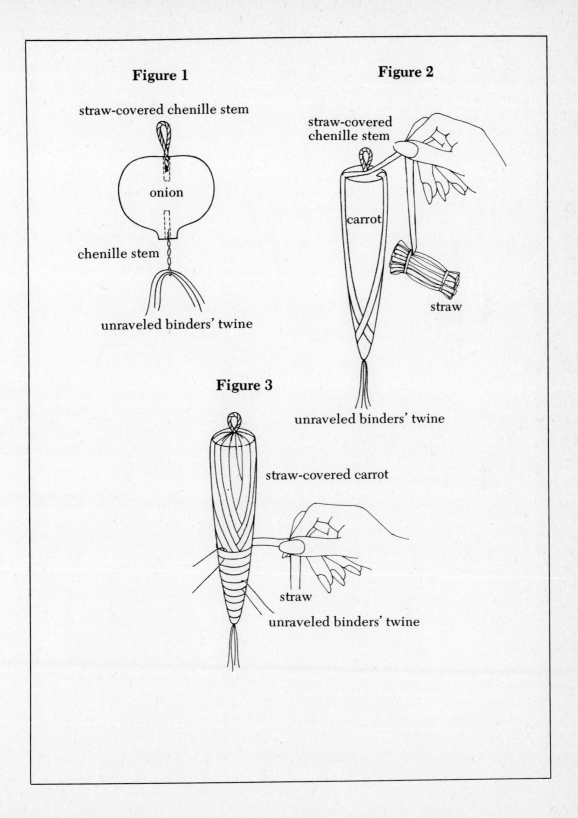

Figure 1

straw-covered chenille stem

onion

chenille stem

unraveled binders' twine

Figure 2

straw-covered
chenille stem

carrot

straw

unraveled binders' twine

Figure 3

straw-covered carrot

straw

unraveled binders' twine

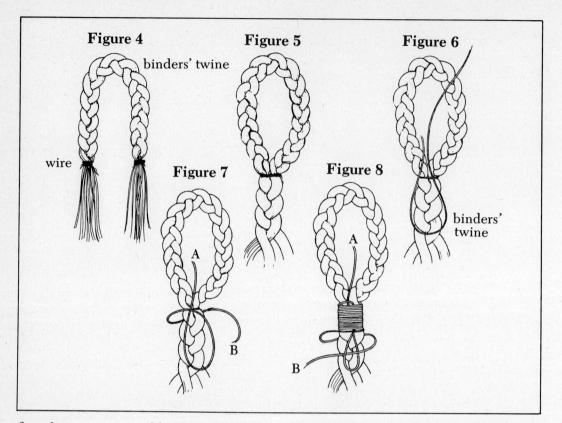

Figure 4

binders' twine

wire

Figure 5

Figure 6

binders' twine

Figure 7

A

B

Figure 8

A

B

from bottom to top, adding in strands of unraveled binders' twine for rootlets (Figure 3) as you wrap. Glue end of wrapping to top of carrot.

7. Cut binders' twine into fifteen 8-foot lengths. Find the midpoint of these pieces and measure off 6 inches on either side. Wrap bundle with a piece of wire at one 6-inch mark. Then divide bundle into three groups of five and braid until other 6-inch mark is reached. Wrap with another piece of wire (Figure 4). To form loop for hanging, remove both wires, fold braided section in half, and rewrap at bottom with a single wire (Figure 5). Then, divide remaining twine into three groups of ten and braid. Wrap bottom of braid with a piece of wire.

8. To wrap braid below hanging loop, cut a piece of binders' twine about 24 inches

long. Hold ends over braid as shown in Figure 6. With end A about 3 inches long, bring end B over A and around braid below loop (Figure 7). Evenly wrap twine around braid for a distance of about 2 inches below loop, keeping bottom of A in small open loop (Figure 8). When wrapping is completed, bring B through loop of A. Pull ends A and B to tighten knot and wrapping. With darning needle, run ends A and B into braid. Trim ends evenly.

9. Before adding vegetables, hang completed string so that spacing will be easier. For each vegetable, cut 8-inch piece of twine and fasten to hanger at top with lark's-head knot (see macramé knots in "Helpful Hints"). Add vegetables to string by threading darning needle with twine ends and weaving them into braid.

Mexico

Papier-Mâché Sun Face

Since before the conquest of Mexico, the tiny village of Tonala, which is not far from Guadalajara, has been famous for its beautiful pottery. The clay from which this pottery was made was supposed to have had curative powers, and shards of it were carried as amulets by women in both Mexico and Europe. The patterns that decorate these pieces are reminiscent of seventeenth-century Persian-style painting and consist of finely drawn flowers and leaves, animals, and geometrics of all kinds. Decorative animal figures painted with these typical patterns are equally popular among Tonala potters.

Also in Tonala is a papier-mâché factory that produces work resembling, in design, the Tonala pottery. The forms for the papier-mâché pieces are all made in homes around the area, collected by trucks, and then brought to the factory for painting and finishing. The resulting pieces are truly beautiful, with their glossy glazes and exquisitely painted animated bird and animal designs.

Since the sun is among the most popular symbols in Mexican designs, we have chosen it as our project design. We have made it of cardboard, covered it with instant papier-mâché, and then painted it in simplified Tonala designs, using acrylic tube paints.

Materials

2 pieces corrugated cardboard, each 20 × 20 inches
white glue
4 inches wire, lightweight
paper plate, 10 inches in diameter, heavy-duty
newspaper
Sculptamold *or* **other instant papier-mâché**
gesso *or* **latex wall paint, in white**
acrylic tube paints, in yellow, black, red, and green, or colors of your choice
high-gloss plastic spray

Tools

pencil
ruler
craft knife
small bowl
paintbrushes, medium
sandpaper, fine grade (optional)
watercolor brushes, small and medium
rags

Procedure

1. On one piece of corrugated cardboard, draw 1-inch grid and enlarge outline of design pattern (see "Helpful Hints"). With craft knife, cut out pattern and glue to second piece of cardboard, crossing the grains of the cardboard. Allow glue to dry. Following outline of first pattern, cut out second shape. About 1 inch into sun face and between any two rays, punch two holes so that they are about ½ inch apart. Then, on the back, make a loop for hanging by pushing wire through holes and twisting ends together.

2. Center paper plate, upside down, on cardboard and draw around it. Apply glue to top rim of plate and glue to cardboard.

3. In small bowl, mix glue with water to the ratio of 2 parts glue to 1 part water.

4. Tear newspaper into pieces measuring about 1 × 2 inches. Dip pieces of paper into glue-and-water mixture, and glue them over edges of sun rays, overlapping each piece by about ¼ inch. To prevent air bubbles and creases, smooth each piece completely with fingers. Continue gluing paper around all rays, and then work over tops of rays, over edges of plate, and up to curve on plate. Let dry.

5. Following package instructions, mix small amount of Sculptamold or other instant papier-mâché and build up features on paper plate, making certain that center of forehead aligns with loop on back. Allow drying time.

6. Cover entire sun face with two more coats of papier-mâché, using a contrasting paper for the second layer so that no areas of sun will be skipped.

7. Paint a coat of undiluted glue over sun and set aside to dry completely.

8. Paint sun with gesso or white latex paint. When dry, sand if necessary and apply second coat.

9. Apply a base coat of yellow to sun; when dry, use pencil to draw in features and designs on border and rays. Then, using watercolor brushes, paint in features and all designs, following color code on pattern or in colors of your choice. All facial feature lines and outlines are done in black.

10. Spray completed sun with one coat of plastic spray; let dry.

11. Thin black paint with water and brush over entire sun. As paint is just beginning to dry, wipe off high spots with cloth. Black paint will remain in low areas, giving an antique look to the piece.

12. When antique coat is completely dry, spray sun with two or three additional coats of plastic spray, allowing adequate drying time between each application.

Design Pattern

each square = 1 inch

Color Code:
A = black
B = red
C = green
D = yellow

Rush-style Stool Seat

For thousands of years, stools and chairs were the signs of high rank and were the possessions solely of rulers; those belonging to the Egyptian rulers some three thousand years ago were outfitted with seats of woven rush, which is one of the earliest evidences of the ancient craft of rush weaving. Eventually, this simple technique became very popular in England and in the rest of Europe, where it was used to make floor coverings and seats for provincial and cottage furniture. In fact, one could say that rush seats were made wherever rush was found, primarily around the rivers and marshes of the world.

Originally, most rush weavers were roof thatchers who turned to rush weaving during the inclement weather. Today, most rush seating is factory-made, but in some remote country villages here and there, it is still practiced.

The best kind of rush bears small brown flowers near the top and reaches a height that is between four to ten feet. It is cut in July before it becomes woody, dried in the sun, and stored for later use. When it is time for the weaving and braiding, the rushes must first be dampened so that they are soft and supple.

It is possible to obtain rush from mail-order houses specializing in natural-seating materials. However, if you have some rope on hand and a stool frame without a seat, you can weave a seat in the same old and easy way that rush work was done in the early days.

Materials
stool frame, with 12 × 12-inch opening
approximately 120 feet of rope, ¼ inch in
  diameter
1 tack

Tools
work gloves
tack hammer
ruler

Procedure
1. Before weaving seat, keep the following points in mind:

    a. With hands protected by gloves,
pull rope tightly and maintain even
tension as you work.

    b. Lay strands evenly, side by side,
and always remember to cross points
at right angles.

    c. If you must leave work temporar-
ily, secure rope by wrapping several
turns around adjacent stool leg so
that completed weaving will not
slacken off.

    d. As the center is filled with weav-
ing, it will become more and more
difficult to get rope bundle through
opening; eventually, you will have to
pull length of cord through opening.

    e. When stool frame is square, work
is continued until all four sides are
covered. When an oblong frame is
used, a point will be reached at
which the shorter sides will have
been filled but a small space will
remain at the center. Fill this space
by weaving back and forth in a figure
8 until seat is completed.

2. To begin work, tack one end of rope to
underside of back rail on frame, as shown
in Figure 1. Referring to Figure 1, begin
first round of weaving as follows:

    1. Over and around rail at A; over

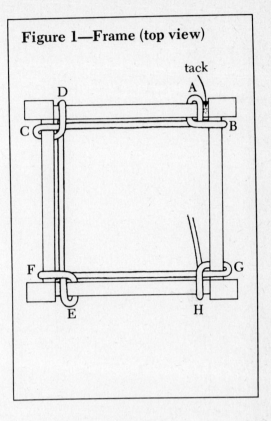

Figure 1—Frame (top view)

and around rail at B.

    2. Across opening and around rail at
C. Over and around rail at D.

    3. Across opening and around rail at
E. Over and around rail at F.

    4. Across opening and around rail at
G. Over and around rail at H, across
opening, and next to starting point A.

3. Repeat process for entire seat, laying
strands next to each other as each
weaving pattern is completed (see step
1b).

4. When weaving is completed, cut end
so that it is about 12 inches long. Wrap
end several times through bottom strands
at center of weaving. Secure with overhand knot (see macramé section in
"Helpful Hints"), and tuck end into center of seat between top and bottom strands.

England

Raffia Mat

Braiding with raffia is one of the earliest known forms of human activity. When man was living closer to nature, he made the things he needed from the plants that grew around him. Rushes, reeds, cane, roots, bark, and twigs were transformed into housing, clothing, and utensils of all kinds. Every museum contains materials attesting to this kind of ingenuity shown by so-called primitive man. Raffia still works as well today as it did thousands of years ago, and the original working techniques are probably still the best.

The most beautiful raffia grows on Madagascar and is made of the ribs of the leaves of the raffia palm. In general, there are two kinds of raffia—white, which is wide and comes in strands up to seventy feet in length, and yellow, which is narrower and shorter in length. Both take ordinary household dye well. Raffia is generally worked dry; if it is *very* dry, however, it is easier to work with dampened hands.

With raffia, the simple braid can become the basis for all shapes and sizes of mats for the table and floor, for shoe soles and tops, for baskets and bags, and for countless other items. The only basic needs for any raffia project are the raffia and a large needle.

Materials
4¼ pounds raffia
household dye, in red orange

Tools
blunt needle, with large eye
hook, doorknob, *or* **C-clamp**
ruler
scissors

Procedure
1. To prevent raffia from tangling while dyeing, open hank and tie raffia together at intervals along the length. Following directions on package for dyeing linen, dye one pound of raffia with red orange dye. Air-dry raffia before braiding.

2. Begin braiding the mat, using about eighteen strands of the dyed raffia. First, tightly wrap ends together several times with a piece of orange raffia. Thread end of wrapping piece through needle and run into wrapping to secure. Slip bundle over a hook, tie it to a doorknob, or fasten to workbench with C-clamp.

3. Divide bundle into three groups of six strands and braid, pulling fairly tightly to make braid about ¾ inch wide. To add new pieces for length, simply braid them in, leaving ends projecting. These ends will be trimmed later. Keep braid even in width and, for added firmness, twist strands while braiding. (Figure 1 shows braiding process.) When you have braided several feet of raffia, turn braid on its side and, starting from the center, coil into a definite oval. Braid or unbraid as necessary to make oval that measures about 5½ inches long and 3 inches wide. This will become center oval of mat.

4. To sew braids of coil together, use more red orange raffia and large blunt needle. Begin stitching at center of oval. With needle sloping upward, join inner braid to next one by pushing needle through center of first braid and bringing it out through center of second braid. Then, leaving a small space before starting next stitch, go back through center of second braid into center of first braid and out on top. Using this stitch pattern and sewing as invisibly as possible, join all braids in oval shape.

5. Bind together ends of eighteen strands of natural raffia, and divide into three groups of six strands each. Braid in the same manner as described in step 3 until you have enough braid to form next oval, which should be 2½ inches wide when laid around center oval. Bind ends with a strip of natural raffia and sew to orange section as described in step 4. The width of the rows on mat in photograph are as follows: center orange, 3 inches; natural, 2½ inches; orange, 1½ inches; natural, 3 inches; orange, 1 inch; natural, 2½ inches. You may complete your mat in this way or in style of your choice. When changing colors or ending mat, finish ends neatly by binding off with a strip of raffia and sewing down. Trim all projecting ends of braids when mat is done.

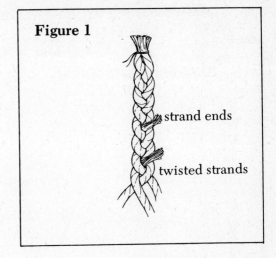

Figure 1

strand ends

twisted strands

Mid-Europe

Wicker Lampshade

Whether you call it rattan, cane, or wicker, it is all the same material and it comes from the core of the cane, or rattan, palm grown primarily in the Indian archipelago. Actually, the rattan palm is not a tree at all but a climbing plant whose shoots grow to lengths up to six hundred feet. When the outer leaves and thorns have been peeled away from the stems, a glossy surface remains. This surface is removed by machine and used in the making of chair seats. The pulp, or center cane, is cut to different thicknesses to become baskets and furniture. None of the material is wasted, for the leftovers from this process are used to make matting, ropes, and furniture stuffing.

Cane is numbered up to size 12 and from then on it is sold by the diameter. As a rule, you will work with two grades of cane. The frame of an object will be constructed of heavy thick cane, referred to as stakes, while the weaving will be done with thinner, more pliable cane, called weavers.

Whatever you make from wicker will be sturdy and long-lasting. By soaking the canes first, you can work them into a multitude of shapes. Our lampshade makes a good project for the beginner, since it requires only a simple over-and-under weaving.

Materials

8½ ounces #3 cane, for weavers
18 pieces #6 cane, each 18 inches long,
  for stakes
1 round wine bottle, gallon-size, without
  handle

Tools

clothespin
rubber band *or* string
ruler
sharp scissors *or* craft knife
awl *or* knitting needle

Procedure

1. Form all cane into a coil, fasten ends with a clothespin, and soak in lukewarm water for 5 to 10 minutes.
2. With rubber band or string, tie nine pairs of stakes to neck of bottle (Figure 1). Keeping pairs of stakes evenly spaced, begin weaving at top, going over and under each pair of stakes with weavers. You will find it easiest to work at edge of table, resting bottle against it. Press rows closely together with fingers of left hand after each round of weaving. When you come to the end of a weaver, begin a new one under a stake (Figure 2).
3. When diameter of shade measures about 5 inches (approximately 6 inches down from top), divide the pairs of stakes into single stakes and continue weaving up to point where bottle starts to curve inward (Figure 1). At this point, remove rubber band or string and take out bottle. Resume weaving until shade is desired size, shaping it as shown in photograph. Cut ends of stakes to about 4 inches beyond last row of weaving and point them with scissors or a craft knife.
4. Before working borders, soak stakes in bowl of lukewarm water for 5 minutes.

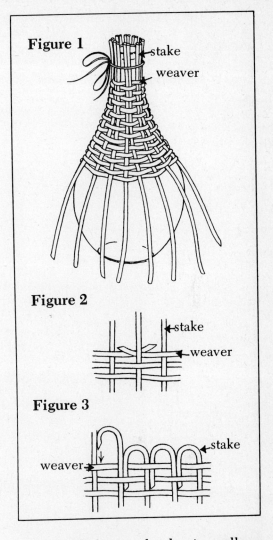

Figure 1

stake
weaver

Figure 2

stake
weaver

Figure 3

weaver
stake

5. To work bottom border in scallops, insert end of each stake alongside next stake (Figure 3). Use awl or knitting needle to open the way for stake and to help push in place. For top border, cut off every other stake just above weaver and work remaining stakes into scallops in same manner as bottom border was done.
6. When shade is completed and dry, use craft knife or sharp scissors to cut, on the diagonal, any projecting weaver ends. Don't cut ends too short or they may work out from behind the stakes and show.

Tree of Life

One of the earliest symbols of rebirth and fertility is the tree of life. Originally, the idea was brought to Spain probably by the Moors and from there it went to Mexico with the Spanish Conquest. The earliest—and still the most popular—motif on the tree represented Adam and Eve in the Garden of Eden, amidst treelike serpents, stylized apples, and angel-faced crescent moons. Until about 1918, the tree was a part of every Mexican wedding and was included in the wedding photographs.

The Mexican people have always accepted death as a part of life, so that it is not surprising that there is also a tree of death. It is, however, just as happy as its counterpart, bearing white skeletons with carmine lips, crowned skulls, and always flowers. On the Day of the Dead, Mexican women carry it, as well as food, to the cemetary to enjoy with departed family members.

Made in all sizes, these imaginative trees are really fun to see—there's always so much to enjoy! Our tree of life is made with cardboard and is covered with instant clay.

Materials

**4 pieces corrugated cardboard, each 19 ×
19 inches**
white glue
1 Styrofoam ball, 5 inches in diameter
wire, lightweight
Celluclay _or_ Claycrete
**5 pieces cardboard tubing, each
approximately 1¼ inches in diameter,
2 inches long**
**2 cardboard cones, each approximately
2½ inches in base diameter, 7 inches
long**
1 Styrofoam ball, 1 inch in diameter
**cardboard, medium-weight (such as shirt
cardboards)**
soft cotton string
gesso
**acrylic tube paints _or_ tempera paints and
plastic spray, in green, yellow, blue,
red, pink, brown, black; or colors of
your choice**

Tools

tracing paper
pencil
ruler
carbon paper
craft knife
needle _or_ other sharp pointed tool
pen cap (optional)
sandpaper, medium grade (optional)
paintbrush, medium
scrap piece of Styrofoam
watercolor brushes, small and medium

Procedure

1. On tracing paper, draw 1-inch grid and
enlarge right side of pattern for tree
frame (see "Helpful Hints"). On one
piece of corrugated cardboard, place
traced pattern over carbon and transfer
design. To complete design, flip pattern
over and, matching edges, transfer left
side of pattern. Cut out with craft knife.

2. Apply white glue to cutout frame, and,
crossing grain of boards to strengthen
frame, glue frame to second piece of cardboard.

3. Using first cutout as guide, cut out pattern on second piece. Repeat procedure
with remaining two pieces of cardboard
so that resulting piece is four layers thick.

4. Cut 5-inch-diameter Styrofoam ball in
half. Cut slot in center of curved surface
of one half of Styrofoam ball, to form base
for frame. Push tab of frame into slot.

5. Cut twenty pieces of wire, each about
1½ inches long. Twist small loop at one
end of each piece and push other ends
through frame into positions for each
flower (see pattern).

6. Following package directions, mix a
cup of Celluclay or Claycrete. Fill corru-
gations in all edges of frame and spread
around areas where wires have been inserted. Dip fingers in water to smooth.
Apply a thin layer of clay onto base.

7. To make candleholders, cut slot as
wide as frame thickness and 1 inch long
on one side of each of four cardboard
tubes. In remaining tube, cut two slots to
same dimensions, one on each side, for
center candleholder. Glue tubes in place
on frame (see pattern). Spread clay
around lower edges of tubing.

8. For Madonna dress, cut two slots, each
1 inch long and as wide as frame thickness, on opposite sides of one cardboard
cone. Cut 1½ inches off top of cone. Slide
cone over inverted V on frame. For mantle, cut 3 inches off base of second cardboard cone. Cut slot, 1¾ inches long and
as wide as frame thickness, on each lower
side of mantle cone. Cut 1-inch-diameter
Styrofoam ball in half. Push half of Styrofoam ball into small end of mantle cone,
forming top of head. From medium-

weight cardboard, cut halo pattern for Mary and glue around head. Cover Styrofoam ball with thin layer of clay and model face if desired. Slide mantle cone onto first cone. Working from inside the cone, glue small strips of cardboard under slots in mantle. Then, working on outside of cone, fill slots with clay so that they are flush with mantle.

9. From medium-weight cardboard, cut Babe holder and halo. From corrugated cardboard, cut three body shapes of Babe and glue together. Spread a thin layer of clay on holder. Press halo and body into clay. On remaining half of 1-inch foam ball, spread clay on flat side and press onto halo. Rounded side will become face. Fill corrugated edges of body with clay and spread a thin layer of clay over face, modeling hair and features if desired. Swaddling bands can also be modeled if you wish. When clay is dry, attach body to Madonna figure with clay (see photograph).

10. The frame may be considered complete at this point, or you may build it up on the front side with clay, making it rounded. If you wish, add clay, to a depth of about ¼ inch, to centers of frame arms and smooth out to edges. By keeping clay thin, drying time will be speeded up. You can accelerate drying by placing frame near a source of heat or in a warm oven (150 degrees—do not turn oven any higher or Styrofoam will melt).

11. Dip soft cotton string in white glue and decorate bottom of Madonna dress and bottom of mantle, as shown in photograph.

12. From medium-weight cardboard, cut patterns for flowers, leaves, and birds (including bird wings). Cut slots in birds as indicated on pattern. Using a needle, make a hole in each unit that is ⅜ inch down from top edge of flower, bird, and narrow end of leaf. Then cut a 3-inch length of wire for each unit. Push wire through hole, bend at midpoint, and twist wires together. For flowers and leaves, continue to twist wires out to ends. For birds, leave wires open, forming legs. Slide bird wings into slots. Apply a thin layer of clay to one side of flowers, leaves, and birds; model flower centers

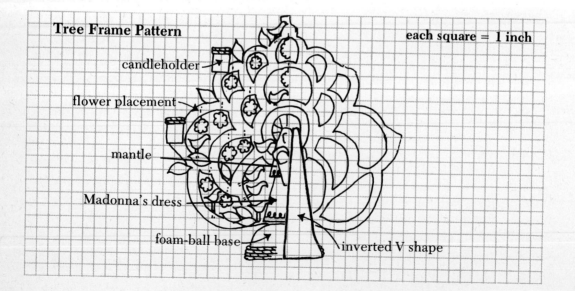

Tree Frame Pattern   each square = 1 inch

candleholder

flower placement

mantle

Madonna's dress

foam-ball base

inverted V shape

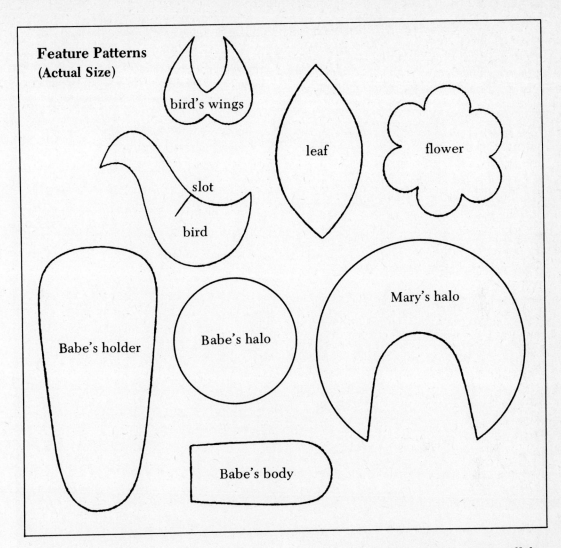

Feature Patterns
(Actual Size)

bird's wings

slot

bird

leaf

flower

Babe's holder

Babe's halo

Mary's halo

Babe's body

with a pen cap pressed into the clay, and define petals with a pencil point. Allow clay to dry completely.

13. If necessary, sand frame and all pattern pieces; then apply a coat of gesso to all parts. You can speed this process by dipping flowers, birds, and leaves into gesso and then pushing wires into piece of Styrofoam to hold figures while drying. One coat of gesso is sufficient, but a second coat will give an even better result. Paint with media of your choice—acrylic or tempera. If you use tempera, a

final coat of clear plastic spray will be necessary. Paint as shown in photograph or in any other way you wish; allow drying time for paint.

14. To assemble candleholder, note position of birds and leaves on frame. At these spots, use a needle or sharp pointed tool to make holes in frame for wires. Force wires into frame (see pattern). Touch up frame where necessary. Thread wire on flowers through wire loops in frame, loop or twist wires to hold flowers securely in position, and cut off any excess.

Owl Basket

All baskets are multipurpose, but this Swedish basket had two special uses. During the winter, it was hung on the loom to hold bobbins, and at berry-picking time, it served to hold the day's gatherings. Baskets of this kind were made with vertical wooden staves, each of which was ended with a carving of an animal or flower.

In Sweden, basketmaking never achieved the popularity that it did in other countries and it was never practiced as an art form. The principal weavers were the poor, the disabled, the blind, and the aged, and weaving was often their only livelihood. It is for this reason that basketmaking was never practiced by the Swedish peasants—a basket weaver was considered to be only one step away from the poorhouse.

Most Swedish baskets were utilitarian in purpose and were used to hold fish, salt, roots, and vegetables. Large straw baskets were used to hold grain. Materials other than straw were also used to make the baskets—twigs, roots, and woven strips were all utilized, depending upon the area from which the basket originated.

Our easy-to-make owl basket is especially attractive when used as a potted-plant holder.

Materials

8 pieces pine, each ½ × 1½ × 9 inches,
   for owl staves
wood stain, in shade of your choice
1 wooden circle, ⅜ × 7¼ inches, for base
white glue
reed:
   7 ounces #6, for weavers
   1 piece #6, 21 inches long, for handle
   6 pieces #6, each 31 inches long, for
      handle
   4 ounces #3, for handle wrapping
thin brads, ¾ inch long

Tools

brown wrapping paper
pencil
ruler
scissors
masking tape
coping saw
craft knife *or* pen knife
small set of woodcarving tools *
cloth
drill with ¼-inch bit
pail *or* large pan of water
awl

*Japanese-made beginner sets are available inexpensively at art-supply and craft stores.

Procedure

1. On brown wrapping paper, draw 1-inch grid and enlarge pattern for owl stave (see "Helpful Hints"). Cut out pattern, tape over each pine piece, and draw outlines. Using hard, sharp pencil, indent design pattern for owl into wood. With coping saw, cut around outline of owl and bottom peg on each stave. With craft knife or pen knife, make incised lines around eyes and on wing outlines. Carve away edges of chest next to wings and round the chest area. Cut straight down into wood on bottom lines of beak. Slope

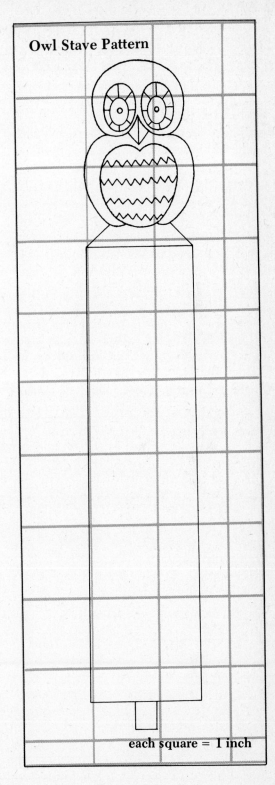

Owl Stave Pattern

each square = 1 inch

top of chest back to beak, and slope neck areas to curve shoulders. Round outer edges of bird body from front edge to sides but keep back of stave flat. Texture head and wings by carving off small pieces of wood or by using small U-gouge. Use craft knife to incise "feathers" on bird chest. Shape top of beak by cutting straight down on two outlines next to eyes; then remove a chip on each side of nose by cutting on a slant from beak center down each side. Round off front edges of the staves, and shape bottom end into a ¼-inch-diameter dowel. Following manufacturer's instructions, stain front and back of owls. With cloth, wipe off stain on high areas of carving.

2. Drill eight equally spaced holes, each ¼ inch in diameter, around circular base for staves (Figure 1). Glue staves in holes, slanting staves slightly forward.

3. In lukewarm water, soak all seven ounces of #6 reed for 5 to 10 minutes.

4. Following Figure 2 and using two pieces of #6 reed, begin weaving around staves at base. Continue weaving up to base of owls. On top row, twist the two weavers around each other between staves. At end of top row, use craft knife or pen knife to point ends of weavers, and then push ends down between weaving at staves.

5. Stain the 21-inch piece of #6 reed. Allow drying time. In lukewarm water, soak all #6 handle reeds and all #3 reeds for wrapping.

6. Point ends of the six unstained handle reeds, and push three of them down into weaving alongside any owl stave. Insert other three alongside the next stave so that all six reeds are between a pair of staves. Arch all reeds up over basket to form handle, divide into groups of three again on other side of basket, and insert,

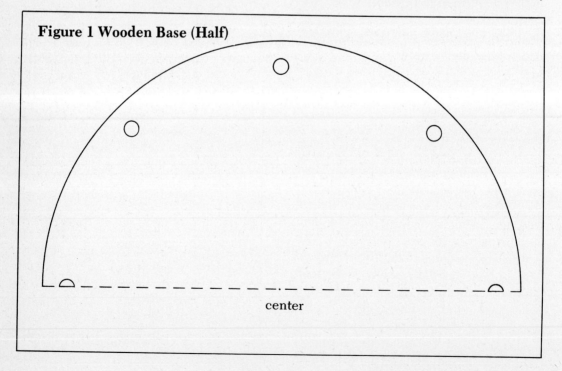

Figure 1 Wooden Base (Half)

center

Figure 2

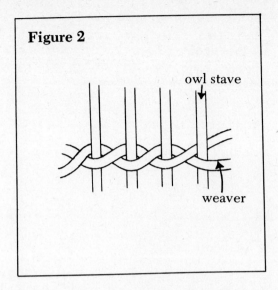

owl stave

weaver

Figure 3

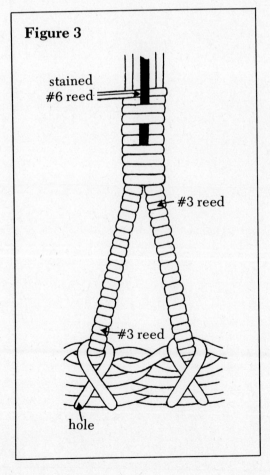

stained
#6 reed

#3 reed

#3 reed

hole

as described above, between the opposite pair of staves.

7. About 4 inches up from start of handle, draw together the six reeds, side by side (Figure 3). At this point, push a ¾-inch brad through all reeds, thus holding them in one parallel row. Continue to join reeds with brads across length of handle, leaving 4 inches of handle open at other side of basket.

8. At second row of weaving below left side of divided handle, use an awl to make a hole through front of weaver. Point end of a 2-yard-long #3 reed and, from front, thread a short length through hole to inside of basket. Push end into weaving to secure it. Following Figure 3, bring other end up around right side of left handle, behind handle, and down to the right, forming a cross below left side of handle. Two rows below top edge, push end of reed through weaving to inside of basket. Bring reed from back to front and then wrap left side of handle up to point where divided sections are joined. To end wrapping, cut off wrapping reed, leaving about a 2-inch end. Point end and push it between top handle reeds. Repeat same procedure on right side of handle and on divided handle portions on other side of basket.

9. Place stained #6 reed on top of handle reeds, above divided sections. Point end of a #3 reed and push through handle to secure. Following Figure 3, wrap #3 reed over both brown reed and handle with about four turns, covering 2-inch ends left from previous wrapping. Continue to wrap handle, passing wrapping cane twice under brown cane and then twice over brown cane for entire length of handle. To end wrapping, point end of wrapping reed and push through handle.

China

Dragon Pillow

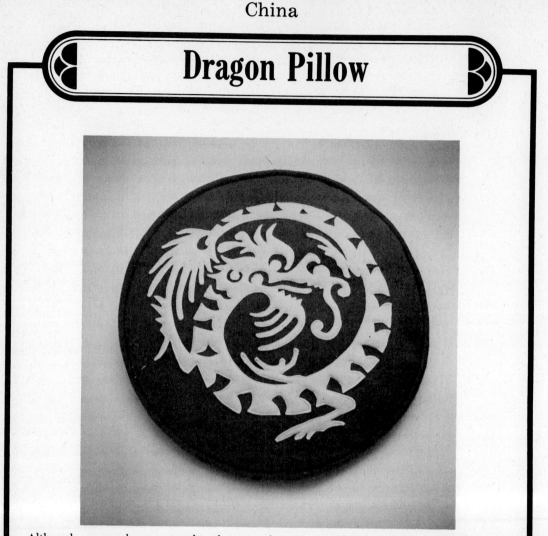

Although no one knows exactly when or where it originated, the art of making paper cutouts has long been used in China. There, a festival just isn't a festival without paper cutouts pasted on gates, pillars, and walls. The designs used in these cutouts predict wealth, joy, success, health—all the best wishes possible.

The design on this pillow is a reproduction of a *hua yang*, or cut-paper design. In China, *hua yangs* serve as preliminary embroidery patterns for the decoration of such articles as children's clothing and footwear.

The dragon of our design is symbolic of thunder and is, therefore, considered a moving and exciting power. It symbolizes the emperor, eternity, and authority, and it represents both the spring season and rain. At the same time, it admonishes against greed and avarice. According to legend, the dragons dwell in the clouds, to which they ascend, from earth, in spiral writhing motions. When two dragons fight, rain is supposedly created. In form, the dragon is actually a composite creature, having the head of a camel, the horns of a deer, the eyes of a rabbit, the ears of the water buffalo, the neck of a snake, the belly of a frog, the claws of an eagle, the scales of a carp, and the paws of a tiger. Other symbolic *hua yang* designs, along with their meanings, are given at the end of this project.

Materials
1 piece felt, 12 × 12 inches, in white
½ yard felt, 72 inches wide, in red
4 feet cording, #100
Dacron stuffing
thread, in red

Tools
brown wrapping paper
pencil
ruler
dressmakers' carbon
tracing wheel
scissors
sewing-machine cording or zipper foot

Procedure
1. On brown wrapping paper, draw 1-inch grid and enlarge design pattern (see "Helpful Hints"). Using dressmakers' carbon and tracing wheel, trace pattern on white felt. Cut out felt on outlines.

2. From red felt, cut two circles, each 14½ inches in diameter. Also cut a strip, 1½ inches by slightly more than 4 feet, to cover cording.

3. Center dragon cutout on red pillow cover, and machine-stitch along outlines.

4. Cover cording with felt strip. Pin all around edge of pillow front, right sides together. Then, with cording foot or zipper foot, machine-stitch. Join ends of cording by hand.

5. With right sides together, stitch front to back of pillow, leaving open a section for stuffing.

6. Turn pillow cover right side out and then stuff. Sew opening together by hand.

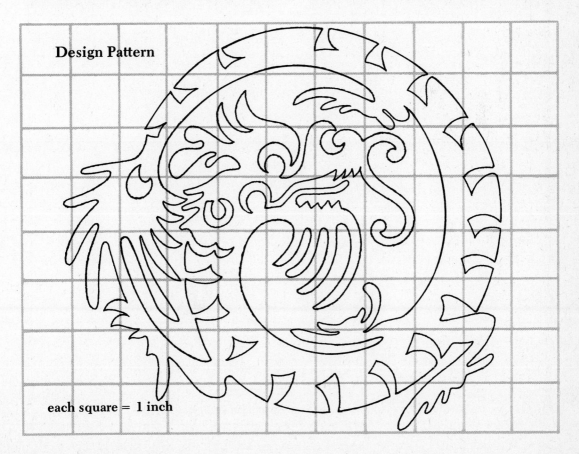

Design Pattern

each square = 1 inch

Hua Yang Patterns

1. Phoenix singing to rising sun depicts "talent succeeds at the proper time."

2. *Shou* and five bats indicate "age, wealth, health, and virtue."

Hua Yang Patterns

3. *Hsi* and butterfly indicate "joy and wedded bliss."

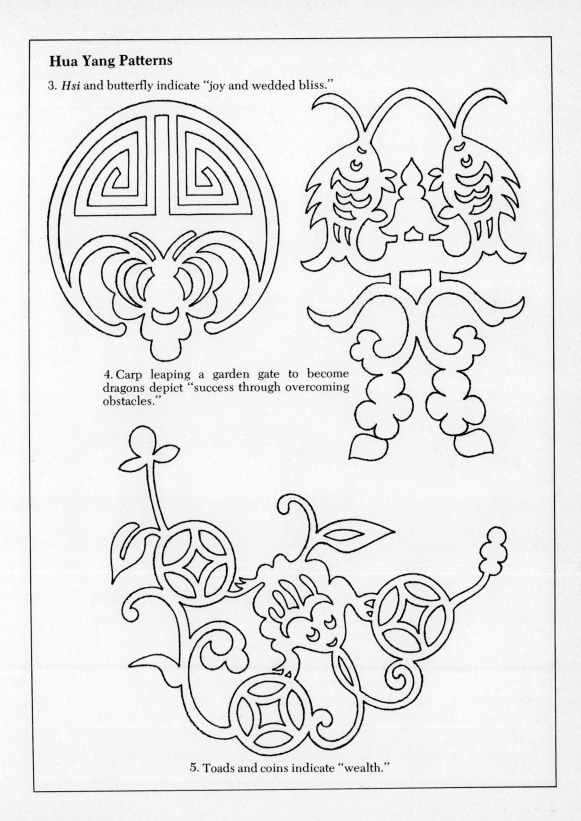

4. Carp leaping a garden gate to become dragons depict "success through overcoming obstacles."

5. Toads and coins indicate "wealth."

Poland

Wycinanki

A *wycinanki* is a form of cut-paper folk art created by the Polish farmland people during the nineteenth century. The designs, which were hung in the home or were used to decorate stables and barns, featured natural or religious objects, geometric shapes, or scenes. *Wycinanki* designs are either multicolored, as exemplified by the three designs shown in the photograph, or done in one color, such as the design featured in Chapter 7.

Materials

paper, in colors of your choice
white glue *or* spray adhesive
board *or* paper, for mounting

Tools

scissors

Procedure

1. Choose predominant color for design and fold paper of this color in half.

2. Study outline of main portions of design so that you will be able to cut freehand, or, if you wish, draw outline in pencil.

3. Working from edge of paper opposite fold, cut around outline of main portions, through both layers of paper.

4. Unfold *wycinanki* and spread for mounting.

5. If you would like to achieve a three-dimensional effect, dot back of design with white glue and position on mounting paper or board. If you would prefer to have *wycinanki* glued flat, use spray adhesive.

6. Cut details from paper of different colors and glue to main design as before.

Design Pattern (Half)

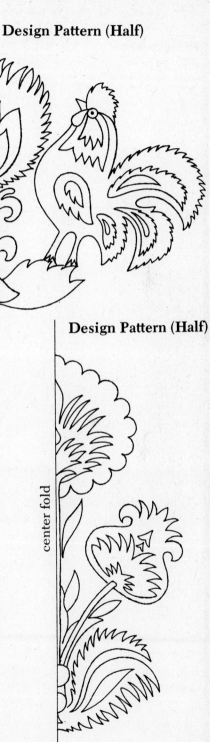

Design Pattern (Half)

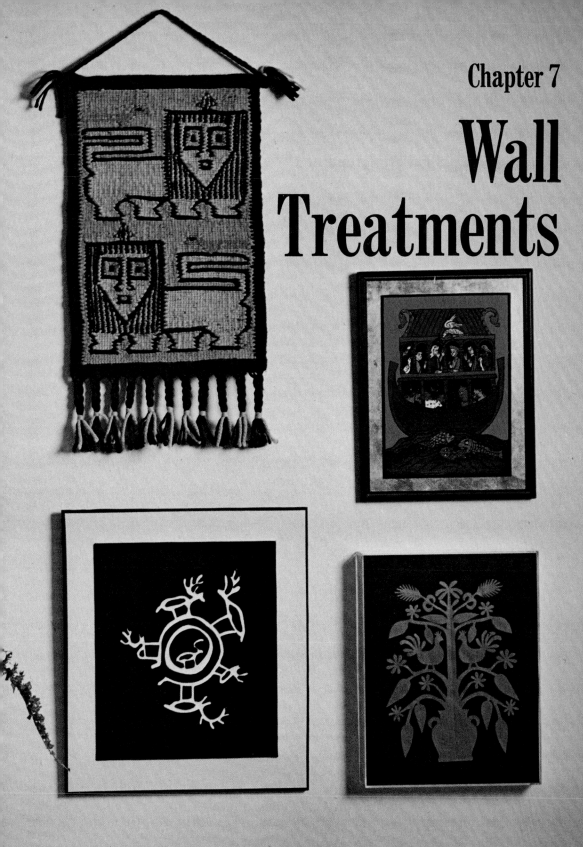

Chapter 7

Wall Treatments

Mexico

Festival Banner

If you are ever lucky enough to be in a village in Mexico while preparations are being made for a fiesta, it is more than likely that you will see most of the village girls snipping away at folded lengths of brightly colored tissue paper, producing lacy designs of animals, flowers, dancing figures, saints, and even skeletons. No holiday, fiesta, or wedding is complete without these long colored banners gaily decorating the streets, churchyards, and patios. All part of the "here today, gone tomorrow" philosophy of the Mexican people, these fragile—and often beautiful—paper decorations are only for the moment, but the memory lasts and lasts. These traditional and typical decorations are one of the most charming of the popular minor arts.

Our festival banner design is authentic, and because we would like it for tomorrow, too, it has been cut out of felt instead of paper and then mounted on a wooden strip.

Materials
½ yard felt, 72 inches wide, in hot pink or
   color of your choice
1 wood strip, ¼ × 1 × 18 inches, *or* 18-
   inch section of wooden yardstick
2 screw eyes *or* brads
wire, lightweight, for hanging

Tools
tracing paper
brown wrapping paper
ruler
pencil
scissors
straight pins
dressmakers' carbon
tracing wheel

Procedure
1. On tracing paper, draw 1-inch grid
and enlarge design pattern (see "Helpful
Hints"). Cut out on outline. Note that
large designs on pattern are separated by
bands of flowers or by diamonds. If you
would like your banner to be longer or
shorter than pattern, adjust length by
adding or subtracting these sections.
2. Measure width of felt to find center
and mark down length of fabric. Allowing
enough fabric at top to form slot for wood
strip, pin pattern to felt on left side of
center line.
3. Slip carbon under pattern and use
tracing wheel to transfer pattern to fabric.
After tracing one side completely, flip
pattern over and complete transfer of design, working from back of pattern.
4. With sharp scissors, cut out fabric on
outline. Refer to photograph and note
cutout design areas. To start cutouts,
push scissor point through fabric in
middle of design area and then snip
around on outline. Complete all cutting
in this manner.
5. To form slot for wood strip, fold top
section of felt in half and machine-stitch.

6. To prepare banner for hanging, slide
wood strip through slot, add a screw eye
or brad at each end, and attach wire.

Design Pattern (Half)

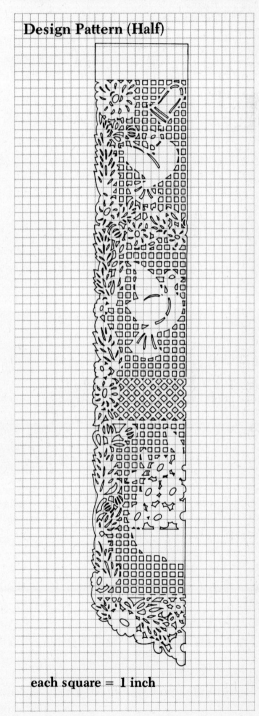

each square = 1 inch

Ofrenda

Ofrendas are the incredible yarn paintings made by the Huichol Indians of Mexico. True ones—complete with blazing colors and symbolic designs—might even be called small spectaculars. To make an *ofrenda*, the Huichols mix wild beeswax with resin, soften the mixture in the sun, and then apply it to a piece of wood or hardboard panel. Strands of brightly colored yarns are then pressed into the wax.

The Huichol Indians have been able to retain much of their pre-Hispanic culture intact, for they live in the rugged mountains of north central Mexico. On their yearly pilgrimage to San Luis Potosi, in the north central desert, they gather peyote, a strong hallucinogenic cactus root, which, when eaten, enables them to commune directly with their gods. Then, all surrounding elements of life talk to them, revealing their wisdom and granting them their well-being. The bright colors of the *ofrendas* as well as many of the designs are representative of the colors and designs seen in these euphoric states.

In this project, glue has been substituted for beeswax. The design is of "Our Mother Dove Girl, the Mother of Maize," who, in Huichol legend, brought them maize.

Materials
hardboard:

    1 piece, ⅛ × 6 × 20 inches, for yarn painting

    1 piece, ⅛ × 9 × 23 inches, for mounting board

pine:

    2 pieces, each ½ × 1½ × 23 inches, for frame

    2 pieces, each ½ × 1½ × 9 inches, for frame

gesso *or* paint, in white

paint, in black

white glue

tapestry yarn, 3-ply (approximate amounts):

    24 yards, in hot pink

    7 yards, in yellow

    3 yards, in green

    4 yards, in black

    3½ yards, in white

Tools
paintbrushes

brown wrapping paper

ruler

pencil

carbon paper

scissors

miter box and saw

hammer

nailset

brads, each ½ inch long

sandpaper, medium grade (optional)

Procedure

1. With gesso or white paint, paint 6 × 20-inch hardboard. (Design colors will be much stronger when applied over white.) When board is dry, paint edges black.

2. On brown wrapping paper, draw 1-inch grid and enlarge pattern (see "Helpful Hints"). Place pattern over carbon on 6 × 20-inch board, and trace design and border outline onto the board.

Design Pattern

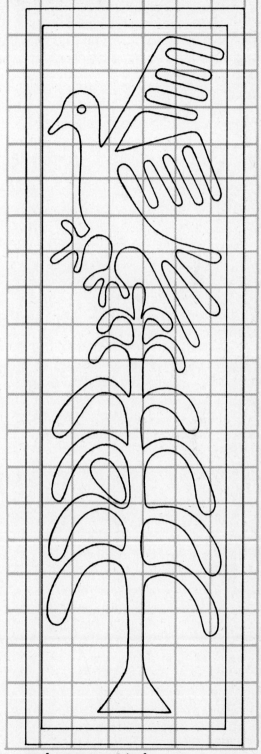

each square = 1 inch

3. With brush, paint glue around ½-inch border area of design. Cut end of hot pink yarn straight across. Twist end and place strand along top edge of board. Keeping corners square, continue to glue yarn around remaining edges of board. When one row of border is completed, cut yarn and twist end before gluing down. Before adding each new yarn piece, remember to cut end straight across and to twist ends at beginning and end. As you fill design, glue rows of yarn closely together and do not let yarn twist or overlap. Add second row of hot pink as closely as possible to the first, holding yarn taut with one hand as you position it with the other. Then, to complete border, add two rows of yellow yarn and two rows of green. (Most *ofrendas* show three colors bordering the edges.)

4. Paint glue on dove outline and glue black yarn around figure.

5. Paint glue on outer edge of black yarn outline and work row of yellow around it.

6. Paint eye area with glue and work with black yarn, starting from the outside and spiraling inward.

7. Paint glue on dove body and fill with white yarn, working from outer design edge to center.

8. Paint glue on outline of maize stalk and work with black. Glue a row of yellow outside black outline. Paint body of maize stalk with glue and fill in with green. Work top tassel with yellow.

9. Work background areas one section at a time (such as area above bird head and upper wing). Select an area, paint with glue, and then apply yarn, starting at outer edge of area and filling with one continuous strand of yarn. You can form a subtle pattern by gluing yarn in swirling patterns on background sections.

10. Assemble a box frame for the *ofrenda* by mitering corners of pine strips with a miter box and saw (see woodworking section in "Helpful Hints"). Glue and, with nailset and brads, join strips at corners. Glue and nail 9 × 23-inch hardboard over frame and sand edges if necessary. Paint frame black.

11. Center *ofrenda* on hardboard, and lightly mark corner placements with pencil. Paint even layer of glue on back of *ofrenda* and glue to hardboard, matching corners to marks. Weight overnight to ensure obtaining good glue bond.

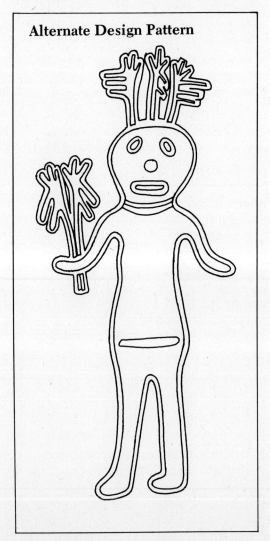

Alternate Design Pattern

Alternate Design Patterns

198

Alternate Design Patterns

Ethiopia

Lion Tapestry

Imagine shopping in a great marketplace with row after row of merchants displaying every kind of merchandise available under the sun. Then imagine great squares packed with people and camels. From just such a spot as this in Ethiopia, you would probably see tapestries and rugs that look a great deal like our project. Made of heavy handspun yarn, these pieces are handwoven into patterns that often include lions, birds, and houses. This work is striking in its strong and simple design qualities and the use of natural handspun wool. In some pieces, dyed wool is used, but since the wool is unbleached, the colors are still subtle.

The loom used for our project was fashioned from a beach backrest. However, you may improvise one with a picture frame, a rug frame, or some canvas stretchers—the only requirement is that the opening be about 18 by 24 inches. Support the frame by lashing or nailing sections of yardsticks or other stock to the back, following the setup diagram.

Materials

66 yards heavy cotton string, seine twine, *or* other material suitable for warp, in black or color of your choice
4 yards string
scrap yarn
white glue
rug yarn, 3-ply (approximate amounts):
   24 yards (or ⅝ ounce), in black
   43 yards (or 1½ ounces), in hot pink
   76 yards (or 2 ounces), in gray
   3 yards, in yellow green
thread, in black
13½ inches dowel, ⅜ inch in diameter
5 yards yarn, in black, for hanging cord (optional)

Tools

beach backrest with canvas removed *or* other frame, about 18 × 24 inches, and support stock for loom
nails *or* rope
ruler
scissors
table fork
pencil
2 wood strips, each about ¼ × 1 × 19 inches, *or* 19-inch sections of wooden yardstick
masking tape *or* tacks
crochet hook (optional)
needle

Procedure

1. If you are going to make a loom from a beach backrest, set backrest in its most upright position. Stabilize by nailing or roping support rod to bottom of frame, as shown in Figure 1. If you are going to use another sort of frame as the base for your loom, support it by lashing or nailing sections of yardsticks or other lumber to it, following the setup shown in Figure 1.
2. On the top rod of the loom, mark off

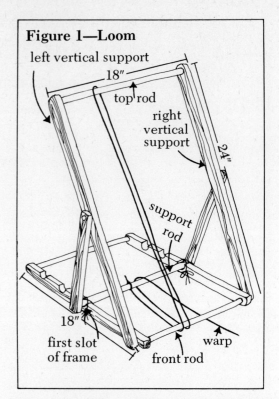

Figure 1—Loom

left vertical support
18″
top rod
right vertical support
24″
support rod
18″
first slot of frame
front rod
warp

the center 12½ inches; you will warp your piece within this measurement, following the example of the two warped threads shown in Figure 1. Begin by tying one end of warp thread to far left of support rod. Bring warp under front rod, over top rod, under front rod again, and under and over support rod. This completes two warp threads. Continue in this manner until there are sixty-six warp threads within the 12½-inch space; then tie off warp at right end of support rod.

3. Cut two pieces of string, each about 2 yards long. At bottom of frame, wrap one string around left vertical support of frame. With ends of string, weave one row of twining stitch across warp threads. To weave twining stitch, refer to Figures 2 and 3. Hold weaver around first warp thread. Hold end A in front and bring B under A and then behind second warp thread (Figure 2). The next stitch goes in

Design Pattern

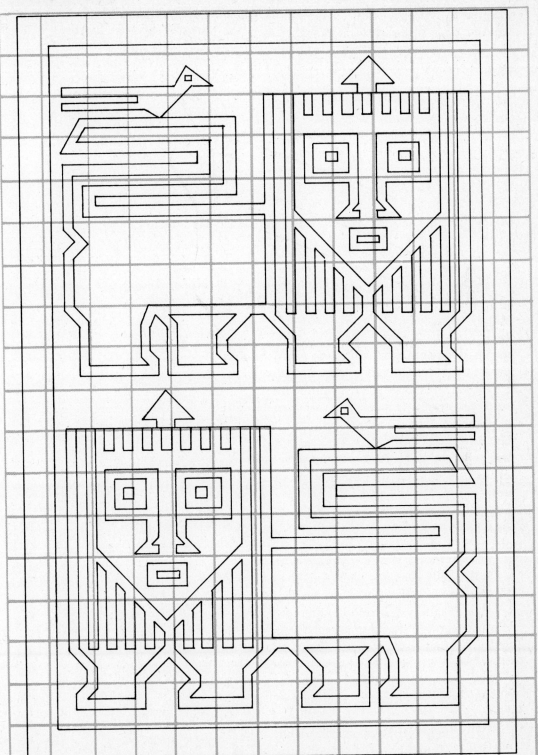

front of the warp thread. Continue weaving across warp threads in this way and, at end of row, tie string to right vertical support. With tines of fork, push row even with front rod. Repeat a row of twining as closely as possible to top rod.

4. Above bottom row of twining, use scrap yarn to weave five or six rows in tabby weave. To do this, use simple over-and-under weaving on alternate warp threads for all rows. Depending on yarn length, either weave each row separately or back and forth continuously. These rows will even the warp threads and will be removed when piece is completed. Keep weaving straight, and use fork tines to push each row down as it is completed.

5. Draw 1-inch grid and enlarge design pattern (see "Helpful Hints"). Color-code each pattern area, following photograph for keying. On back of pattern, glue each wood strip lengthwise on outer side edges of pattern. Hold pattern, face up, behind warp threads. Slip wood strips in front of vertical supports of frame, and tape or tack to frame. Pattern sheet is now visible through warp threads and can be easily followed while weaving.

6. Before you begin to weave, keep the following points in mind:

a. The twining weave is worked with one thread that has been folded in two (*not* in half) to form two working ends (Figures 2, 3, and 4). Figure 3 shows how to start turn at end of row *within* pattern. At outer edges of weaving, the weaver that passes behind the last warp is wrapped around outer warp twice before starting next row.

b. To start new threads of same color, lap new thread over the old and work

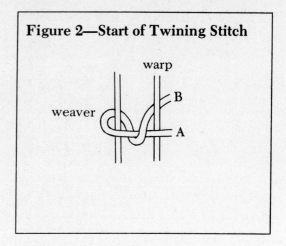

Figure 2—Start of Twining Stitch

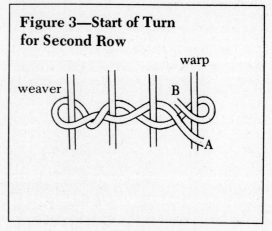

Figure 3—Start of Turn for Second Row

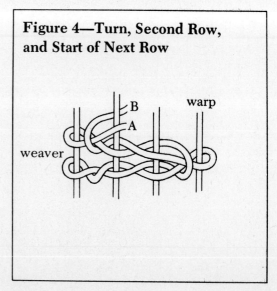

Figure 4—Turn, Second Row, and Start of Next Row

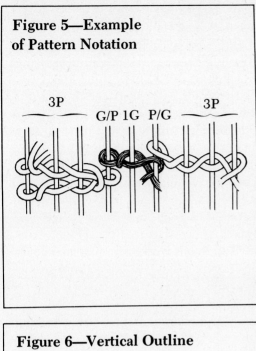

Figure 5—Example of Pattern Notation

3P G/P 1G P/G 3P

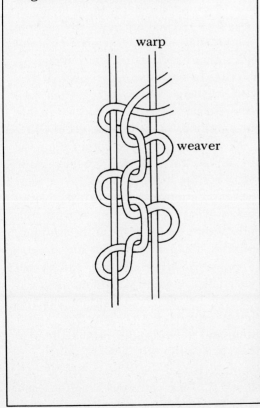

Figure 6—Vertical Outline

warp

weaver

in (see step 8). To avoid buildup resulting from adding a new piece of yarn, always fold weaving threads so that the ends are uneven in length.

c. You can set in pattern first and then fill in background later, but weaving will be more even if you work it row by row. If you work a section at a time, a crochet hook will be helpful for weaving in close spots.

d. To hide yarn ends, draw them through to the back, weave over them, and then cut them off. Or, you may use them as part of the warp threads.

7. To set in pattern, begin work at bottom and start from the right-hand side. With black yarn, weave six rows of twining.

8. See Figure 5 for guidance on how to add new colors and example of a pattern notation. Letters have been assigned to denote colors on pattern notation; they are as follows: B=black, G=gray, and P=pink. Note that pattern-notation example shows two letters appearing above a warp thread in some cases. This indicates that two threads of different colors are to be looped around same warp, thus making a sawtoothed pattern. Starting from left, weave five rows in following pattern: 3 B, 1 G/B, 58 G, 1 B/G, 3 B.

9. To set in horizontal outline for bottom of lion feet, start from right and work one row as follows: 3 B, 1 G/B, 4 G, 1 B/G, 9 B, 1 G/B, 3 G, 1 B/G, 9 B, 1 G/B, 3 G, 1 B/G, 9 B, 1 G/B, 3 G, 1 B/G, 9 B, 1 G/B, 1 G, 1 B/G, 3 B. Repeat for next row, reversing pattern notation and working from left to right.

10. Refer to Figure 6 for vertical outlining stitch. Vertical outline is worked between and around two warp threads. Since other colors share the same threads, the outline will appear saw-

toothed. In the following pattern notation, black is used only for vertical outlining. Work next row as follows: 3 B, 1 G/B, 4 G, 1 B/G, 1 P/B, 7 P, 1 B/P, 1 G/B, 3 G, 1 B/G, 1 P/B, 7 P, 1 B/P, 1 G/B, 3 G, 1 B/G, 1 P/B, 7 P, 1 B/P, 1 G/B, 3 G, 1 B/G, 1 P/B, 7 P, 1 B/P, 1 G/B, 1 G, 1 B/G, 3 B. Then, following design pattern, shape legs by weaving complete rows up to top of legs (total of 9 rows pink).

11. To set in pattern for mane, see Figure 7 for two-color twining stitch. Bring pink in front of starting warp, leaving tail to be woven in later. Bring black under, then over, pink between starting warp and second warp, under pink between second and third warps, and then continue twining in normal manner. The sawtooth effect of B/G and P/B immedi-

ately before and after the two-color twining section in the following notation is achieved by vertical outlining stitch. Weaving pattern for mane from left edge is as follows: 3 B, 1 G/B, 1 G, 1 B/G, 1 P/B, 23 two-color twining B and P, 1 B/P, 1 P/B. To complete rest of lion body and side borders, follow design pattern. After four rows of two-color twining have been completed, begin to shape lion's face. Rows of two-color twining must be decreased in increments of two, in order to maintain zigzag pattern of black and pink.

12. Top lion is worked in same manner as first except that it will face in the opposite direction.

13. To make holder for rod so that tapestry can be hung, remove string twining from top of tapestry. Continue weaving with black for 2 inches, or as far up as warp allows. Then remove weaving from loom by cutting warp threads on top rod and support rod. Turn top 2 inches of weaving to back and sew down. If you wish to hang your weaving from tabs rather than a solid piece, divide warp into eleven groups of six threads each. Using black yarn, weave every other group as far up as warp allows. Then remove weaving from loom. Knot unwoven warp ends on top into pairs and whip down to back of weaving. Fold tabs in half, with ends of tabs on the back of the hanging, and whip down, forming slot for rod.

14. Remove string twining and scrap-yarn tabby weave at bottom edge of weaving. Divide lower warp threads into eleven groups of six each. Braid each group and tie with pink yarn. Trim ends of braid evenly. Slip dowel through top opening. If you wish, braid six 30-inch pieces of black yarn and attach at each end of rod to make a cord for hanging.

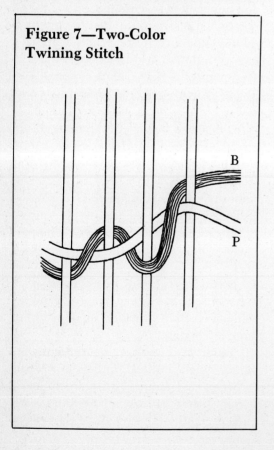

Figure 7—Two-Color Twining Stitch

Europe

Glass Painting

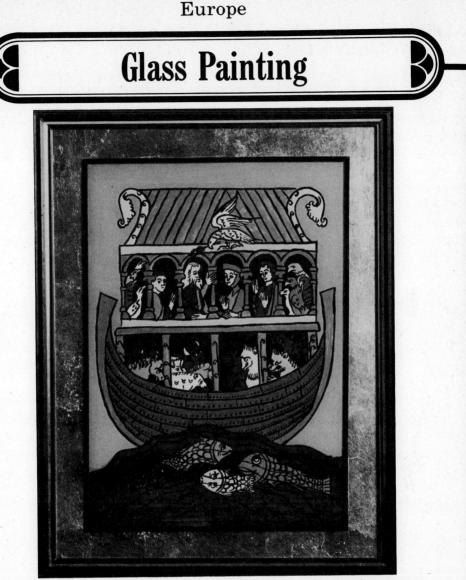

In the late eighteenth and nineteenth centuries, a new art form—glass painting—appeared in mid-Central Europe. First done by glaziers and printers, the technique was soon taken up by peddlers who painted their way from village to village. These anonymous artists did votive paintings for both churches and homes as well as portraits and scenes from everyday life. The latter category was devoted largely to giving pictorial thanks for escaping and/or surviving tragedies of all kinds, ranging from fires to falls off horses to serious illnesses. Polish painters added robbers and brigands as subjects.

Glass painting became exceedingly popular in areas other than Central Europe as well, finding devotees in England, China, France, Mexico, and the United States.

The Noah's Ark scene selected for our project is adapted from a thirteenth-century French Bible. Since it involves no shading, it makes a simple start for glass painting. Whatever designs you choose, remember that your painting will appear in reverse when completed. The painted side will be hung against the wall, which protects your painting.

Materials
frame, 11 × 14 inches, with glass included

cardboard, in size to fit frame, in white, for backing

acrylic tube paints, in black, red, purple, yellow, blue, green, and white, or colors of your choice

self-adhesive auto stripping, ⅛ inch wide, in black

gold-leaf sizing, quick-drying

gold leaf

Tools
glass cleaner

soft cloths

tracing paper

ruler

pencil

felt-tipped pen

scrap paper

watercolor brushes, small and medium

Procedure
1. Remove glass from frame, clean thoroughly with glass cleaner and soft cloth, and dry. To avoid leaving finger marks on glass surface, handle glass only on edges.

2. On tracing paper, draw 1-inch grid and enlarge design pattern (see "Helpful Hints"). With felt-tipped pen, go over design lines on pattern.

3. Turn pattern over and place glass on top. (Design will be reversed when glass is turned over.) To avoid smudging glass while painting, rest your hand on piece of scrap paper placed over glass. Using small watercolor brush and black paint, paint all design outlines on glass. Border the edges of design with black paint or auto stripping. Allow outlines to dry completely.

4. Using watercolor brushes, paint all design areas as you wish. Lay in pigment

Design Pattern each square = 1 inch

quickly and do not go over with more paint or paint will lift. Paint that overlaps outlines will not be visible from other side. Allow paint to dry thoroughly.

5. To apply gold leaf to glass, first paint sizing on border areas surrounding design. Following manufacturer's directions, apply gold leaf on top of sizing. Carefully and firmly press gold leaf on glass but do not rub. Wait at least one hour, and then carefully rub off excess gold leaf with clean soft cloth. If too much gold leaf comes off, resize area and apply again.

6. On the front side of glass around the inside edges of gold leaf, add auto stripping if you wish, mitering the corners.

7. Replace glass in frame, with painted side on back of glass. Slide cardboard backing in place over painted side of the glass, and then hang completed painting by whatever method you choose to use.

Lapland

Reindeer Corral

Because the reindeer provides food, clothing, tools, and transportation to the nomad Lapps, it is not surprising that this vital force be the essential design element on the "magic" drums of the land. In pre-Christian times, these drums were the principal instruments of Lapland's shamanism. In those days, the Lapps believed that they were accompanied on their wanderings by the gods. With the aid of their drums, they could talk to these gods and ask their help. When the Lapps were officially converted to Christianity, these drums were seized and either burned or carried off to Europe as oddities. Around seventy are still in existence.

Using the juice of the red alder bark mixed with saliva, the Lapps painted the skin of these drums with the faces of all the gods, symbols of evil things, and representations of all the things that a Lapp might have questions about—the tent, the storehouses, the reindeer, the fishing, and so on. The intentions of the gods and the offerings they sought were relayed to the Lapps via this drum. To get this information, a sorcerer would place a small piece of bone on the skin. As he beat the drum, the bone would move to the various figures, thus indicating the answers.

The reindeer corral on our wall hanging is the essential design element of the magic drum. A number of other designs from the drum are given in the alternate patterns.

Materials

1 piece chipboard *or* hardboard, ⅛ × 11½ × 13¼ inches, for cutout board

1 piece plywood, ¼ × 15½ × 17½ inches, for backing board

gesso (if chipboard is used)

wood primer

paint, in black and white

contact cement

2 screw eyes

wire, for hanging

Tools

brown wrapping paper

ruler

pencil

masking tape

carbon paper

coping saw (to cut hardboard) *or* craft knife (to cut chipboard)

sandpaper, finishing grade

paintbrushes

Procedure

1. On brown wrapping paper, draw 1-inch grid and enlarge design pattern (see "Helpful Hints"). Tape pattern over carbon on chipboard or hardboard and trace design. Remove pattern.

2. Using coping saw on hardboard or craft knife on chipboard, cut on outline of *all* design areas, including shaded sections. Sections cut from shaded areas will be used later, so save them.

3. With finishing paper, sand cut edges on board.

4. If you are using chipboard, apply a coat of gesso. Then seal all wood with primer. Allow to dry.

5. With black paint, paint board and cutout pieces reserved from step 2. Paint edges of plywood board black and one side white. When paint is thoroughly dry, center black board on white board and lightly mark corner placements with pencil.

6. Following manufacturer's directions, spread contact cement on back of black board, and glue to white board, matching corners to marks.

7. Reposition cutout pieces and glue in place.

8. To hang project, add screw eyes to back of board and attach a length of wire.

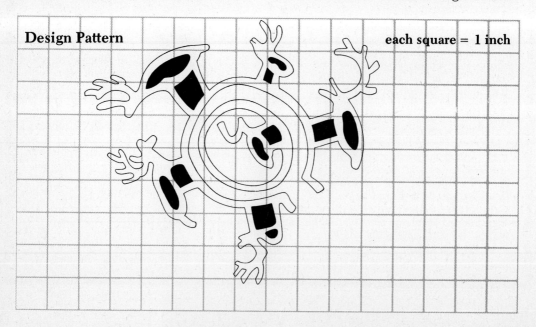

Design Pattern　　　　each square = 1 inch

Poland

Wycinanki

A *wycinanki* is a distinctive folk-art creation that originated in the small rural communities of Poland. Basically, it is a paper cutout of stylized figures and symbols, reflecting Polish culture and beliefs. Never predrawn, these marvelous creations are cut out spontaneously with ordinary knives or sheep-shearing scissors.

Whatever the origins of the art of *wycinanki* cutting, the effect is charming. Because of all the cutout areas, these designs can be applied to rounded surfaces, such as those of Easter eggs or even rocks. Although the multicolored designs are often cut from a glazed paper, any kind of paper can be used to make them, and a plastic spray will protect them from wear and tear. Three additional *wycinanki* designs can be found in Chapter 6.

Materials
paper, in color of your choice
white glue *or* spray adhesive
board *or* paper, for mounting

Tools
scissors

Procedure
1. Fold paper in half.
2. Since *wycinankis* are traditionally cut freehand, study the design outlines on right half of pattern and fix outline in mind. If you would prefer to cut on a predrawn outline, go ahead and draw one. If you wish to use more than one color or more than one design in your *wycinanki*, see step 7.
3. Working from edge of paper opposite fold and going through both layers, cut around pattern outlines, cutting away background to broad outline of design.
4. Cut fine details and add finishing touches to shape design.
5. Unfold *wycinanki* and spread for mounting.
6. If you would like to add a third dimension to your cutting, dot back of *wycinanki* with white glue and position on mounting board or paper. If you would prefer your *wycinanki* glued flat to mounting, use spray adhesive instead of white glue.
7. To make multiple-color designs, first cut main parts of design and glue to mounting; then cut details from other colors and glue on main design. Multiple patterns can be made by folding paper more than once and then cutting design. Three additional *wycinanki* designs can be found in Chapter 6 (see group photograph and patterns). These all provide good examples of multiple-color designs.

Design Pattern (Half)

center fold

New Mexico, United States

Straw-Inlay Cross

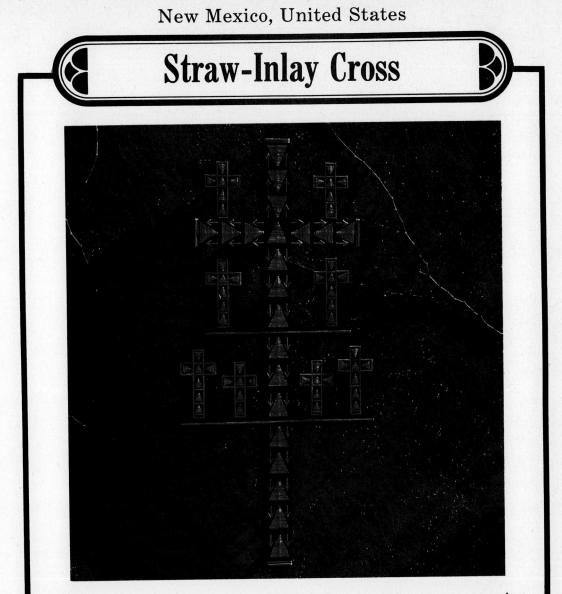

Wherever man grows grain, he eventually finds uses for the golden stems, weaving them into baskets, hats, shoes, even fertility symbols. The list is endless, as it seems that every country has adapted and varied straw work for its own purposes.

The project we have worked with straw designs is from New Mexico's colonial period. Brought to the area by Spanish artisans, straw decorating became the poor man's gilding in New Mexico and was used to ornament panels, boxes, wooden candleholders, picture frames, shelves, and wooden crosses. The technique required that dried straw and cornhusks be cut into fine pieces and then be glued to wooden objects with a rosin–soot mixture, which also colored the wood surfaces black. The straw was always used in its natural color and was pasted on in geometric or floral designs.

The multiple cross in this project is authentic—the original dates probably to the 1700s. Seven other styles of straw-inlay crosses are illustrated at the end of the project.

212

Materials

pine, for large cross:

 1 piece, ¾ × 2¾ × 40 inches, for
  upright

 1 piece, ¾ × 2¾ × 17¼ inches, for top
  arm

 1 piece, ½ × ¾ × 15 inches, for middle
  arm

 1 piece, ½ × ¾ × 20 inches, for bottom
  arm

pine, for medium crosses (two on middle
 arm and two on bottom arm):

 4 pieces, each ¼ × 1¼ × 3¾ inches, for
  E pieces in Figure 2

 4 pieces, each ¼ × 1¼ × 7¼ inches, for
  A pieces in Figure 2

 4 pieces, each ¼ × 1¼ × 4¾ inches, for
  C pieces in Figure 2

 12 pieces, each ¼ × 1¼ × 1¼ inches,
  for B and D pieces in Figure 2

pine, for small crosses (two on top arm
 and two on bottom arm):

 4 pieces, each ¼ × 1¼ × 3¾ inches, for
  C pieces in Figure 2

 4 pieces, each ¼ × 1¼ × 6 inches, for A
  pieces in Figure 2

 4 pieces, each ¼ × 1¼ × 2¾ inches, for
  E pieces in Figure 2

 12 pieces, each ¼ × 1¼ × 1¼ inches,
  for B and D pieces in Figure 2

white glue

flat paint, in black

bag of nesting straw*, manila tagboard, or
 straw-colored paper

satin-finish liquid plastic

2 screw eyes, small (optional)

wire, for hanging (optional)

Tools

coping saw

pencil

ruler

chisel

paintbrushes

craft knife or single-edged razor

rustproof container

tracing paper

paper or cardboard

sandpaper, finishing grade

*Available at feedstores.

Procedure

1. Following Figure 1 for steps 1 through 3, find center of length of top arm and mark. Draw a line 1¾ inches to either side of it and saw each to a depth of ¼ inch. Chisel out wood between outside cuts to form a slot 2¾ inches wide. Repeat cutout process 7¾ inches down from top of upright, fitting arm into it to make sure it fits.

2. At center of middle and bottom arms, saw similar slots and chisel out wood. On upright, measure 7½ inches down from lower edge of first slot and make a second slot to the same dimensions for middle arm. Set arms into upright slots to check for proper fit.

3. To make slots on top arm to hold two small crosses, measure off 2½ inches from each end of arm and chisel out a slot to measure ¼ inch deep, 1¼ inches wide, and ¾ inch long, measuring down from top edge of arm. Repeat process on middle and bottom arms, locating outer edges of outer slots 1¼ inches in from each end of arms. Outer edges of inner slots on bottom arm should be located 5½ inches in from ends of arms.

4. Glue all arms to upright.

5. Paint entire cross black.

6. Keep pieces for small and medium crosses separate by marking each with letter that corresponds with dimensions given in materials list. Place pieces for small crosses in one pile and those for the medium crosses in another. Following Figure 2, make four small crosses and

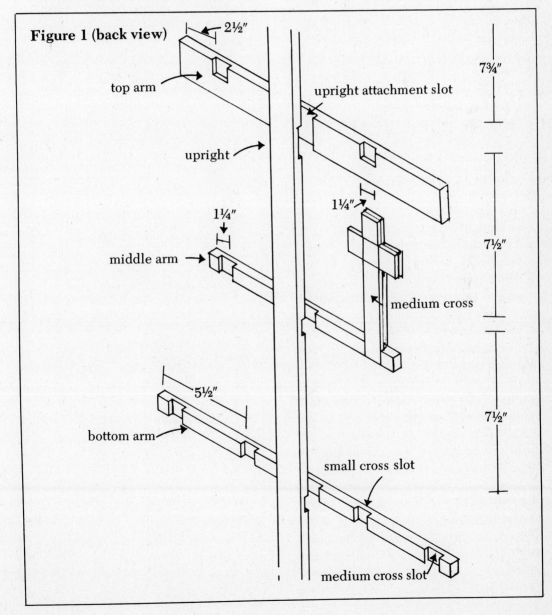

four medium crosses as follows:

    a. Glue B to one end of A.

    b. Glue one D piece to each end of C.

    c. Glue C to A below B.

    d. Glue E to A below C. Bottom section of A will fit into slot on large cross, and lower edge of E will rest on the arm, as indicated in Figure 1.

7. Paint small and medium crosses black. Do not glue to large cross until straw decoration is completed.

8. To prepare straw, use craft knife or razor to cut off joints of straw pieces and then select pieces of approximately the same length. Place selected straw in rust-proof container, and either cover with boiling water and soak for 20 minutes to

Figure 1 (back view)

2½"

top arm

upright attachment slot

7¾"

upright

1¼"

1¼"

middle arm

medium cross

7½"

5½"

bottom arm

7½"

small cross slot

medium cross slot

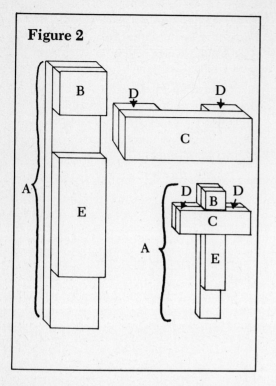

Figure 2

10. To assemble each stairstep motif, glue the center of each step to a length of straw. The length of this straw "holder" may be the same as the vertical dimension of one motif or it may be longer so that it can hold more than one motif at a time. In the latter case, simply weight the motifs until you are ready to glue them to the cross and then cut them apart. If you

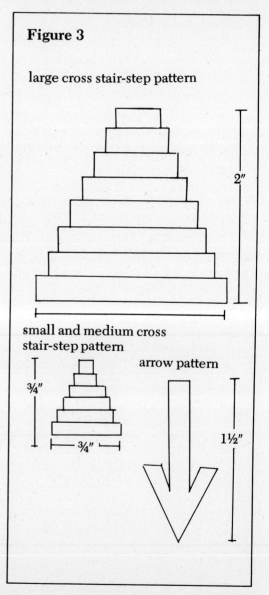

Figure 3

large cross stair-step pattern

2"

small and medium cross stair-step pattern

3/4"

3/4"

arrow pattern

1½"

work with at once or place in water and soak overnight. Then place piece of straw on hard, flat surface, such as glass, and flatten by pressing down with fingers. As each new piece of straw is required, repeat flattening process. Then, as you work, use razor or knife to cut straw pieces in half lengthwise, forming strips approximately the same width of stairsteps shown in Figure 3. If using manila tagboard or straw-colored paper instead of straw, simply cut into strips.

9. To make straw stairstep patterns for small and medium crosses, trace motif in Figure 3 on paper or draw on cardboard. Do not cut out pattern. Lay strip of straw over bottom step of pattern and cut to correct length. Lay straw over step above and cut to correct length. To complete motif, cut strips for remaining steps (six in all). Cut enough straw to make fifty-two of these stairstep motifs altogether.

are using short holders, glue each motif to the cross as you finish assembling it. To glue, cover the entire back of each motif with white glue and, following Figure 4, place in proper position on small and medium crosses. Cover with wax paper and weight with a book. Allow to dry.

11. To make stairstep motifs for large cross, repeat steps 9 and 10, using Figure 3 as pattern and cutting enough lengths of straw to make twenty-one motifs. When ready to glue motifs to cross, follow Figure 4 for proper positioning and glue in same manner as before.

12. To cut straw pieces to make arrow motifs, use Figure 3 as a pattern. Miter the ends of the arrowhead pieces to form a point and glue to another length of straw to form a shaft. Make forty arrows in all and then, following Figure 4 for proper positioning, glue in place on cross.

13. To outline front edges of small and medium crosses (see Figure 4), cut straw to full length of each edge and miter corners; glue in place. (Remember that straw will vary slightly in width, but this variation will add to the charm of the finished design.)

14. When all design patterns have been glued in place, glue small and medium crosses to large cross, following Figure 4 for proper positioning.

15. Paint entire unit with five or six coats of clear satin finish, allowing each coat to dry thoroughly (approximately 6 hours) and sanding lightly with finishing paper before applying next coat. Straw will appear inlaid under coats of plastic finish.

16. To hang cross, evenly space screw eyes on back of top arm and add wire.

Figure 4

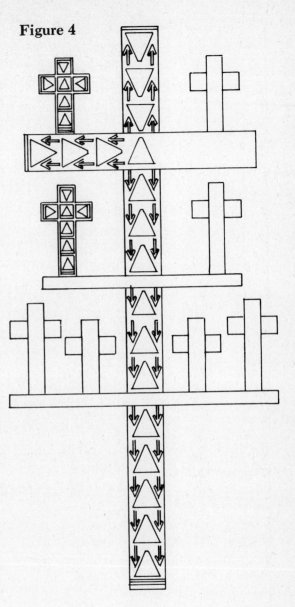

Alternate Design Patterns

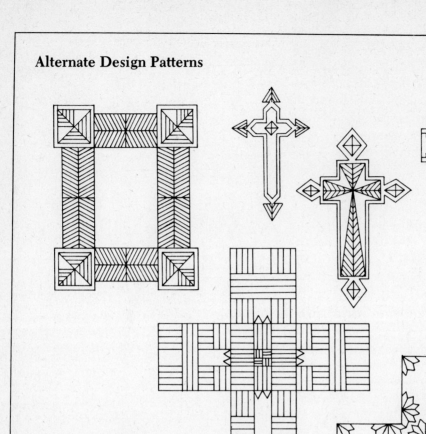

Mediterranean

Branch with Spider Web

With the strong emphasis in today's art on free form and the use of natural materials, this macramé wall hanging will fit perfectly into any contemporary home. For the base, choose a large tree limb that has many intertwining branches. After you have completed the main section, have fun designing your own spider web patterns on the branches. Be sure to read the macramé section in "Helpful Hints" before you begin and refer to it while you are working to learn the structure of the various macramé knots.

Materials

tree limb, with many intertwining branches
460 feet cord, type of your choice, for main section, plus enough extra for spider webs and bell chains
dye, in royal blue, aqua, and chartreuse
12 inches dowel, ¼ inch in diameter
1 circle of wooden embroidery hoop, about 4 inches in diameter
approximately 26 small bells

Tools

scissors
ruler

Procedure

1. Cut eight 280-inch lengths of cord, and, following manufacturer's directions on package, dye them chartreuse. Cut two 280-inch lengths and two 340-inch lengths; dye them royal blue. Cut four 280-inch lengths and two 340-inch lengths; dye them aqua. Dye extra cord in chartreuse, royal blue, or aqua to make spider web patterns and bell chains.

2. *Row 1:* Using part of branch as holding cord, fold one of the 340-inch royal blue cords so that outer cord is 200 inches and inner cord is 140 inches and tie onto branch with lark's-head knot (see macramé section in "Helpful Hints"). Fold a 280-inch royal blue cord, the eight chartreuse cords, and the second 280-inch blue cord in half and, in that order, tie on branch in lark's-head knots. Tie the second 340-inch royal blue cord onto branch folded so that outer cord is 200 inches and inner cord is 140 inches. Divide cords into groups of four. Fold a 340-inch aqua cord in a lark's-head knot over both groups of royal blue cords so that the outer cord is 200 inches and the inner cord is 140 inches. Fold a 280-inch aqua cord over each group of chartreuse cords. Check cord lengths. There should be both a 200-inch aqua and a 200-inch royal blue cord on each end of branch. All other cords should measure 140 inches.

3. *Row 2:* Using dowel as knot-bearing cord, make a row of horizontal double half hitches.

4. *Rows 3–17:* On both outside groups, make square-knot sennits by tying two square knots with aqua cords over blue cords, three square knots with blue cords, one square knot with aqua over blue cords, three square knots with blue, two square knots with aqua over blue, three square knots with blue, and one square knot with aqua over blue.

For each of the four inner groups of cords, tie two square knots with aqua over chartreuse. With chartreuse, tie twelve half knots to form twisting sennits.

Tie a square knot with aqua over chartreuse, three square knots with chartreuse, and one square knot with aqua over chartreuse.

5. *Rows 18–19:* Make one row of horizontal double half hitches, using first cord on left as knot-bearing cord; make one row of horizontal double half hitches, using first cord on right as knot-bearing cord.

6. *Rows 20–43:* For both outside groups, make three square knots with royal blue cords and then make one square knot with aqua cords over royal blue. Repeat this procedure six times. To make diamond patterns in inner groups, follow these steps:

    a. Using first cord in each group as knot-bearing cord, hold cord on the diagonal to the lower right and knot next two cords in diagonal double half hitches. Hold last cord in each group on the diagonal to the lower left and knot preceding two cords in diagonal double half hitches. You should now have a V-shaped pattern with the two knot-bearing cords in the center.

b. Bring left knot-bearing cord across right knot-bearing cord and hold on the diagonal to the lower right. Then make diagonal double half hitches with next two cords. Keeping the right knot-bearing cord on the diagonal to the lower left, make diagonal half hitches with preceding two cords. You should now have an X shape in each group, with knot-bearing cords on outside.

c. Tie the left knot-bearing cord (which is now on the right) of each group in a diagonal double half hitch over the right knot-bearing cord of the next group to connect groups.

d. Continue diamond pattern by completing another X shape in both the first and fourth groups (steps 6a and 6b) and another V shape in both the second and third groups (step 6a).

e. Using two outermost cords of entire inner section as knot-bearing cords and holding them on the diagonal to the lower center, make diagonal double half hitches with two cords adjacent to them.

f. Crossing the two centermost cords of group 2 so that the left knot-bearing cord is over the right and holding the right knot-bearing cord (now on the left) on the diagonal to the lower outside edge, make a row of diagonal double half hitches. Reverse procedure for group 3, cross-ing the right knot-bearing cord over the left. There should now be an inverted V shape across the entire inner section.

g. Using top part of embroidery hoop as knot-bearing cord, tie a row of double half hitches over hoop. Cords must be kept in order; do not skip or lose any cords.

h. To make top half of diamond shape within hoop, cross over each other two centermost cords of entire inner section and hold them on the diagonal to the lower outside edges. Make two rows of diagonal double half hitches. For bottom part of dia-mond, make one row of diagonal double half hitches, holding two outermost cords on the diagonal to the lower center, crossing two knot-bearing cords at center, and making a second row of diagonal double half hitches.

i. Knot cords over bottom of hoop with double half hitches in the same manner as described in step 6g.

j. Using two outermost cords as knot-bearing cords and holding them on the diagonal to the lower center, make a row of diagonal double half hitches. There should now be a V shape across the entire inner section.

k. Hold third cord from each end of inner section on the diagonal to the lower outside edges and tie adjacent two cords in diagonal double half hitches.

l. Follow steps 6a and 6b to make an X shape in inner groups 1 and 4. Make an inverted V shape in groups 2 and 3 by holding two centermost cords of each group on the diagonal to the lower outside edges and tying adjacent cords in diagonal double half hitches in same manner.

m. Connect groups 1 and 2 by tying cord on left in group 1 in double half hitch onto cord on right in group 2. Repeat procedure to connect other three groups.

n. Make an X shape in each of the four groups, following steps 6a and 6b.

7. *Rows 44–45:* Using outside right aqua cord as knot-bearing cord, make one row of horizontal double half hitches. Using outside left aqua cord as knot-bearing cord, make another row of horizontal double half hitches.

8. *Rows 46–62:* Repeat steps 4 and 5.

9. *Rows 63–66:* With the four inner groups of cords, make four rows of alternating square knots. Begin to form an inverted triangle shape by making four square knots in first row. For second row, drop outermost three cords on each side and tie three square knots; for third row, drop outermost six cords on each side and tie two square knots; for fourth row, drop outermost nine cords on each side and tie one square knot.

10. *Rows 67–68:* Using both outside aqua cords as knot-bearing cords, hold them on the diagonal to the lower center and make one row of diagonal double half hitches. At center, loop right knot-bearing cord around left knot-bearing cord and, holding them on the diagonal toward the upper outside edge, work second row of diagonal double half hitches. Drop both aqua cords. These will be cut off and run into back of work when piece is completed.

11. *Rows 69–70:* Make two rows of vertical double half hitches.

12. *Rows 71–100:* Work royal blue and chartreuse groups in a thirty-knot half-knot sennit, making five twists.

13. With aqua cords, tie four alternating half hitches and tie in bell with double half hitch. Repeat procedure two times and tie four additional alternating half hitches at the ends. Tie off ends with overhand knot.

14. Add spider web pattern to tree limb wherever you wish. Follow photograph as a guide and adapt instructions to the shape of your tree limb. For each web, make spokes first by cutting a length of cord for each spoke you wish to have. With branches serving as knot-bearing cords, tie one end of each cord to any branch and the other end to a branch nearby, using a horizontal double half hitch. Make web portion by tying one end of additional cord lengths to a branch that more-or-less intersects branches bearing spokes. Where web cords intersect spoke cords, tie horizontal double half hitches with web cords. Tie the other ends of web cords to another branch. Cut off ends of cords and run them into backs of knots.

15. Cut cord reserved for bell chains to about twice the desired lengths. Fold in half and tie onto branches in lark's-head knots. Make chains of alternating half hitches and tie in bells (see step 13).

United States

Macramé Wall Hanging

The origin of the word *macramé* has been disputed by many. Some say that the word comes from an Arabic term describing trellis work, while other sources say that it is derived from an Arabic word meaning "kerchief" or "shawl." The term has now come to mean any form of knotting, including anything from a fringed edge on a woven garment to a decorative wall piece.

This geometric, formal design is a striking example of contemporary macramé work and you will find it's a satisfying project to undertake. The macramé section in "Helpful Hints" will familiarize you with knotting procedures; be sure to read it before beginning.

Materials

1,757 feet cotton pulley cord
household dye, in fuchsia and tangerine
37 inches dowel stock, 1¼ inches in
 diameter
2 wooden knobs, to fit ends of 1¼-inch-
 diameter dowel
paint, in orange
white glue
21½ inches dowel, ⅜ inch in diameter

Tools

scissors
saw
drill with ⅜-inch bit
paintbrush
ruler
T-pins
plywood board *or* foam rubber backing
hook (optional)

Procedure

1. Following manufacturer's directions on package, dye 924 feet of cord in fuchsia and 833 feet in tangerine. Cut fourteen 45-foot lengths and two 71-foot lengths from fuchsia cord; cut fourteen 45-foot lengths from tangerine cord. Cut 1¼-inch-diameter dowel into two lengths, one measuring 19½ inches and the other, 17½ inches. Paint 19½-inch dowel and wooden knobs orange. With the ⅜-inch bit, drill 1-inch-deep hole in center of each knob and in each end of 1¼-inch-diameter dowel. Cut two 2-inch lengths of ⅜-inch-diameter dowel, for doweling knobs to large-diameter dowel. Then, referring to doweling procedure in the woodworking section of "Helpful Hints," glue and dowel knobs in place.

2. *Row 1:* Fold one 71-foot fuchsia cord so that one side measures 48½ feet and the other side measures 22½ feet. Using painted dowel as holding cord, tie fuchsia cord to dowel in lark's-head knot, with 48½-foot side of cord on the outside.

Fold a 45-foot length of fuchsia cord in half and tie to dowel in lark's-head knot. Fold two 45-foot lengths of tangerine cord in half and tie to dowel in lark's-head knot. You now have one group of four fuchsia cords and one group of four tangerine cords. Continue tying cords across dowel in this manner, alternating groups of four fuchsia and four tangerine cords until you have tied seven groups of fuchsia and seven groups of tangerine. Fold remaining 45-foot fuchsia cord in half and tie onto dowel in lark's-head knot. Fold 71-foot fuchsia cord so that one side is 48½ feet and the other side is 22½ feet and, with longer side on the outside, tie onto dowel in lark's-head knot.3.

3. *Rows 2–7:* Make a six-knot square-knot sennit in each group of four.

4. *Rows 8–11:* Using first cord on the right side as knot-bearing cord, make four rows of horizontal double half hitches.

5. *Rows 12–16:* With four-cord groups, make five rows of alternating square knots.

6. *Rows 17–20:* Using first cord on left side as knot-bearing cord, repeat step 4.

7. *Rows 21–24:* Divide cords into five groups of twelve. Using centermost four cords of each group as knot-bearing cords, make a four-knot square-knot sennit in each group of twelve.

8. *Rows 25–28:* Repeat step 4.

9. *Rows 29–38:* Make ten rows of double alternating square knots in groups of four. This is done by making two rows of square knots instead of one before altering position of knot.

10. *Rows 39–42:* Using first cord on left side as knot-bearing cord, repeat step 4.

11. *Rows 43–52:* Repeat step 7, making a nine-knot sennit instead of a four-knot.

12. *Rows 53–56:* Repeat step 4.

13. *Rows 57–71:* Make fifteen rows of triple alternating square knots in groups

of four. This is done by making three rows of square knots before altering position of knot.

14. *Rows 72–75:* Using first cord on left as knot-bearing cord, repeat step 4.

15. *Rows 76–80:* Repeat step 5.

16. *Rows 81–84:* Repeat step 4.

17. *Rows 85–90:* Repeat step 3.

18. *Rows 91–96:* Using first cord on left as knot-bearing cord, repeat step 4.

19. *Rows 97–100:* Repeat step 7.

20. *Row 101:* Using ⅜-inch-diameter dowel as knot-bearing cord, make one row of horizontal double half hitches.

21. *Rows 102–103:* Using first cord on left as knot-bearing cord, make two rows of horizontal double half hitches.

22. *Row 104:* Using remaining 17½-inch dowel (1¼-inch diameter) as knot-bearing cord, make one row of horizontal double half hitches.

23. For each tassel, cut eight 27-inch lengths of cord and one 12-inch length for holding cord. There will be eight fuchsia tassels and seven tangerine tassels altogether. To make each tassel, pin ends of holding cord to workboard. Fold the eight cords in half, and tie onto holding cord in lark's-head knots. In groups of four, make one row of square knots. Unpin holding cord and tie ends together in a bow, bringing first group of square knots around to meet the fourth group. Working around tassel, make three rows of alternating square knots. Untie bow and thread holding cord on one side through lark's-head knot on opposite side, to connect sides of tassel.

24. Matching colors, slip a four-cord grouping from macramé piece down into center opening of each tassel. Push tassel up till it is about 2 inches below dowel. Using the holding cords as knotting cords, tie a square knot over the four-cord grouping above tassel top. Thread ends of holding cord down through center

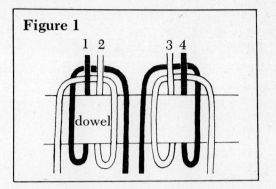

Figure 1

opening of tassel, and, inside the tassel, make another square knot over the four-cord grouping, adjusting tassel so that the two square knots do not show. Apply glue to knot of tassel top; trim ends evenly and tie in overhand knots.

25. From tangerine cord, cut two 161-inch lengths and two 80-inch lengths. Hold the four cords, side by side, with the two 161-inch cords on the outside. Measure off 28 inches from the ends and tie overhand knot at this point. Loop knot over hook or pin to workboard. Using the two long cords as knotting cords, make a 21-inch-long square-knot sennit to serve as hanging cord.

26. Between a knob and the outermost lark's-head knot, attach one end of hanging cord to top dowel as follows: Place the four cord ends behind one end of dowel (Figure 1). Bring cords 1 and 2 up over dowel, behind cord ends, across each other, and back to the front. Repeat for cords 3 and 4. Pull cord ends until the first square knot in 21-inch-long sennit is met. Continue the square-knot sennit for desired length. Repeat procedure to attach other end of hanging cord.

27. Following procedure in step 23, make two tangerine tassels for ends of hanging cord, each with eight 20-inch cords and an 8-inch holding cord. Slip sennit end into center opening of each tassel, and, following directions in step 24, attach tassels to sennit at each end.

Northwest Africa

Dahomey Wall Hanging

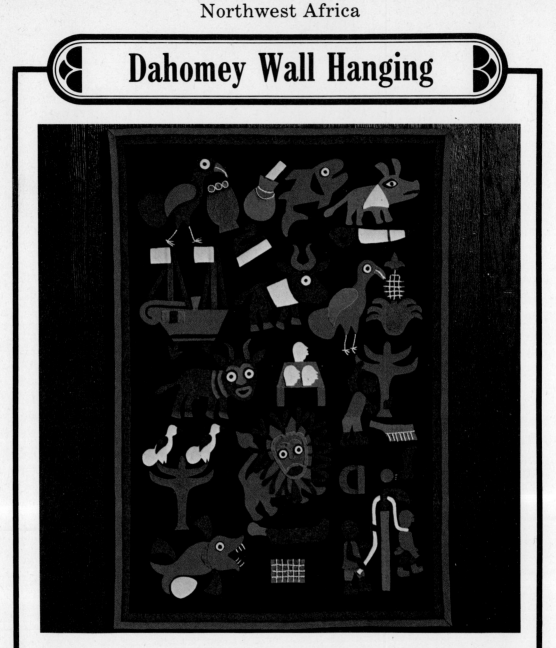

Before the conquest of the French in 1894, Dahomey had, for more than two hundred years, been the most highly organized and wealthy of the kingdoms of the West African Guinea Coast. Here was to be found the richest art of the whole continent.

Art flourishes yet in the kingdom. Patiently appliquéd wall hangings such as ours perpetuate the deeds of ten generations of proud Dahomean kings. The drum represents King Gan Yehesson, the lion symbolizes King Gele, who trafficked in slaves only a century ago, and the fish at the lower left represents his son. You will probably agree that the bold appliqué style used in this hanging presents a unique and attractive family tree.

Materials

felt:

1 piece, 6 × 36 inches, in red
1 piece, 9 × 36 inches, in yellow
3 pieces, each 9 × 12 inches, one each
  in white, green, and blue
1 piece, 27 × 36 inches, in black

spray adhesive

1 skein cotton embroidery thread, in
  white

1 wood strip, ¼ × 1 × 27 inches, *or* 27-
  inch section of wooden yardstick

acrylic paint, in black

Tools

scissors
ruler
brown wrapping paper
pencil
straight pins
newspaper
crewel needle
paintbrush, small or medium

Procedure

1. For border strips, cut two pieces from red felt and two from yellow felt, each measuring ½ × 36 inches. Then cut two more pieces from each color, each measuring ½ × 27 inches.

2. On brown wrapping paper, draw 1-inch grid and enlarge pattern figures (see "Helpful Hints"). Cut out patterns. Refer to color photograph and note color from which each figure is cut. Designate on each pattern piece the color from which it is to be cut. Then pin all patterns to be cut from same color felt to appropriate felt piece. Mark around figures on felt and cut out, leaving patterns still pinned to felt for ease in identification.

3. Miter corners on border strips, and place strips upside down on newspaper. Spray strips with adhesive and glue them to edges of black felt, forming frame.

4. Unpin patterns and, following photograph, arrange felt figures on black background but do not glue on yet.

5. Turn each cutout upside down on newspaper, spray with adhesive, and glue to background. To keep spacing even, glue on one figure at a time.

6. Embroider in details, such as legs and beaks, using white embroidery thread in outline or stem stitch (see embroidery-stitch section in "Helpful Hints").

7. Paint wood strip black and allow drying time. Then glue hanging to strip.

Patterns   each square = 1 inch

Leather Curtains

The fringed leather curtains in our project are certainly reminiscent of the Old West, having the look of the garments worn by Daniel Boone and Davy Crockett. At the same time, they are just as suggestive of casbahs and the Arabian Nights. Whatever the mood you wish your curtains to set, the warmth, rich texture, and natural aroma of the leather will turn the many hours needed to make this project into especially pleasant ones.

Materials
sueded split cowhide, in size to fit
   pattern (see step 1)
leather cement
beads, in style and number of your choice
wooden drapery rings, in style and
   number of your choice, for hanging
   curtain
wood stain, in shade of your choice
curtain rod, in size to fit window

Tools
brown wrapping paper
pencil
ruler
metal straightedge
craft knife
leather punch
sandpaper, medium grade
wire suede brush (optional)

Procedure
1. Before purchasing leather to fit your window, make paper pattern for top section, or heading, of curtain. The curtain heading may be as deep as you wish, and the width should be your window measurement plus about 6 inches to allow for sag when curtain is hung. Also figure amount of leather required to make fringe, which can be pieced for length. Take your pattern and measurements with you when you purchase leather. Select a skin and check pattern for fit on leather. (By doing this, you will minimize waste and ensure that skins you buy will match each other in color.) Buy as many skins as are necessary. Then, on a hard, flat surface, such as glass or marble, and using a metal straightedge and craft knife, cut leather piece for curtain heading to proper dimensions.
2. To make horizontal slits in heading, refer to Figure 1 for pattern to follow.

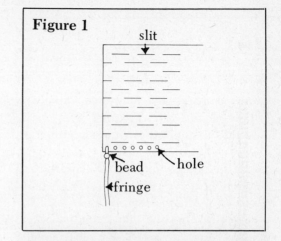

Figure 1

slit

bead   hole

fringe

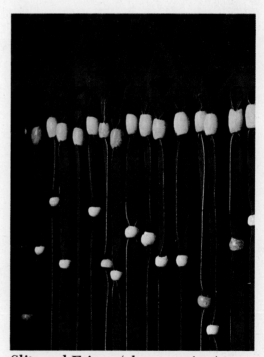

Slits and Fringe (close-up view)

Measure and mark first slit 1 inch from top and 1 inch in from left edge. Do not cut yet. Mark slit 2 inches long and continue across heading, marking 2-inch slits at 1-inch intervals. (Our curtain measures 81 inches at top; if your window size is smaller, you may wish to space slits closer together.) Keep in mind that you will need a drapery ring for each slit that is cut in top row. You can adjust the number accordingly. Mark first slit in second row about 1 inch below first row, starting from outer edge of heading. Continue to mark slits at 1-inch intervals across second row. Measure and mark rows of slits for entire curtain heading in this way, alternating position of first slit for each row. Be sure that slits on outer edges of heading start and end on second row from top and bottom.

3. Place leather on hard, flat surface. Align metal straightedge with each marked slit, and cut on lines with craft knife.

4. To make fringe, measure, mark, and cut ½-inch-wide strips from leftover leather. To lengthen fringe, you can piece strips together by skiving one end of both pieces and then gluing them together. (*Skiving* is a process of reducing the thickness of leather. When two pieces have been skived at the ends and then pieced, the join is hardly visible as the thickness of each end is reduced to a minimum.) To skive strips, use an extremely sharp craft knife and work on a hard, flat surface. Hold blade flat on leather ½ to ¾ inch from end of each piece, and lift handle to form a slight angle. Keeping blade almost horizontal to leather, stroke blade into leather, making shallow cut. Move blade forward to outside edge of leather. After thinning ends of pieces to be joined, cement skived ends together with leather cement.

5. On lower edge of curtain top, ½ inch from bottom, make marks 1 inch apart for holes for fringe (Figure 1). With leather punch, make a test hole on scrap leather and draw through it a piece of fringe to make sure that hole holds fringe snugly. Then punch all holes into curtain top.

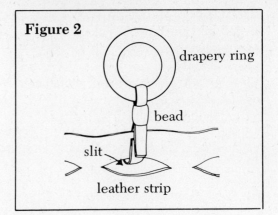

Figure 2

drapery ring

bead

slit

leather strip

6. Cut one end of fringe to a point, skive for about ¾ inch, and thread about 1 inch through hole from front to back. Cement end to back of fringe strand. (If any glue spills on leather, scrape off excess and rough up spot with small piece of sandpaper. Finish with a wire suede brush if necessary.) Slide bead up fringe strip and position over glued area (Figure 1). Add as many beads to fringe strips as you wish; this project shows twelve beads per strip.

7. To prepare drapery rings, remove screw eyes and stain rings. From scrap leather, cut a strip measuring ½ × 6 inches for each ring. Following Figure 2, pass strip through ring and thread both ends through a bead.

8. To attach ring to curtain top, both strips extending beneath bead will be glued over and through top row of slits. Cut end of one strip to 1 inch in length; cut the other to 1½ inches. Following Figure 2, position longer strip on front side of curtain above first slit and cement in place, pushing the extra ½ inch through slit and cementing to back side of heading. Cement 1-inch strip over end previously cemented.

9. Slide rings onto rod, and then trim ends of fringe evenly if it is necessary.

China

Priest Cords

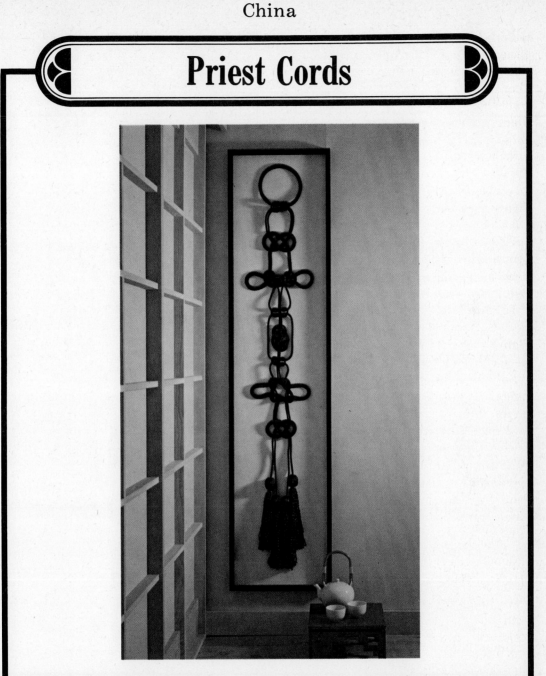

Priest cords—examples of Chinese expertise in the art of ornamental knotting—are series or lines of decorative, flat knots that are tied on silk cords. Unlike macramé, the individual knots are made to stand alone rather than in a continuous group of knots. Like macramé, however, they make striking wall hangings.

Although priest cords were originally done with silk, we have substituted cotton sash cord. It is available in heavy weights, can be unraveled, and takes well to dyeing.

Materials

approximately 130 feet uncoated cotton
  sash cord, ¼ inch in diameter
string *or* scrap yarn
dye, in black or color of your choice
thread, in color to match dye
4 Styrofoam balls, each 1 inch in
  diameter
pine:
  2 pieces, each ¾ × 1½ × 72 inches
  2 pieces, each ¾ × 1½ × 17½ inches
nails
1 piece wallboard or lightweight
  plywood, ¾ × 17 × 71 inches
flat enamel paint, in white and black
wire, heavyweight

Tools

scissors
Styrofoam workboard, approximately 2 ×
  12 × 18 inches
T-pins
needle
crochet hook, any size
miter box and saw
hammer
paintbrush
drill

Procedure

1. Cut two pieces of cord, each 45 feet in
length. Then cut 32 feet of cord into six-
teen 2-foot lengths. Unravel four of the 2-
foot lengths and, with string or scrap
yarn, tie them together several times
around entire length of bundle to prevent
tangling. Repeat for remaining 2-foot
cords, to make four bundles in all. These
will be used later for tassels.
2. Following manufacturer's directions
on dye package, dye cords and bundles.
After drying, untie string or scrap yarn
that was holding bundles together but
keep bundles separated from each other.

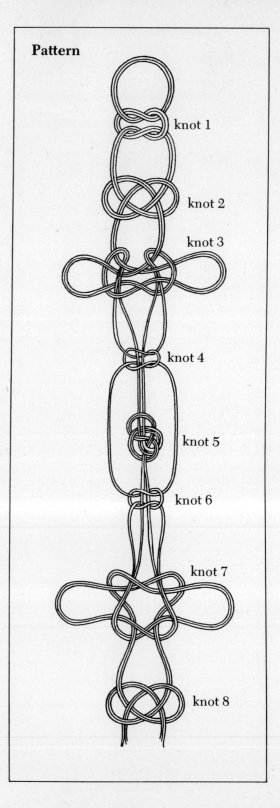

Pattern

knot 1

knot 2

knot 3

knot 4

knot 5

knot 6

knot 7

knot 8

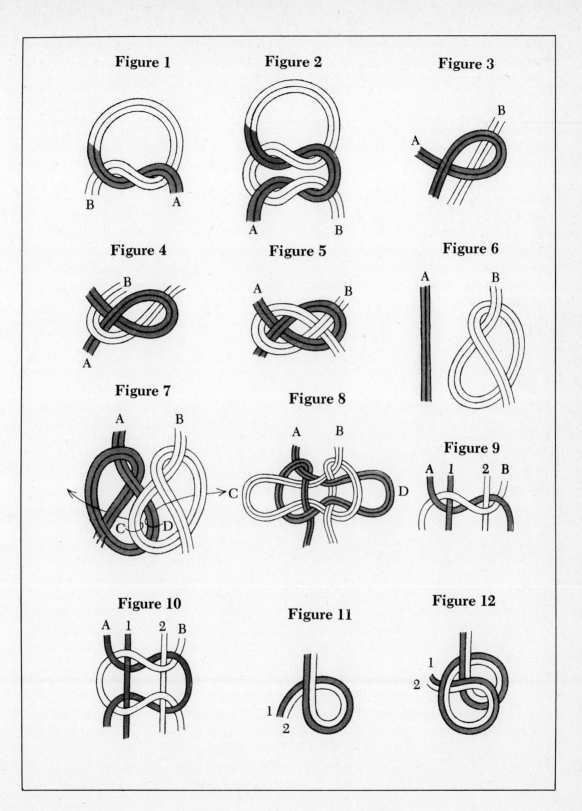

Figure 1

Figure 2

Figure 3

Figure 4

Figure 5

Figure 6

Figure 7

Figure 8

Figure 9

Figure 10

Figure 11

Figure 12

3. Fold the two 45-foot cords in half. Line up cords side by side on workboard and pin centers to top of board. The first three knots will be tied with two double-thickness cords. Whip two cords together for a distance of about 10 feet on both sides of pin. Form a circle with cords (see pattern).

4. *Knot 1 (square knot):* Following Figure 1, bring cord B over cord A and under left side of circle while bringing cord A under cord B and over right side of circle. Following Figure 2, bring cord B over cord A and then under right side of loop, while bringing cord A under cord B and then over left side of loop. Keep cords flat and tighten knot.

5. *Knot 2 (Josephine knot):* Following Figure 3, make a loop in cord A and place it over cord B. Following Figure 4, bring cord B over lower end of cord A and then under upper end of cord A. Following Figure 5, bring cord B over upper loop of cord A, under upper end of cord B, and then over lower loop of cord A. Pull cords enough to secure knot, but keep them flat and even.

6. *Knot 3 (noninterlocking overhand knots):* Following Figure 6, loop cord B to the right and bring it under and then over itself. Following Figure 7, loop cord A to the left and bring it over and then under itself. With thumbs and index fingers of both hands, grasp cords at points C and D and, following direction of arrows, pull outward. Pull and tighten knot, as shown in Figure 8.

7. *Knot 4 (square knot over center cords):* If you have whipped your two cords beyond this point, separate them so that you have two single cords on either side. Then, keeping center cords 1 and 2 held taut, repeat step 4, following Figures 9 and 10 (also refer to Figures 1 and 2).

8. *Knot 5 (flat Turk's-head knot):* Working with cords 1 and 2 as one cord (see pattern) and following Figure 11, loop cord to the right and under itself. Following Figure 12 and using same cord, form another loop in the same manner and place second loop over first. Following Figure 13, bring cord end over top of cord. Following Figure 14, bring cord end under top of first loop, over top of second loop, under bottom of first loop, and over bottom of second loop. Tighten knot, keeping cords flat.

9. *Knot 6 (square knot over center cords):* Keeping two center cords held taut, repeat step 4, following Figures 9 and 10.

10. *Knot 7 (True Lovers' knot):* Whip cords 1 and A together and cords 2 and B together for a distance of about 5 feet. Following Figure 15, loop cord B downward and bring end over, under, and then over loop. Following Figure 16, loop cord A through cord B, bringing end under and over cord B; bring cord A over, under, and over itself. With thumbs and index fingers of both hands and following direction of arrows in Figure 17, grasp cords at points C and D and pull outward. Following Figure 18, tighten knot.

11. *Knot 8 (Josephine knot):* Repeat step 5.

12. If necessary, remove the stitching from below knot 8 so that you have four cords. Decide upon how much space to leave between knot 8 and tassels, and insert T-pin in each cord to mark this length. With a crochet hook, punch a hole all the way through the center of each Styrofoam ball that will be large enough for cord to pass through. Slip ball up to pin on each cord and, following Figure 19, knot below ball. Above ball and following Figure 20, use a length of leftover cord to tie center of one of the bundles of

unraveled cords securely to each cord. Evenly distribute cords around ball and, following Figure 21, tie securely below it. Trim ends of tassel evenly. See Figure 22 for completed tassel.

13. Using a miter box and saw, miter the corners of pine. Nail frame together and paint black. Paint wallboard or plywood piece white and nail to back of pine frame. Position completed cord piece on wallboard and determine which knots need to be fastened down to board for support. Drill two holes through board at these places, one above cord and one below. For each set of holes, bring a piece of wire up through one hole, around cord, and down through the other hole. Then twist wires together in back.

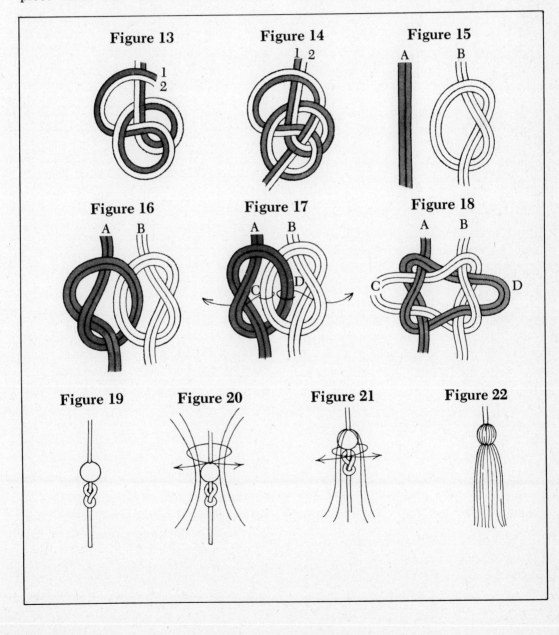

Chapter 8

Helpful Hints

General Notes on Enlarging Patterns

Most of the project design patterns in this book will have to be enlarged to meet project specifications. To enlarge those already marked off in squares, count the number of squares and rule off the same number on a sheet of brown wrapping paper, making each square measure 1 by 1 inch (Figure 1). Then copy the design, square by square, onto your grid. To enlarge an *alternate* design pattern, first determine how large you wish to make it. Then compute the percentage of enlargement this represents and square off pattern and your grid accordingly. For instance, if design in book measures 6 by 8 inches and you wish to make it 12 by 16 inches, the percentage of enlargement is 100 percent, or double. To achieve this, then, rule off book design in ½-inch squares and make your grid with 1-inch squares.

Mechanical devices that can be used for enlarging designs are pantographs, which are readily available at any art-supply house, and photostat machines.

General Notes on Transferring Patterns

For most of the projects in this book, you will be transferring patterns from paper

Figure 1—grid

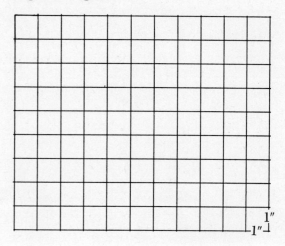

to whatever material you are working on. While there are many methods of transferring, the best methods are those that you find easiest to do. Project directions will specify which method to use, but if you prefer one of the following methods, by all means use it. Remember to enlarge all patterns that are marked off in squares before transferring.

Outlines: Cut out pattern and tape to material with masking tape. Draw around outline with pencil; remove pattern. Cut or saw out piece.

Intricate designs: In general, place carbon paper, face down, on working material and tape pattern over it. Go over all lines with a hard, sharp pencil or ball-point pen. Remove pattern. Retrace lines where necessary. Since carbon paper usually comes in small sheets, you may have to tape several pieces together.

To avoid having to use carbon paper, you can blacken the back side of a pattern with pencil lead. Then tape the pattern, face up, to the working material and go over all design lines with a hard, sharp pencil. Remove pattern. The penciled back will have transferred the lines.

For wood and metal pieces, tape pattern to surface, face up, and go over all lines with a pencil or ballpoint pen, pressing hard enough to indent the surface. Remove pattern. Check to make sure all lines have been indented; retrace where necessary.

For fabric, dressmakers' carbon and tracing wheel (packaged together or separately and sold in fabric shops, variety stores, and department stores) can be used. Place dressmakers' carbon, face down, over fabric, tape pattern over it, and go over all lines with tracing wheel. Remove pattern. The design lines will appear as tiny dots on the fabric. Go over all lines with indelible felt-tipped pen. If ink is not indelible, it will run when the fabric is washed.

What is referred to in this book as a "hot-iron transfer pencil" is another excellent device for transferring patterns to fabric, particularly to loosely woven fabrics on which tracing-wheel dots do not show up well. To use the hot-iron transfer, or hectograph, pencil, make your pattern on tracing paper so that the design lines will show through to the other side of the paper. Working on back side of paper, draw over all lines with transfer pencil. Then, with transfer-pencil lines

against fabric, tape pattern to fabric and iron over paper with a hot iron.

For lightweight fabrics, you may be able to use your window as a light box. To do this, tape fabric with pattern placed underneath it to a window that receives a lot of sunlight. Draw over the lines that show through to the fabric.

General Notes on Woodworking
Many of the projects in this book are made with wood. If you have never worked with wood before, don't be intimidated by it. Just like everything else, it is a skill that is learned only through practice. Your lumberman is a good source of information and will be happy to answer your questions. The following tips will help you to get started. For further information, consult any one of the excellent handyman manuals on the market.

Purchasing Wood
If project instructions do not specify type of wood to use, the choice is up to you. Lumber is categorized as either hardwood or softwood. Hardwoods include oak, maple, birch, mahogany, teak, and ebony. Soft woods include redwood, pine, fir, and spruce. Plywood, used in many projects in the book, is made from sheets of wood that have been glued together. Very thin sheets of wood are called veneer sheets.

A trip to the lumberyard might be a bit confusing for someone who hasn't done it before. Wood pieces come in set thicknesses and widths and are sold by the length. Dowels are round rods of hardwood. You can purchase dowels cut in lengths ready for use, or you can buy full-length doweling in 3-foot lengths. The diameter of doweling runs from 1/8 inch to 1 inch, graduating from 1/16 inch to 1/8 inch.

Another fact to remember when purchasing wood is that because of the milling process, the actual size of the lumber will be slightly less than what was requested. For instance, a "2 by 4" will actually be 1⅝ × 3⅝ inches. However, this has been accounted for in the projects, so don't be concerned when you find your wood pieces smaller than those required in the materials lists. Unmilled, rough lumber is also available, if you wish.

Once you have purchased your lumber, check to make sure that the sawed ends and edges have been smooth-cut. If necessary, lightly rasp ends and edges with a fine wood rasp. This will prepare lumber for proper fitting and gluing.

Sawing Wood

There are many different types of saws, each of which is suited to make a different type of cut. The following are just some of the many types. Become familiar with them, and learn what they can and cannot do.

Coping saw (Figure 2): A handsaw with a U-shaped metal frame, a short,

Figure 2—Coping Saw

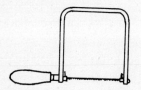

slender blade, and a handle, which, by turning the blade, can cut intricate shapes and curves in wood. It can also be used to make inside cuts. To do this, first drill a hole in the area to be cut out. Remove the blade, insert it in the hole, and reassemble the saw around it. The lim-

iting factor of a coping saw is that it can make inside cuts that are no more than the distance between its frame and the blade.

Crosscut saw (Figure 3): A handsaw used to cut across the grain of wood.

Figure 3—Crosscut Saw

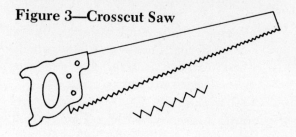

Hacksaw (Figure 4): A handsaw with a long U-shaped frame and a removable blade usually used to cut metal. Pointed hacksaws can be used for making cuts in tight places.

Figure 4—Hacksaw

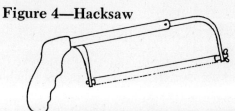

Jigsaw (Figure 5): Basically, a power version of a coping saw. However, it can be used when deeper cuts are necessary.

Figure 5—Jigsaw

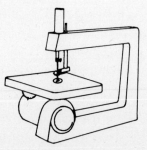

Keyhole saw (Figure 6): A handsaw with a tapered blade used to cut inside curves, slots, and holes. It, too, has removable blades.

Figure 6—Keyhole Saw

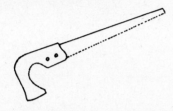

Miter (or back) saw (Figure 7): A handsaw used with a miter box (see *"Mitered joints"*) to cut angles on wood.

Figure 7—Miter Box and Saw

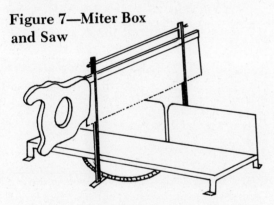

Rip saw (Figure 8): A handsaw used to cut with the grain of wood.

Figure 8—Rip Saw

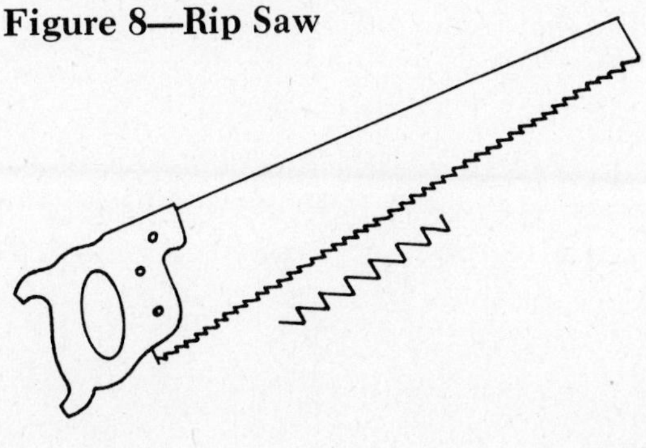

Saber saw (Figure 9): A hand-held, keyhole-type power saw used for straight and curved cuts and to cut slots and holes.

Figure 9—Saber Saw

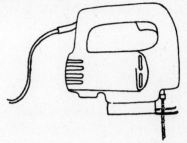

When sawing wood, your objective should be to make even, true, and square cuts. Here are a few pointers to keep in mind:

• Before sawing, draw a line on best side of wood, designating length to be cut. When placing wood on work surface, align drawn line with surface edge so that area to be cut off extends beyond surface.

• Use a straight piece of wood, at least as long as the cut to be made and either 2 × 2 or 2 × 4 inches, as a guide for cutting. To do this, place guide alongside drawn line and clamp guide to work surface. Rest saw blade against wood piece and cut.

• Always saw with best side of wood facing up.

• For plywood cuts, draw cutting lines on both sides of wood and score with a sharp chisel before sawing. This helps prevent splintering. A fine-toothed saw is best for cutting plywood.

• When sawing out grooves or slots (grooves are cut partway through wood, while slots are cut all the way through), start by drilling a series of small holes within the area to be removed. Be careful to drill only within these confines. If depth of groove has to be controlled, use a drill-stop (either purchased or homemade). After drilling, cut out final groove or slot with keyhole saw, thin rasp, carving knife, or chisel. The flat side of a chisel or half-round pattern file will be helpful for dressing and finishing sides.

Working with Wood

Some additional tools that may be needed for woodworking are a hammer, screwdriver, pliers, wrench, file, rasp, chisel, center punch, a nailset, vise, clamps, awl, and drill and bits. Hammers and screwdrivers, of course, are used for driving nails and screws. Pliers and wrenches can be used to tighten or loosen bolts and for a multitude of other purposes. Files are used to smooth metal or wood edges. They come in flat, half-round, triangular, and square shapes. Rasps are most often used to file wood. Chisels are used to cut slots and grooves. Awls and center punches can be used to make starting holes for drill bits or nails, while nailsets are used to countersink nails. A vise or clamps will hold wood securely in place while it is being worked on. An awl is used to make holes in wood before setting in nails or screws. A drill may be a hand drill or a power drill and is used to drill holes into wood or metal. Attachments for sanding, grinding, and buffing are available for most electric drills.

Joining Wood Pieces

There are many ways to join wood pieces. Basically, however, you will be able to assemble any of the projects in this book by using either butt joints or mitered joints.

Butt joints (Figure 10): The simplest

Figure 10—Butt Joints

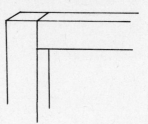

kind of joints, these are made by cutting the ends of the pieces to be joined so that they are square and then holding the two pieces together by some sort of fastening device, such as nails, screws, or dowels.

Mitered joints (Figure 11): These are usually used when a more attractive and

Figure 11—Mitered Joints

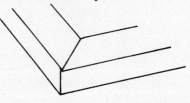

stronger joint is desired. They are made by cutting the ends of two wood pieces to corresponding angles with a miter box and saw. The two pieces are then joined by nails, screws, or dowels. A miter box is a U-shaped wood trough with slotted sides that guide the saw into the correct angle (Figure 12). Miters can also be cut with power tools, such as a table saw.

Figure 12—Miter Box

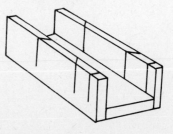

In most of the woodworking projects in this book, the fastening devices used are nails, screws, nuts and bolts, dowels, or glue. Read the following information for some helpful tips on working with these.

Nails: Basically, there are five types of nails—common nails, wire nails, box nails, finishing nails, and casing nails. Common nails have large, round, flat heads and are used for rough, heavy work. Wire nails have much shorter, thinner shanks and are used on thin wood. Box nails, which also have thin shanks but are longer than wire nails, can be used for light, rough woodworking. Finishing nails have thin heads that can be set below a wood surface. Casing nails are slightly thicker and have cone-shaped heads; these are used for interior trims.

Most nails are sold in "penny size," designated by the letter *d*. The smallest nail sold by penny size is labeled 2d and is 1 inch long. A 3d nail will be slightly longer. Any nail smaller than size 2d is called a brad or tack. These are sold by shank length.

Here are some points to keep in mind when nailing:

- To avoid splitting wood, either blunt nail end with hammer before driving it in or drill a hole that is slightly smaller than the nail in the wood first and then drive in the nail.
- Never recklessly bang on the nail with your hammer, attempting to drive it in with just a few blows. Take your time or you may split the wood. Work slowly and accurately.
- Hammer in nails as far in from the ends of the board as is possible.
- Try not to nail through or near knots in wood, since knots are weak sections.
- In some cases, you will need to counter-sink nails. This means that the nailhead is to be driven below or flush with the wood surface. To do this, hold nailset over nail and stroke with hammer. Fill holes with wood putty to make flush with wood surface.
- When nailing wood temporarily (this is often done to check fit of pieces), pound nail into wood just far enough to hold pieces together and no farther. To remove a temporary nail, place a wood block alongside nail and under curved claws of hammer. Using block for leverage, pull out nail with hammer claws.

Screws: The advantages of using screws are that they have strong holding power and can be easily removed.

There are many varieties of screws. For woodworking, however, make sure that you are using wood screws. Usually made of steel or brass, wood screws are categorized by the diameter and length. A #2 wood screw is the smallest; a #24 is the largest. Those with straight-slotted heads come with flat, round, or oval heads. Flat-headed screws are the most commonly used on these projects since they can be countersunk.

Before inserting screw in wood, either punch a hole in the wood with an awl or ice pick or drill a hole smaller than the diameter of the screw; then drive in the screw with a screwdriver.

Nuts and bolts: These are used when an even stronger holding power than screws provide is desired. The advantage to using them is that you can easily disassemble the pieces. Nuts are purchased to match with bolts. Bolts must be long enough to go completely through the wood and still extend far enough beyond the other side to allow for screwing on the nut. To do this, a hole is drilled in the wood the size of the bolt shank, the bolt is inserted, and the nut is twisted on the protruding end to hold it in place.

Hinges: These are used to attach doors and lids of boxes. Unless otherwise specified, butt hinges (Figure 13), which are

Figure 13—Butt Hinge

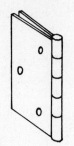

the most widely used type of hinge, should be used for projects in this book. For cabinets and cupboards, however, piano hinges (Figure 14) are specified, for they will add strength and durability to the piece. Hardware stores usually stock piano hinges in long lengths. If you cannot have piano hinge cut to size there, use a hacksaw to shorten it to the required length. Always cut at the joint of the hinge and then file the edges smooth.

Figure 14—Piano Hinge

In many cases, to attach hinges, you will have to mortise the wood to the size of the hinge butt. To do this, draw around outline of butt and, with a chisel, hollow out a space to the same depth as butt. With an awl, make holes for screws of hinge, set in butt, and drive in screws. Remember that hinges should be fitted before wood has been stained, painted, or finished.

Dowels: The use of dowels is an effective way to add strength and support to a joint. Ready-to-use dowels are available in standard lengths, with a rounded end and spiral scoring across the length. Although there are several methods of doweling, the *open-hole* method, which is fairly easy and effective, will be sufficient for the projects in this book. Even so, it must be done carefully and accurately to obtain best results. Here are some points to remember:

• If your dowel has not been scored, do so before gluing. Score spirally or straight down the length, using the corner of a file. This scoring will allow the glue to ooze out of the hole once the dowel has been inserted, thus preventing a glue build-up. Glue build-ups may very well result in difficulty when trying to drive in dowels. Before inserting dowels, it is also a good idea to round the ends slightly with a file or sandpaper.

• When drilling holes for dowels, the wood pieces to be joined must be firmly held together in their correct positions. Clamping or temporary nailing will do the trick. Choice of method is optional, and, in some cases, it might be a good idea to use both methods. Never try to hold pieces together with your hand. The slightest tilt or shift of one piece will throw the dowel holes out of alignment.

• Locate dowel positions according to pattern and center-punch each position to start point for drill bit.

• Since narrow drill bits are easier to control than wider ones, use a ⅛-inch bit to establish position, angle, and depth of dowel holes. Then, switch to bit for required diameter of hole and complete hole.

• To help ensure straight drilling, line up the drill against a carpenter's square. Precision doweling jigs, which are clamped onto the wood and hold the bit or drill in position, can be purchased, if you wish, for this purpose.

• To control depth of drilled dowel holes, you can use a dowel as a simple drill-stop or depth gauge. To do this, first drill a hole through the length of a dowel whose diameter is larger than that of the drill bit. Then cut dowel so that when it is slid up the bit and resting against the chuck, the exposed portion of the bit will equal the desired depth of the hole. The dowel thus forms a sleeve, preventing the drill from entering the wood deeper than desired. A commercial drill-stop may also be purchased from hardware stores.

• After drilling has been completed, leave wood pieces clamped together and remove wood chips.

• To glue dowels, apply drop of glue to ends of dowels and to dowel holes.

• To drive dowels in position, pound in with wooden mallet. Using a metal hammer may cause dowel end to split. If you must use a metal hammer, place a wooden block between it and the dowel end. This will help drive dowel in even with surface and will prevent marring.

• If dowel protrudes beyond surface, cut off projection with blade of coping saw or fine-toothed hacksaw. To prevent possible scuffing of wood while being sawed, place a piece of cardboard or thin sheet metal (such as a piece of flattened coffee can) around the dowel and cut with saw blade laid flat against it. Then, working with the grain, file or sand dowel flush with surface.

• Wipe off all excess glue with damp cloth.

Glue: Some projects can be assembled by gluing. Be sure first to remove all wax, grease, oil, or paint from surface to be glued. Then apply glue to surface, and clamp pieces together until glue has dried completely.

Clamps: While there are several types of clamps used for various gluing operations and for holding steady an object being worked on, the projects in this book call for either pipe clamps (Figure 15), which are also known as bar clamps, or C-clamps (Figure 16). Pipe clamps are used for holding work that is long, up to 6 feet in length. Blocks of scrap lumber, referred to as cushion blocks, are always inserted between the project and the clamps to prevent denting of the wood.

Figure 15—Pipe Clamp

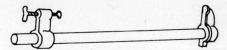

Figure 16—C-clamp

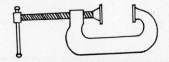

If you're confronted with the problem of clamping an object to a wide board and your clamp is not large enough to reach the object, improvise with two clamps and a strong steel bar or piece of wood. The bar or wood should be long enough to span the width of the board and strong enough for the job involved. Place the bar or wood across object to be clamped, with ends extending to edges of board. Apply two C-clamps, one at each end, to pull bar downward, exerting sufficient pressure to hold object firmly in place.

Sanding Wood

Sanding is necessary to smooth wood surfaces, particularly cut edges. In this book, it is done by hand, using abrasive materials—collectively referred to as sandpaper—that have been backed with cloth or paper. Among the many different types of sandpaper, those best suited for woodworking are aluminum oxide, flint, and garnet papers.

Most of the projects in the book that require sanding will specify what grade of sandpaper to use—coarse, medium, fine, or finishing (very fine). Coarse sandpapers, used to sand cuts, range in number size from about 12 to 50. Medium sandpapers range from about 60 to 100, fine sandpapers from about 120 to 180, and finishing (very fine), used between coats when finishing wood, from about 220 to 600. When purchasing sandpaper, look for the number or word classification on the back of the sheet.

When you are ready to sand, keep three basic points in mind.
- Always sand with the grain of the wood. Sanding across the grain will tear the wood fibers.
- If using more than one grade of sandpaper for the same surface, sand with the coarser grade first and then with the finer grade.
- Apply an even amount of pressure over the entire surface. You can wrap sandpaper around a block of wood or use a sanding block to ensure even pressure.

- For inside curves and circles, wrap sandpaper around a large-diameter dowel and sand surface. If a great deal of sanding is necessary, first use a half-round file and then switch to sandpaper.

Finishing Wood

After you have assembled the project and sanded the wood smooth, you are ready to finish the wood. If there are spaces around nails or small cuts or holes in the wood surface, use wood putty to fill them and then sand the surface smooth. Although projects will designate how to finish your piece, there are basically three choices. You may have a painted surface, a natural-finish surface, or a stained surface.

Painted surfaces: Before painting, the first step is to seal the wood with sealer or shellac. This is done to hold wood fibers in place and to keep them from rising. If you do not seal the wood, you will have to apply more coats of paint.

There are essentially three categories of paint for wood use—water-base, oil-base, and lacquer. All three come in flat, semigloss, or gloss finishes and a variety of colors. Water-base paints are easy to apply, fast-drying, and can be cleaned up with water. Oil-base paints are slower-drying, longer-lasting, and require paint thinner to be cleaned up. Lacquers are fast-drying and require lacquer thinner for cleanup. Remember that since lacquer will raise any finish, do not apply it over anything but lacquer. Before applying lacquer to wood, prime the surface with lacquer primer.

Apply as many coats of paint as are needed, sanding between coats and allowing drying time. Be sure to follow manufacturer's directions for best results.

Natural-finish surfaces: With this method, the natural quality of the wood is retained. Apply either clear varnish or clear lacquer, following manufacturer's directions on the product.

Stained surfaces: Oil-base or water-base stains come in a wide variety of shades, from mahogany to oak, maple, and walnut. Before you apply the stain, test it on scrap wood first to see how much time and stain is required to achieve the color you desire. Then apply to piece, allow to develop the proper amount of time, wipe away residue, allow to dry thoroughly, and finish with clear varnish. Always follow manufacturer's instructions given on the product.

General Notes on Metal Tooling
There are three projects in the book that require metal tooling—the Sun Fern Stand, the Metal- tooled Cabinet, and the Bakota Ancestor Figure. Read the following instructions before starting any of these projects.

Gathering Materials and Tools
Equipment required for metal tooling is minimal. You probably already have many of these items at home.

Metal: For the projects in this book, you will need tooling aluminum or tooling copper. Both are sold by the foot from rolls that are 12 inches wide. You will probably want some extra to practice on first. While the methods of tooling aluminum and copper are the same, aluminum is softer than copper and should, therefore, be handled with greater care.

Before tooling copper and before applying finish, you must remove the black coloring caused by oxidation. A fine grade of steel wool is best for this purpose. (While you are handling copper, avoid touching it any more than is necessary, as skin oils will further oxidate the material.)

Work surface: For smoothing and flattening backgrounds, it is necessary to work on a perfectly smooth surface, such as a glass or Masonite sheet. Make sure that the surface is perfectly clean and has no tiny grit particles on it. For embossing design, you will need to work on a padded surface. A piece of felt, a magazine, or a newspaper pad will do nicely.

Pattern preparation: For transfer of design, masking tape is used to tape pattern to metal and a ballpoint pen or fat-lead drawing pencil is used for tracing.

Tooling instruments: The best instruments to use for metal tooling are clay-modeling tools, available in a variety of

Figure 17—Modeling Tools

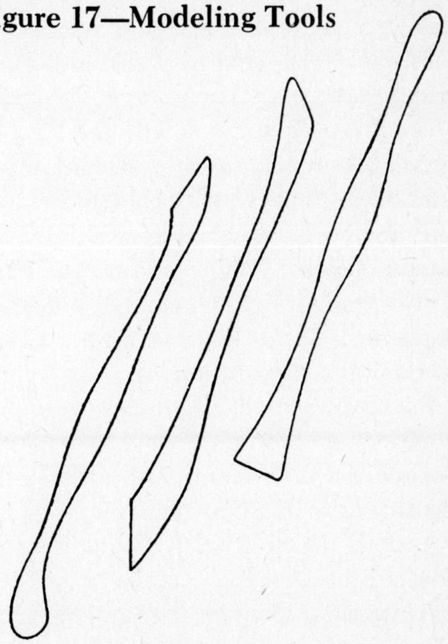

shapes (Figure 17). If you have a leather-modeling tool, give it a try, using the pointed end for lines and the spoon-shaped end for larger areas. Make sure, however, that it has no nicks on its surface or it will scratch the metal. If it is nicked, smooth it with a pink desk eraser or emery cloth.

Backgrounds of designs and other areas will be flattened after design has been tooled. Pink desk erasers, bone folders, or wood smoothing tools can be used for this purpose. Pink desk erasers are particularly good because they can be sanded down to fit the area to be smoothed.

Materials for filling back of design: If your tooling is deeply embossed, you must fill in the back of the metal with modeling clay, Sculptamold, or a mixture of sawdust and white glue.

Materials for finishing: To avoid leaving fingerprints on completed pieces, wear a pair of cotton gloves while finishing. Also have on hand a supply of lint-free cloths, cotton swabs, and clean sponges.

To finish copper, you will need a clear lacquer spray to prevent oxidation. If you wish to antique your copper piece, you will need a bottle of liver of sulfur (sulfurated potash). While you are working with it, keep it in an enamel or porcelain container. Store it in a colored-glass bottle with a tight-fitting lid.

To clean tooled aluminum, you may use lacquer thinner, alcohol, or vinegar. To antique aluminum, you will need a fast-drying black spray paint for metal.

Tooling the Design
It is wise to practice tooling on scrap metal first to master the technique. As you practice, you will probably find that you will have to repeat each procedure, working first on the back and then on the front. To begin, follow these steps:

1. Place metal on flat work surface. Tape pattern securely to front side of metal with masking tape. Go over design lines with ballpoint pen or pencil, pressing firmly enough to leave a clear impression on the metal. Turn metal over to make sure all lines appear on the back. Remove pattern.

2. Place metal face down. With modeling tool, push forward design areas to be raised.

3. Working with metal face up, use modeling tool to retrace design lines. Flatten background areas with an eraser, bone folder, or wood smoothing tool.

4. If tooling is deeply embossed, you will need to level off the back side of the metal. If you don't, any kind of pressure exerted on the metal will cause it to dent. Fill in these areas with modeling clay, Sculptamold, or a mixture of sawdust and white glue. Draw a straight edge across the back to remove any excess filler.

Finishing Copper
Copper can be finished in any one of the following ways. Before finishing, however, polish it thoroughly with fine steel wool to remove all dirt and fingerprints. Wear cotton gloves.

Natural finish: After you have polished copper until it is as bright as possible, spray two or three coats of lacquer over piece. Allow drying time between coats.

Antique finish: Liver of sulfur is the most commonly used antiquing solution for copper, for it causes rapid oxidation. To make a weak solution, add a pea-sized lump of it to a quart of warm water. For a stronger solution, add more. Test solution on a scrap of clean copper to see how much time is required for it to develop to the color you want.

To apply solution to copper, use lint-free cloth, cotton swab, or steel wool. When the desired color has been reached, wipe off solution with a sponge that has been saturated in water or vinegar. After copper has dried, polish areas to be highlighted with fine steel wool. Wipe off dust and steel-wool particles, and spray a coat of lacquer over piece. Allow to dry.

Opalescent finish: Hold copper over an open flame till it has an opalescent quality. Spray with clear lacquer.

Finishing Aluminum

Finished aluminum pieces may be left plain or antiqued. To antique, clean aluminum with a soft lint-free cloth that has been saturated in lacquer thinner, alcohol, or vinegar. Wear cotton gloves. Spray aluminum with a coat of fast-drying black paint for metal. Wipe off raised areas with a cloth that has been dipped in the solvent recommended for your paint.

General Notes on Macramé

Macramé, ever growing in popularity, is simple and fun to do. The four macramé projects in this book—Macramé Plant Holder, Macramé Doormat, Branch with Spider Web, and Macramé Wall Hanging—illustrate the diversity of this age-old craft.

Basically, there are five steps involved in doing a macramé project—computing the required length of cords, gathering the materials and tools, setting up, working the design, and finishing off.

Read the following information and practice each knot before beginning any of the macramé projects. You'll find them much easier to do if you first master these basic skills.

Computing Required Length of Cords

In macramé work, there are three types of cords. The *holding cord* is the horizontal cord (usually at the top) upon which all other cords are tied. *Knot-bearing cords* are the cords upon which the knots are tied, and *knotting cords* are the cords actually knotted.

For the macramé projects in this book, cord lengths have already been computed for you. If you are working on your own design, however, you will have to compute lengths yourself. To compute the length for the holding cord, simply add 6 inches to the width you desire your completed piece to be. To determine the length of the knotting cords, decide upon the length you wish your finished piece to be. Multiply this figure by 3½ or 4. Since each cord will be folded in half to form two cords, multiply the result by 2.

In many designs, the outermost cords serve as the knot-bearing cords. They should, therefore, be about 1½ times the length of the knotting cords. Check design before cutting cord lengths, and make sure you tie longer cords in correct position.

Total computed cord lengths to find amount of cord needed. Although this method of computing is a bit generous, it is far better to have cord lengths that are too long than too short. And, remember, you can always use leftover cord for your next macramé project.

If you have *under*estimated cord lengths, there are several ways to add on cord. The least noticeable way is the best way, and the method you choose will depend on the design. New cord can be added in the center of a square knot or a horizontal double half hitch by knotting over both new and old cords for a short distance, dropping the short cord and then continuing to knot over the new cord. The ends of both new and old cords will be cut close to work when completed.

To add to other types of knotting, drop the short end of the cord, pin a new cord in place to workboard, and continue knotting over the new cord. When piece is finished, tie cords together on back or run ends into knots on back of piece.

If neither of these methods works, splice new and old cords. For twisted cord, such as sisal, splice at an angle, place one cord over the other, twist together, and glue. For woven cord, such as parachute cord, pull out about 1 inch of filler from new and old cords to form hollow tubes, wrap one end tightly with masking tape, apply white glue to the tape, and insert into other cord tube.

Gathering Materials and Tools

Macramé equipment is relatively inexpensive and easy to come by. One trip to a good hardware store might very well take care of everything you will need.

Knotting materials: Practically any type of cord can be used for macramé as long as it is strong enough to take knotting and pulling but, at the same time, is not too elastic. Popular materials are cotton twine, jute, mason cord, parachute cord, seine twine, sisal, hemp, and pulley cord. Keep in mind the overall design plan, and decide whether you want to use a light or heavy cord. For all practice work, use heavy cords so that errors will

be easily seen. Tie a sampler of selected cord to see how much cord will be taken up by the knots and to determine the number of cords per inch. Knotting thick cord usually takes up more length than thin cord.

Work surface: When working on large macramé projects, such as wall hangings, you will need to pin piece down while working on it. Styrofoam sheets, beaver boards, plywood boards, cardboard cartons, or any other flat, sturdy surface that will take pins easily are suitable. If you are working a three-dimensional project, such as a plant holder, suspend the piece from a sturdy hook.

Holding devices: T-pins, hatpins, or pushpins are used to hold piece to work surface and to separate knots. Small C-clamps can be used to hold wooden dowels or holding cords to work surface. They may also be used to anchor cord while you are measuring it.

Finishing aids: To run ends of a finished knot into back of piece, you will need a blunt, large-eyed needle. If necessary, use an awl or ice pick to open a passageway and then pull ends through with a pair of pliers.

Miscellaneous: You will need a ruler or yardstick for measuring cord lengths, a pair of sharp, heavy-duty scissors for cutting cords, rubber bands for securing cord bundles, small pieces of masking tape if you wish to number cords for easy reference, a pencil to draw guidelines on work surface, white glue for splicing cord lengths and for sealing knots, and a pair of cotton gloves to protect your hands while working. If you wish to dye cords for your project, use ordinary household dye before beginning work.

Setting Up

Before you begin work on the design, gather all equipment you will need and follow these steps.

1. If you wish to dye cord, follow manufacturer's directions on package; then allow cord to dry.

2. Cut knot-bearing cords and knotting cords into appropriate lengths and tie ends of cords in overhand knots (Figure 18).

3. Cut holding cord 6 inches longer than piece will be wide when completed and make an overhand knot at each end. For large macramé pieces, pin through each overhand knot, attaching holding cord to work surface (Figure 19). If you are using a dowel, cut to length you wish, tie first row of knots, and then fasten to work surface and table with C-clamps. For three-dimensional projects, suspend cords from a hook by tying holding cord around hook in a simple knot or bow.

4. Fold each knotting cord in half and tie onto holding cord in lark's-head knot (Figures 20 and 21). When doing a design that requires many rows of horizontal double half hitches, fold outermost cords and knot-bearing cords so that one side will be same length as knotting cords and other side will be longer. Tie onto holding cord in lark's-head knot so that the longer cord is on the outside.

5. Starting about 8 inches below lark's-head knot, bundle each cord in a figure-eight pattern and secure with rubber band. This is done by bringing cord in front of index and third fingers, around to the back of ring and last fingers, around to the front of ring and last fingers, and then around to the back of index and

third fingers. Continue for length of cord, slip bundle off fingers, and secure with rubber band around center crossing. As you work, simply pull out cord from bundle.

6. Attach a small piece of masking tape to end of each cord and number consecutively. For the projects in this book, cord

Figure 18—Overhand Knot

Figure 19—Holding Cord Pinned to Work Surface

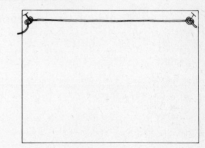

Figure 20—Knotting Cord Tied Onto Holding Cord

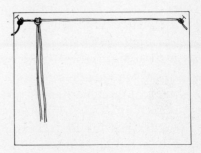

1 is the first cord on the left of the piece.

7. To guide you as you are working, draw lines on work surface to correspond with finished width of piece. Pin ends of finished rows to work surface to keep work even. Pin knots to boards where necessary to keep knots in place.

Working the Design

Designs are usually worked in rows of knots. Although there are hundreds of knots and variations, the following knots will give you a good head start and enable you to do the macramé projects in the book, as well as countless others. Remember to pull each knot tight. Make knots as uniform as possible and keep vertical and horizontal rows even.

Lark's-head knot (Figure 21): Fold cord into loop and place loop over holding cord. Fold loop back over holding cord, insert ends into loop, and pull through. Pin at both sides of knot.

Figure 21—Lark's-head Knot

Horizontal double half hitch (Figure 22): Use first cord on either right or left side of piece as knot-bearing cord and hold it parallel to holding cord, resting over knotting cords. Bring cord 2 up, over, and around knot-bearing cord, insert it between knot-bearing cord and itself, and pull through. Repeat with same cord. Drop cord 2 and repeat procedure for all other knotting cords, keeping knot bearer taut and knots neat and uniform. Pin knots to secure. At the end of the row,

pin last knot and reverse direction of knot-bearing cord, making horizontal half hitches across piece. You now have two rows of horizontal double half hitches, with knot-bearing cord in its original position.

Figure 22—Horizontal Double Half Hitch

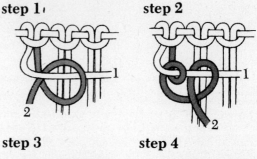

Vertical double half hitch (Figure 23): Use first cord on either side as knotting cord and all other cords as knot bearers. Bring knotting cord behind cord 2 and then up, over, and around it. Insert end between cord 2 and itself and pull through. Repeat on same cord. Repeat across the piece, using same knotting cord and making two knots on each knot-bearing cord. Hold knot-bearing cords taut. When you come to the end of the row, reverse knotting cord and knot across piece, as before. You now have two rows of vertical double half hitches, with knotting cord back in its original position. You will notice that the color of the knotting cord will be the color of entire row of knots and that two rows of knotting will actually look like four rows.

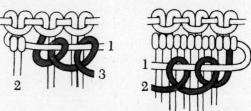

Figure 23—Vertical Double Half Hitch

Figure 23—Vertical Double Half Hitch

Diagonal double half hitch (Figure 24): Use the first cord on the left as knot-bearing cord and hold it on the diagonal to the right. Bring cord 2 up, over, and around knot-bearing cord. Insert end between knot bearer and itself and pull through. Repeat with same cord. Drop cord 2. Continue for all other knotting cords until you have done half the group. Drop knot-bearing cord and pick up first cord on right side of group. Using this cord as knot-bearing cord and holding it on the diagonal to the left, follow same procedure to knot right-side cords. When you come to the center, knot the left knot-bearing cord over the right knot-bearing cord. You can continue to hold knot-bearing cords on the diagonal to form X shapes, or you can stop at this point to create patterns of chevrons or V-shapes.

Figure 24—Diagonal Double Half Hitch

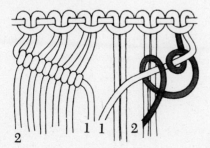

Figure 24—Diagonal Double Half Hitch

Square knot and half knot (Figures 25 and 26): A square knot is composed of two half knots. Use the outer two cords as knotting cords and inner two cords as knot-bearing cords. The first part of the knot is made by bringing cord 1 behind cords 2 and 3 and over cord 4, while bringing cord 4 over cords 2 and 3 and behind cord 1 (Figure 25). Pull tight. The second part of the knot is made by bringing cord 1 behind cords 2 and 3 and over cord 4, while bringing cord 4 over

Figure 25—Part-1 Half Knot or Part 1 of Square Knot

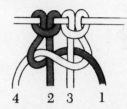

Figure 25—Part-1 Half Knot or Part 1 of Square Knot

cords 2 and 3 and behind cord 1 (Figure 26). Pull tight. Either part of the square knot is known as a half knot.

Square knots and half knots can be tied in horizontal rows or vertical rows. The vertical rows are called *sennits*. Half-knot sennits twist. The direction of this twist will reverse when you switch to using the other half of the square knot. When the first part of the knot is made (Figure 25), the sennit twists to the left. When the

Figure 26—Part-1 and Part-2 Half Knots or Part 1 and Part 2 of Square Knot

Figure 26—Part-1 and Part-2 Half Knots or Part 1 and Part 2 of Square Knot

second part of the knot is made (Figure 26), the sennit twists to the right.

Although square knots are usually tied with four cords, any number of cords can be used.

Alternating square knots (Figure 27): Make a row of square knots. On next row, leave cords 1 and 2 free and make square knot in next group of four cords. Continue to make square knots across row. The third row will be a repetition of the first. Many variations in alternating square knots can be achieved by lengthening or shortening space between rows or by knotting more than one row of square knots before alternating.

Figure 27—Alternating Square Knots

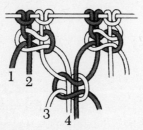

Alternating half hitches (Figure 28): First, use cord 1 as knot-bearing cord and cord 2 as knotting cord. Bring cord 2 up, around, and under cord 1. Next, using cord 1 as knotting cord and cord 2 as knot-bearing cord, bring cord 1 up, around, and under cord 2. Continue alternating in this manner.

Figure 28—Alternating Half Hitches

Overhand knot (Figure 18): Make a downward loop in cord and bring end behind and through. To position knot, put a pin in work surface, tighten cord around pin, and remove pin.

Finishing Off

Thread ends through eye of needle and run through knots on back of piece. Trim off excess cord and place a drop of glue on cord end. If you have trouble running cords through back, make a passageway with an ice pick or awl and use pliers to pull cord through.

General Notes on Embroidery Stitches

While there are literally hundreds of embroidery stitches, the following directions will enable you to do the stitches called for in the projects of this book.

Chain stitch (Figures 29 and 30): Used mostly for outlining or filling. Bring needle and thread through fabric at point A (Figure 29). Holding thread down with thumb, bring needle down and through at point B and up again at point C. Make sure needle is above loop of thread. The distance between B and C will be the length of the stitch. For next stitch, bring

Figure 29—Chain Stitch

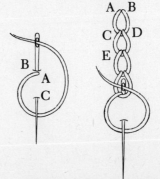

Figure 30—Completed Chain

needle around, holding thread down with thumb, and insert needle down and up again at points D and E (Figure 30). Continue in this manner for desired length of chain.

Closed herringbone stitch (Figure 31): Used often as a border stitch. Bring needle up at A, down at B, up at C, and down at D. You now have a complete X shape. Bring needle up at E, down at F, up at B (using same hole as before), and down at H. Bring needle up a D, down at J, up at F, and down at L. Continue in this manner.

Figure 31—Closed Herringbone Stitch

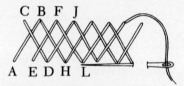

Couching stitch (Figure 32): Used to tie down decorative threads. Draw thread or threads to be couched through from wrong side of fabric, at the right-hand end of design line to be covered, and lay along design line. Taking tiny, straight up-and-down stitches, bring couching thread up at point A, down at B, up at C, and down at D. Continue in this manner until you come to the end of the line. Bring ends of couched thread or threads to wrong side of fabric and fasten.

Figure 32—Couching Stitch

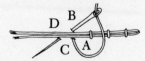

Outline stitch (Figure 33): Used as an outline or filling. Bring needle up at A, down at B, and up at C. The thread should always be kept above or to the left

of the needle. Note that point C is halfway between points A and B. Continue in this manner.

Figure 33—Outline Stitch

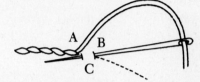

Running stitch (Figure 34): Used for a multitude of decorative and functional purposes. Bring needle up at point A, down at B, up at C, and down at D. Note that the distance between A and B is the same as the distance between B and C. Continue in this manner.

Figure 34—Running Stitch

Satin stitch (Figure 35): Usually done to fill small shapes, such as flower petals. Bring needle up at point A, down at B, up at C, and down at D. Continue in this manner, as shown.

Figure 35—Satin Stitch

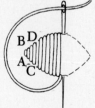

Stem stitch: Used as outline or filling stitch. Done the same way as outline stitch (Figure 33) except that thread is held below or to the right of needle.

Straight stitch: Often used as detail stitch. It is simply one isolated satin stitch. Referring to Figure 35, bring needle up at point A and down at point B.

Bibliography

Andrews, Ralph W. *Indian Primitive*. New York: Bonanza Books, 1960.

Ashley, Clifford W. *The Ashley Book of Knots*. Garden City, New York: Doubleday, 1944.

Better Homes and Gardens. *Handyman's Book*. rev. ed. Des Moines: Meredith Corporation, 1970.

Binder, Pearl. *Magic Symbols of the World*. London: Hamlyn Publishing Group, 1972.

Bossert, Helmuth. *Peasant Art of Europe and Asia*. New York: Praeger, 1966.

Bresden, Kay and Stanley. "Art of the Aborigines." *National Geographic Magazine,* 143, February 1973.

Buehler, A., et al. *Art of the South Sea Islands*. Art of the World Library. New York: Crown, 1962.

Bunt, Cyril G. E. *History of Russian Art*. London and New York: The Studio, 1946.

Bussabarger, Robert F., and Robins, Betty S. *Everyday Art of India*. New York: Dover, 1968.

Butler, Grant C. *Kings and Camels*. New York: Devin-Adair Co., 1960.

Buxton, David. *Travels in Ethiopa*. New York: Praeger, 1967.

Cowles-Gellhorn, E. *McKay's Guide to the Middle East*. New York: David McKay, 1965.

Diaz, May N. *Tonala: Conservatism, Responsibility and Authority in a Mexican Town*. Berkeley: University of California Press, 1966.

Dostl, Rose. "Riches of Tribal Chiefs." *Los Angeles Times Home Magazine*, August 5, 1973.

Finlay, Ian. *Scottish Crafts*. London: George G. Hamap & Co., 1948.

Fodor, Eugene. *Fodor's Guide to Morocco*. New York: David McKay, 1971.

Furst, Peter T. "Myth in Art: A Huichol Depicts his Reality." *Los Angeles County Museum of Natural History Quarterly*. Winter 1968-69.

Gilliard, E. Thomas. "To the Land of the Headhunters." *National Geographic Magazine*, 108, October 1955.

Gink, Karoly, and Kiss, Ivor Sandor. *Folk Art and Folk Artists in Hungary*. Budapest: Corvina Press, 1968.

Girard, Alexander. *The Magic of a People*. New York: Viking Press, 1968.

Gould, Richard A. *Yiwara: Foragers of the Australian Desert*, New York: Charles Scribner's Sons, 1971.

Hansen, H. J. *European Folk Art*. New York: McGraw-Hill, 1968.

Harvey, Marian. *Crafts of Mexico*. New York: Macmillan, 1973.

Harvey, Virginia. *Macramé: The Art of Creative Knotting*. New York: Van Nostrand Reinhold Co., 1967.

Hillier, M. Inez, and Miyazama, Eiji. "Japan's Sky People: The Vanishing Ainu." *National Geographic Magazine*, 131, December 1967.

_____. *Together with the Ainu: A Vanishing People*. Norman: University of Oklahoma Press, 1971.

Holme Charles, ed. *Peasant Art in Russia*. London: The Studio, 1912.

Ickis, Marguerite. *Folk Arts and Crafts*. New York: Association Press, 1958.

_____. *Arts and Crafts: A Practical Handbook*. New York: A. S. Barnes & Co., 1943.

"India's Crafts Today." *Craft Horizons*, 19, July/August 1959.

Johnson, Beverly Edna. "Happenings." *Los Angeles Times Home Magazine*, January 14, 1973.

Johnson, Pauline. *Creating with Paper: Basic Forms and Variations*. Seattle: University of Washington Press, 1966.

Kapp, Kit S., Capt. *Mola Art from the San Blas Islands*. K. S. Kapp Publications, 1972.

Kybalova, Ludmila. *Coptic Textiles*. London: Paul Hamlyn, 1967.

Larousse Encyclopedia of Byzantine and Medieval Art. London: Paul Hamlyn. 1963.

Lederer, Charlotte. *Made in Hungary*. Budapest: Dr. George Vajna & Co., no date.

McDowell, Jack. *Mexico*. Menlo Park, California: Lane Magazine and Book Co., 1973.

McIntire, Virginia. "The Seeing Eye: Primitive Art from Discarded Oil Drums." *Los Angeles Times Home Magazine*, August 26, 1973.

Manker, Ernest. *People of Eight Seasons*. New York: Crescent Books, 1963.

Miege, J. L. *Morocco*. Paris: B. Arthaud, no date.

Newman, Thelma R., Jay Hartley, and Lee Scott. *Paper as Art and Craft.* New York: Crown, 1973.

Norman, James, and Schmidt, Margaret F. *A Shopper's Guide to Mexico.* New York: Doubleday, 1968.

Pericot-Garcia, Luis; Galloway, Johy; and Lommel, Andreas. *Prehistoric and Primitive Art.* New York: Harry N. Abrams, 1967.

Plath, Iona. *Decorative Arts of Sweden.* New York: Dover, 1965.

Ridge, Betsy, and Madsen, Peter Eric. *A Traveler's Guide to India.* New York: Charles Scribner's Sons, 1973.

Schuler, Stanley and Elizabeth Meriweather. *Householders' Encyclopedia.* New York: Saturday Review Press/E. P. Dutton & Co., 1973.

Scobey, Joan. *Rugmaking from Start to Finish.* New York: Lancer Books, 1972.

Soria, Alfonso Soto. "The Hnichols and their Magic World." *Ates de Mexico: Mitos, Ritos, y Hechierias,* 124, Ano XVI, 1969.

Stalder, Valerie. *Lapland.* Tokyo: Kodansha International, 1971.

Sunset Editors. *Macramé.* Menlo Park, California: Lane Magazine and Book Co., 1971.

Tuer, Andrew. *Japanese Stencil Designs.* New York: Dover, 1967.

Volkskunst in Osterreich. Wien-Hannover: Forum Verlag, 1966.

Wardwell, Allen. *The Art of the Sepik River.* Chicago: The Art Institute, 1971.

Weaver, Kenneth F. "The Five Worlds of Peru." *National Geographic Magazine,* 125, February, 1964.

Weyer, Edward. *Primitive Peoples Today.* New York: Doubleday, 1959.

"A Fascinating Craft from Panama: Reverse Appliqué." *Woman's Day,* May, 1966.

Yamada, Sadami, and Ito, Kiyotada. *New Dimensions in Paper Craft.* Tokyo: Japan Publications Trading Co., 1967.

INDEX